Sports Law in Slovakia

Sports Law in Slovakia

Second Edition

Tomáš Gábriš

This book was originally published as a monograph in the International Encyclopaedia of Laws/Sports Law.

Founding Editor: Roger Blanpain
General Editor: Frank Hendrickx
Volume Editor: Michele Colucci

Wolters Kluwer

Published by:
Kluwer Law International B.V.
PO Box 316
2400 AH Alphen aan den Rijn
The Netherlands
E-mail: international-sales@wolterskluwer.com
Website: lrus.wolterskluwer.com

Sold and distributed in North, Central and South America by:
Wolters Kluwer Legal & Regulatory U.S.
7201 McKinney Circle
Frederick, MD 21704
United States of America
Email: customer.service@wolterskluwer.com

Sold and distributed in all other countries by:
Air Business Subscriptions
Rockwood House
Haywards Heath
West Sussex
RH16 3DH
United Kingdom
Email: international-customerservice@wolterskluwer.com

Printed on acid-free paper

ISBN 978-94-035-1744-5

e-Book: ISBN 978-94-035-1793-3
web-PDF: ISBN 978-94-035-1841-1

Printed in the United Kingdom.

The Author

Tomáš Gábriš, Prof. JUDr, PhDr, PhD, LLM, MA, was born on 28 March 1981 in the Slovak Republic. He graduated in Law and History from Comenius University in Bratislava (Slovakia), Central European University in Budapest (Hungary), Trnava University in Trnava (Slovakia), and Tilburg University in Tilburg (the Netherlands). He wrote an LLM thesis at the Tilburg University on behaviour regulation of athletes, under the supervision of Prof. Dr Roger Blanpain and Prof. Dr Michele Colucci. In the past, he has worked in the non-profit sector and as a junior lawyer in Bratislava, Slovakia. Between 2004 and 2019, he was employed at the Faculty of Law of Comenius University in Bratislava, and currently he is a Professor at the Faculty of Law of Trnava University in Trnava. He is also a practicing lawyer, attorney-at-law, licensed by the Slovak Bar Association. He is a member of the Legislative, Legal and Ethical Committee of the Slovak Football Association, member of the Dispute Resolution Chamber of the Slovak Football Association, member of the Legislative and Legal Committee of the Slovak Olympic and Sports Committee, and member of the Scientific Committee of the Sport and Citizenship think-tank. Contact: gabris.tomas@gmail.com.

The Author

Table of Contents

Table of contents

List of Abbreviations

AER	Anti-doping Examination Regulation
ASC	Army Sports Club
AVS	Audiovisual Sport
CAS	Court of Arbitration for Sport in Lausanne
CHF	Swiss Franc
CJEU	Court of Justice of the European Union
Coll.	Collection of Laws
CSSF	Confederation of Slovak Sports Federations
DC	Disciplinary Commission
EBU	European Broadcasting Union
EC	European Communities
EEC	European Economic Community
EHF	European Handball Federation
EU	European Union
EUR	Euro
FIBA	International Federation of Basketball
FIFA	International Federation of Football Associations
FIFPro	International Federation of Professional Footballers
IAAF	International Association of Athletics Federations
IABA	International Amateur Boxing Association
ICAS	International Council of Arbitration for Sport
IHF	International Handball Federation
IIHF	International Ice Hockey Federation
ILO	International Labour Organization
IOC	International Olympic Committee
MSC	Military Sports Club
NATO	North Atlantic Treaty Organization
NHL	National Hockey League
NSC	National Sports Centre
OECD	Organisation for Economic Cooperation and Development

List of Abbreviations

OSCE	Organization for Security and Cooperation in Europe
PEU	Physical Education Unit
SAA	Slovak Athletic Association
SADA	Slovak Anti-doping Agency
SAPC	Slovak Association of Physical Culture
SBA	Slovak Basketball Association
SFA	Slovak Football Association
SFKMA	Slovak Federation of Karate and Martial Arts
SHU	Slovak Handball Union
SIHF	Slovak Ice Hockey Federation
SKK	Slovak Koruna (currency before 1 January 2009)
SOC	Slovak Olympic Committee
SOSC	Slovak Olympic and Sports Committee
SOS	Slovak Olympic Society
SPC	Slovak Paralympic Committee
SR	Slovak Republic
SSF	Slovak Swimming Federation
STA	Slovak Tennis Association
SUSA	Slovak University Sport Association
SVF	Slovak Volleyball Federation
TFEU	Treaty on the Functioning of the European Union
TUE	Therapeutic Use Exemption
UEFA	Union of European Football Associations
UFP	Union of Football Professionals
UK	United Kingdom
ULC	Union of League Clubs
UN	United Nations
UNESCO	United Nations Educational, Scientific and Cultural Organization
USA	United States of America
USD	United States Dollar
VAT	Value Added Tax
WADA	World Anti-Doping Agency
WADC	World Anti-Doping Code

Preface

The present monograph on sports law in Slovakia is the only comprehensive monograph covering this issue in English language.

The issues of the relationship between sports and law in Slovakia, and previously in Czechoslovakia, were already attended to at the turn of the 1970s and 1980s. Those beginnings, however, were marked by the rejection of the concept of so-called sports law. This approach is gradually changing in the Slovak Republic.

The lack of scientific investigation of this issue has been closely related to the general lack of interest in solving the problems of the sports movement in Slovakia, as well as a lack of interest in modernizing Slovak legal scholarship and legal education. However, there is a slow evolution to which this monograph substantially contributed. In a world affected by globalization and Europeanization, legal cultures and legal trends necessarily have to interact, leading to a greater recognition of sports law in Slovakia. Finally, European law does recognize the existence of sports law. This is shown by the case law of the EU Court of Justice (CJEU) and by the introduction of Article 165 into the Treaty on the Functioning of the European Union (TFEU). This fact cannot be overlooked by the Slovak legal scholarship.

This monograph is construed according to a fixed structure designed for national monographs within the International Encyclopaedia of Sports Law. The coverage of topics ranges from European law, administrative law, criminal law, civil law, commercial law, labour law, social security, and competition law, to internal regulation of sports organizations operating in the territory of the Slovak Republic.

Acknowledgements

I would like to thank late Prof. Dr Roger Blanpain and Prof. Dr Michele Colucci, my teachers and the supervisors of my thesis on sports law, defended at Tilburg University, and Prof. Dr Frank Hendrickx, editor of the International Encyclopaedia of Sports Law, for the opportunity to write this monograph.

I would also like to thank those who helped me to successfully complete this difficult work on a topic that was not yet elaborated in detail within Slovakia. Specifically, I would like to thank Dr Lýdia Tobiášová, Dr Lukáš Kvokačka and Dr Miroslav Motyčík, former director of the SADA, for their comments on the chapters that fall within their areas of interest and expertise. I am also indebted to Dr Ladislav Križan, former director of the sports section of the Ministry of Education of the Slovak Republic, for his help in gathering the literature and information quoted in this monograph.

General Introduction

Chapter 1. General Background

§1. Statistics of the Slovak Republic

1. The official name of the country is Slovak Republic (hereinafter 'SR'). With her independence on 1 January 1993, SR became a republic state adopting a political system of parliamentary democracy. SR is divided into eight regions, seventy-nine districts, 138 towns and 2,933 villages, and shares her borders with Czech Republic, Poland, Ukraine, Hungary and Austria. The capital city is Bratislava and has a population of about 428,672 inhabitants. The official language is Slovak. Slovak covers a total land area of 49,034 km^2. The current population of Ghana is about 5,433,385 (out of which 51.4% are women), and the population density amounts to 109/km^2. SR has a diverse ethnic structure with Slovak nationality (85.8%), Hungarian (9.7%), Roma (1.7%), Czech (0.8%), Ruthenian, Ukrainian, Russian, German, Polish and other nationalities (2%). The main currency is Euro (EUR), but until 31 December 2008 Slovak Koruna (SKK) was used. SR is a member of many international organizations such as European Union (EU), North Atlantic Treaty Organization (NATO), United Nations (UN), Organisation for Economic Cooperation and Development (OECD), Organization for Security and Cooperation in Europe (OSCE) and others. The unemployment rate is 14.4% in 2010.

2. Statistics concerning sports are to be found, for example, in the publication by J. Peráčková from 2006.[1] According to information from the National Sport Development Programme for 2001–2010, there were approximately 7,000 sports clubs, Physical Education Units (PEU) and other forms active in Slovakia (registered by the Ministry of Interior), established mainly on the basis of the Act no. 83/1990 Collection of Laws (Coll.) on association of citizens. There are approximately 600,000 people regularly involved in sports, and the vast majority of them carry out their activities voluntarily, without any financial remuneration. The physical training and sports movement is the largest and the most active civic movement in the SR, which, at the national level, consists of 115 superior physical education

1. Janka Peráčková, *The Slovak Republic and Its Sport Sector* (Faculty of Physical Education and Sport 2006).

and sports organizations. The latest numbers speak of approximately 200,000 athletes taking part in competitive sport, which represents approximately 4% of the population.

3. Regarding youth sports, under the same national programme, there are 46,025 athletes involved in over 1,400 registered units for gifted youth. This represents 6% of the population visiting primary and secondary schools, from a total of 803,125 pupils.

§2. Impact of the EU and International Commitments

4. The SR is a party to several international conventions that relate to sport. These treaties originate in the UN, its specialized agency, the United Nations Educational, Scientific and Cultural Organization (UNESCO) or in the Council of Europe. These conventions usually assess the specific nature of sport as not being a purely commercial activity.

5. Protection of the moral and ethical values of sport against excessive commercialization was already enshrined in the International Charter of Physical Education and Sport of UNESCO in 1978. From among the legally binding documents of the Council of Europe, Slovakia is bound by the Convention on Spectator Violence and Misbehaviour at Sports Events and, in particular, at Football Matches (1985), the Convention on the Manipulation of Sports Competitions (2014) and the Convention Against Doping (1989). Within UNESCO, in 2005, another convention – the UNESCO International Convention against Doping in Sport – was adopted, which was also ratified by the SR. The content of these documents has been transposed into the national legislation of the SR.

6. A national regulation within all sectors of the Slovak legal system is undoubtedly influenced by membership in the EU, even though the Treaty of Paris (1952) and the Rome Treaty (1957) establishing communities did not specify any relationship to sports.

7. Neither of the EU secondary legislations – regulations and directives – does specifically provide for sport-related issues. European law should thus apply to athletes and sports clubs to the same extent as to any other entities and activities.

8. From among other documents issued by the EU bodies, decisions are binding only on the parties. One must note, in particular, the first CJEU decision on the relationship between European law and sports – in the case of *Walrave and Koch* (1974), and subsequent decisions in the cases of *Donà v. Mantero*, *Bosman*, *Deliège*, *Lehtonen*, *Simutenkov*, *Kolpak*, *Meca-Medina and Majcen*, or the *Bernard* – which marked the evolution in this field. Within the competition law aspects of sports activities, the decisions of the European Commission play an important role.

9. Regarding the *legally non-binding* documents, these include, in particular, recommendations and opinions, such as the Adonino Report of 1985 and other two reports by Larive (1994) and Pack (1997).

10. It was in the Treaty of Amsterdam (1997) that the sport was finally mentioned in the treaties, albeit only in the final non-binding declarations: Declaration no. 29 explicitly recognized the social value of sport.

11. The first EU conference on sport – in 1999 – identified the commercialization of sport as the biggest threat, yet it emphasized the character of sports, which transcends the economic nature of sporting activities. Similarly, in the Nice Declaration (2000), the specific nature and social function of sport have been particularly emphasized, with the need to maintain training opportunities and the protection of young athletes. These documents were thus seeking to maintain a particular *status quo* and prevent the negative effects of commercialization of sports.

12. A new direction was taken within the EU's policy in relation to sport, only after 2006, when the initiative of France, Germany, Spain and Great Britain, together with the Union of European Football Associations (UEFA), resulted in an Independent European Sport Review. In March 2007, the European Parliament passed a resolution on the future of professional football in Europe. In this resolution, a specificity of football was identified in comparison with other economic sectors, as well as the persistent inequality of women, and the need for the support of domestic players (*home-grown players*) in order to support the development of domestic sport. Attention was also paid to the competition law aspects of the broadcasting of sporting events and ticketing. In the same year, in July 2007, the European Commission adopted a White Paper on Sport, which stressed, in particular, the protection of minors, the fight against doping, racism, violence, money laundering, the need for regulation of broadcasting rights, and the initiation of social dialogue. The White Paper also offered a casuistic definition of the specific nature of sports. The specific nature was seen as: (1) the specificity of sporting activities – separation between men's and women's competitions, limiting the number of participants, efforts to maintain balance in the competition; and (2) the specificity of sports organizations – autonomy, pyramidal structure, construction on a national basis, and the existence of a single federation for each sport industry.

13. The EU definition of specificity largely corresponds to the autonomous view of the sports movement on the specificity of sport. Besides the White Paper, the specificity of sport is also defined in Annex 2 to the Memorandum of Understanding between UEFA and International Federation of Professional Footballers (FIFPro) of 2007.

14. In December 2008, Appendix no. 5 from the European Council meeting in Brussels, reiterated the importance of sport for a European community and acknowledged its special character (specificity).

15. In 2009, finally, the *Treaty of Lisbon* came into force, *which for the first time explicitly expressed the EU's relationship to sport in primary EU law.* According to Article 6 of the Treaty on the Functioning of the EU (TFEU):

> The Union shall have competence to carry out actions to support, coordinate or supplement the actions of the Member States. The areas of such action shall, at European level, be: ... (e) education, vocational training, youth and sport. This means only an auxiliary role to ensure effective action by Member States, thus a *complementary competence*. This is also shown in the wording of Article 165 TFEU, under which the EU cannot harmonize legislation of Member States in this area and the main tools are supportive measures and recommendations.

§3. Sports Law in Slovakia

I. Sports Law and the Nature of Autonomous Rules

16. Scholarly investigation of the relationship between sport and law started in the territory of the SR only in 1970s and 1980s, when this field was first explored by J. Prusák.[2] Subsequently, a longer gap ensued until the turn of the twenty-first century, in particular, at the initiative of M. Králík.[3]

17. The very term 'sports law' is not accepted in Slovakia. It is rejected both in terms of legal scientific literature as well as in legal education.[4] Even abroad, this concept is controversial.[5] Traditionally, in Slovak conditions, the basic argument against the existence of 'sports law' is the view of J. Prusák, published in his book in 1985, where he argues that the *statutes of sports organizations do not meet the standards of law – perceived as a set of standards determined or recognized by the State, and enforceable by the State.*[6] Regarding the nature of the internal norms of sports organizations nowadays, it is worth noting that the Czech and Slovak academics do not admit the legal nature of internal standards, however, they speak, in this respect, of a 'para-legal system'.[7]

18. Already in the period before 1989 (before the change of the regime and of the scientific paradigm in law), there were diverse views on this issue. For example, P. Holländer, in joint authorship with P. Blaho in 1989,[8] expressed the unique view

2. Jozef Prusák, *Šport apråvo (Úvod dodejín, teórie apraxe právnej zodpovednosti všporte)* (Bratislava: Šport 1985).
3. Michal Králík, *Právo ve sportu* (Prague: C.H.Beck 2001).
4. Cf. Pavel Hamerník, *Sportovní právo s mezinárodním prvkem* (Prague: Auditorium 2007), 17–28.
5. Cf. Simon Gardiner, *Sports Law* 97 et seq.(Cavendish Publishing Limited 2nd ed. 2001); Michael Beloff, Tim Kerr & Marie Demetriou, *Sports Law* 3 (Hart Publishing 1999).
6. Prusák, *Šport apråvo*, 89–90.
7. Aleš Gerloch, *Teorie práva*, 71 (5th ed., Plzeň: Aleš Čeněk 2009).
8. Peter Blaho & Pavel Holländer, *Postavenie práva vsystéme metód štátneho riadenia spoločnosti* (Bratislava: Univerzita Komenského 1989).

that non-legal rules such as the rules of socialist coexistence can also be considered a source of law, if they are referenced in an act of Parliament. Holländer subsequently pointed to the legal nature of internal normative guidelines, which, according to a number of authors, are not a source of law. Other authors quoted by Holländer, however, claimed that the internal norms are not legal standards, but they have a certain legal nature. Finally, one of the quoted scholars occasionally regarded some of them as legal acts.[9] A similar problem is the legal nature of the internal rules of professional chambers, for example, Bar Associations. In recent Czech and Slovak scholarly works, one can find the idea that professional chambers have a competence to issue internal regulations, which may be considered legislation.[10] Sports organizations, however, despite some similarities with professional chambers of compulsory membership, are not considered equivalent to these chambers.

19. However, the recently repealed Act no. 300/2008 Coll. on the organization and promotion of sport as well as the new Act no. 440/2015 Coll. on Sports explicitly provide that sports organizations may adopt their own standards, which should be consistent with the standards of international sports federations. Potentially, one may consider this State 'recognition' of internal standards as binding norms. In this sense, internal and legal norms are specifically linked when regulating the system of penalties for doping, where it is assumed that the sentence is imposed by a national association in accordance with international sports rules.

II. Independent Legal Discipline

20. The question of recognition of sports law as an independent branch of law is connected with the problem of the division of law into separate branches of law on the basis of object (employment law, environmental law, or so-called information and communication technologies law) and on the basis of the method applied (administrative law, criminal law, and civil law). In the current system of law, a kind of network structure of law is dominant, which combines horizontal elements (object) with vertical elements (methodology). Should sports law thus be included in this network structure, it should be distinguishable from other branches of law by its object or methods.

21. Methodologically, potential 'sports law' includes elements of both public and private laws, which is characteristic also of labour law. It has a specific object as well – legal relations arising from sports, being an activity of a special nature – just like in labour law, it is the legal relations connected with the performance of work. Regarding the question of whether sporting activities can be considered sufficiently specific to be recognized as different from employment, it is possible to refer to foreign practices of specific legislation regulating sports contracts, as it was

9. *Ibid.*, 141.
10. Zdeněk Koudelka, *Samospráva*, 352 (Prague: Linde 2007).

also proposed in Slovakia in the original bill on sports, which later became the very limited Act no. 300/2008 Coll.[11] (in the meanwhile repealed by the Act no. 440/2015 Coll. on Sports).

22. The principal argument against sports law as a separate legal discipline is that it is a cross-cutting discipline covering relationships that fall within the domain of traditional legal disciplines such as civil law, commercial law, criminal law. For example, in the field of contractual relations in sport, the private law of obligations is applied. In the area of injury and bodily harm, civil or criminal liability is applied. However, the classical regulation is sometimes not applicable in a straightforward way, but given the specific nature of sport, some exemptions are admissible. For example, in competition law, the collective selling of broadcasting rights in a manner that recalls an abuse of market dominance is allowed. Furthermore, the competition between clubs follows a goal that is completely different from creating a dominant position, because the system is construed on matches between approximately equal opponents. Finally, the relationship between sports organizations and athletes also exhibits features that are not explicable by usual structures of civic associations, or business corporations, or by a simple application of labour law. Should we therefore admit that sports law is only a cross-cutting discipline, we must accept that it is necessary, in each discipline of law, to take into account the specificity (specific nature) of sport, justifying a number of exemptions.

23. The specificity of sports is one of the key words of the sports movement, and it is also accepted by the EU in its White Paper on Sport and in the awards of the Court of Justice of the European Union (CJEU). The specificity is thereby not in itself a safeguard for exceptions to the rule, but may only serve as justification for the use of special provisions or special interpretation due to specific circumstances that the law allows to be taken into account. Finally, the recognition of the specificity of sport in the Lisbon Treaty and the explicit EU competence in sports make the existence of sports law legitimate and justified, at least at the level of European law.

III. Principles of Sports Law

24. The specificity of sport in different legal branches of Slovak law can be explained through a set of fundamental principles of sports law. Should we not recognize sports law as a separate discipline, we would be able to recognize only the law applicable to sport.[12] Instead of principles of sports law, we could then speak only of the 'legal principles applicable to sport'. However, the legislation and its

11. Cf. Jozef Čorba, *The Slovak Act on the Organization and Support of Sport; a Missed Opportunity?*, 3(4) Intl. Sports L.J. 65–70 (2009); Ladislav Križan, 'Analýza vybraných ustanovení zákona NR SR č. 300/2008 Z.z. o organizácii a podpore športu a o zmene a doplnení niektorých zákonov', in *Medzinárodná vedecká konferencia Atletika 2008*, ed. Jaroslav Brod'ani, Martin Miškolci (Nitra: KTVS PF UKF, 2008), 17–23.
12. Cf. Richard Parrish & Samuli Miettinen, *The Sporting Exception in European Union Law* 16 (T.M.C. ASSER Instituut 2008).

application take into account the specific nature of sport to an extent which might justify the claims for a separate legal branch. Although, various other areas of life and their rules show certain specificities as well, whether this is to the same extent as in the case of sport remains questionable. So far, we accept the hypothesis that so-called sports law's main principle is the specificity of sport (but not perceived as isolated from the law), manifested in the form of the specific application of law. This takes the form of 'specifically adjusted' principles of sports law. The following main principles may be identified.

A. *Limited Contractual Freedom*

25. Autonomy of the will (individual autonomy) of entities of private law is one of the main pillars of civil law. It is perceived as a principle that no one can find themselves in a legal position against their will, and also, as part of the natural desire to have freedom, to express it freely and to implement it freely. In other words, it is an indication of the possibility of 'auto-determination' and 'self-regulation' of one's own interests.[13] According to some authors, it implies:

(1) liberty and freedom in the choice of legal instrument, type of contract and of contracting partners; and
(2) discretion in determining the content of the act, the content of the contract.[14]

26. This is just one aspect of autonomy in relationships between private entities, the so-called freedom of contract. Autonomy, in a broader sense, also includes:

(1) a free option to own, acquire and enjoy property (ownership freedom);
(2) a free option for the use of property values and rights (freedom of contract); and
(3) the free possibility of the development of human personality and of its creative intellectual activity (freedom of creation).[15]

Moreover, other authors also distinguish the possibility to decide freely on property upon death.[16]

27. At this point, we will only concentrate on the *freedom of contract.* This means that parties are free to choose the form of the contract, the contents of the contract and the question of whether they conclude any contract at all. While both parties dispose of the freedom of contract, in practice, one may question whether

13. Zdeňka Králičková, *Autonomie vůle rodinném právu včesko-italském porovnání* (Brno: Masarykova univerzita, 2003), 33.
14. Ján Cirák et al., *Občianske právo: Všeobecná časť* (Šamorín: Heuréka, 2008), 32–33.
15. Ján Lazar et al., *Základy občianskeho hmotného práva I* (Bratislava: Iura Edition 2004), 15.
16. Jan Wintr, *Říše principů: Obecné a odvetvové principy současného českého práva* (Prague: Karolinum, 2006), 144.

the bargaining position of both sides really is equal.[17] In sport, there are cases when the athlete (especially if he/she is not a superstar) cannot influence the content of the contract and is only a 'weaker party'. He/she only has a choice to sign or not to sign, which may be detrimental to his/her future sports career. Freedom of contract is therefore largely limited by a monopoly (dominant position) of sports organizations. A principle *in dubio contra proferentem* was formulated in this respect, which means that controversial interpretation of the contract is to favour the weaker party. This principle was confirmed by the Constitutional Court of the SR in the finding of 19 June 2008 (I. ÚS 243/07). According to the Court, the vague term is to be interpreted against the party who used it, and this is to be applied as a general method of interpretation of all legal acts.[18] This rule is also stated in §266 subsection 4 of the Commercial Code and §54 subsection 2 of the Civil Code, adjusting the position of consumers. Such a restriction on freedom of contract is not specific only for sports, but comes up in various other sectors. However, a specific *restriction of freedom of contract at the end of the contract,* the so-called principle of contractual stability, is characteristic mainly of sports.[19]

B. *Contractual Stability (Pacta Sunt Servanda)*

28. The principle of contractual stability in sports law is stronger than in traditional civil and commercial law. This stems from the fundamental requirement for stability of the legal relationship between players and clubs, which does not allow the player to arbitrarily terminate the contractual relationship with the club. The same applies vice versa – clubs cannot terminate the relationship with a player. For the same reason, probation periods are not used in sports employment. This exemption is justified by the fact that if, during the season, a rich club could attract top players from rival clubs, this would change the balance of power during the season, which would be detrimental to the whole competition, and particularly, to its attractiveness to spectators. At the international level, this principle is expressed in the International Federation of Football Associations (FIFA) Regulations on the Status and Transfer of Players. These rules in Article 16 explicitly *prohibit the unilateral termination of contracts during the season. After the season,* Article 14 allows a player to terminate the contractual relationship if there is *a legitimate reason (just cause),* for example, if a player played in less than 10% of the club's matches in the season. Even in this case of so-called sporting just cause, however, a player may only terminate the contract within fifteen days after the last match played by his/her club during the season. When a player terminates the contract at the end of the season *for* an unauthorized *reason (without just cause),* he/she will be obliged to pay a compensation calculated, with regard to domestic law, according to the specificity

17. Jonathan Magee, *When Is a Contract More Than a Contract? Professional Football Contracts and the Pendulum of Power*, 4(2) The Ent. & Sports L.J. 2 (2006).
18. Kristián Csach, 'ÚS SR: Výklad contra proferentem a preferencia platnosti právneho úkonu ako všeobecné výkladové pravidlá', www.lexforum.sk/240, 30 Dec. 2010.
19. Simon Gardiner & Roger Welch, *The Contractual Dynamics of Team Stability Versus Player Mobility: Who Rules 'The Beautiful Game'?*, 5(1) The Ent. & Sports L.J. (2007).

of the sport and other objective criteria that include, for example, the remuneration for sporting activities and other benefits that the player receives, costs his/her club has faced with respect to the player, originally negotiated duration of the contract, and whether the termination occurred in the protected period (which is determined by the age of players – the players signed up before the age of 28 years must stay in a contractual relationship for at least three years, players older than 28 years, only for two years).[20]

29. The amount of any compensation may be determined by agreement of the parties concerned. The player and his/her new club, into which the player transfers, are both responsible for the payment. It is explicitly presumed that if there was a dismissal without just cause, a new club urged the player to terminate his/her contract with the previous club. In such a situation, the new club is to be punished with a ban on registering new players for two registration periods.

30. In the event of termination within the so-called *protected period* (three or two years), sporting sanctions may be imposed on the player, generally, a four-month ban on playing official matches. In the case of aggravating circumstances, the penalty can be extended up to six months. Unilateral termination of the contract *after the protected period* does not bring any sporting sanctions. Only a disciplinary sanction may be imposed if the contract is not terminated within fifteen days from the last official match of the club in which the player is registered in a given season.

C. Nullum Crimen, Nulla Poena Sine Lege in the Prosecution of Doping

31. From among other principles that apply in sports law in a way that is different from the ordinary course of (criminal) law, one may mention the principle of *nullum crimen sine lege, nulla poena sine lege.* In the case of the penalty for doping imposed by sports organizations on the basis of Act no. 440/2015 Coll. on Sports (not being a criminal deed nor a criminal sanction), referring to the internal norms of the sports movement, it is questionable whether the sanction is imposed under the law or under the internal norms. While the Act contains a definition of doping rules violation (section 88(3)), the list of banned substances as well as the penalties applicable are only formulated by a hybrid (public-private) organization – the World Anti-Doping Agency (WADA). There is therefore a situation where the penalties and the list of banned substances are formulated by a private organization without specific statutory support.

32. Moreover, even within the autonomous rules of sporting organizations, one may find problematic provisions on sanctioning. In this respect, e.g., many disciplinary rules of various sports associations are in breach of the principle *nullum crimen sine lege, nulla poena sine lege* because they allow for punishment by analogy, when they provide that in case of misconduct which is not directly mentioned in the

20. Cf. the *Andy Webster* case decided by CAS.

rules, it should be punished as a disciplinary offence most similar by its nature. In our opinion, such a provision should be rejected and cannot be justified even by the specific nature of sport.

33. Another problem can be found in provisions of the Code of the WADA, under which the sportsman who has refused to submit to a test for doping three times in twelve months should be sanctioned as a user of doping. Such a punishment seems to breach the presumption of innocence. In fact, however, this is not a penalty for doping or the presumption of guilt, but rather, a penalty for failure to comply with the obligations associated with doping controls.

D. Permissible Limitations of Fundamental Rights and Freedoms

34. Another manifestation of the specificity of sport is the existence of derogations from fundamental rights and freedoms, both at the national and European level. At this point, we pay attention to only some aspects of this problem.

1. Equal Treatment and Limited Freedom of Movement and Establishment in the EU

35. The principle of equal treatment in sports allows for exceptions. Even the White Paper on Sport published in 2007 by the European Commission admits this. In its view, the specificity of sport has resulted in 'separate competitions for men and women', as well as for people with disabilities, or genetically specific individuals. The most famous examples are the scandal about the South African athlete Caster Semenya and questions about the prostheses of Oscar Pistorius. A similar issue is the equal treatment in case of medical adjustments available to athletes, for example, golfers' eye operations.[21]

36. The Slovak Anti-discrimination Act no. 365/2004 Coll. enshrines the principle of equal treatment only in the field of employment and similar legal relations, social security, health care, provision of goods and services and in education. Despite the fact that professional sporting activity in collective sports is not considered employment activity in Slovakia in practice, the Labour Code considers such activity to be dependent work, and prohibition of discrimination should therefore probably apply to sport as well. The Anti-discrimination Act, however, contains in its §8 a general clause, which states that:

> Discrimination is not the different treatment which is justified by the nature of occupational activities or the circumstances under which these activities take

21. Mark Hamilton, *Elective Performance Enhancement Surgery for Athletes: Should It Be Resisted?*, 36(2) Acta Universitatis Palackianae Olomucensis. Gymnica 39 (2006).

place, if the reason is a genuine and determining occupational requirement, provided that the objective is legitimate and requirement is proportionate. (trans. T.G.)
Separate competitions for men and women and other cases of separate sports competitions most probably fall under this exemption.

37. In particular, the question of equal treatment and non-discrimination arises in connection with limiting the number of foreign athletes. The issue of equal treatment between persons of different nationalities results from the efforts of the EU Member States to ensure freedom of movement. Therefore, these two issues – freedom of movement and discrimination based on nationality – are closely linked. This is also true for sports law. The CJEU in the case of *Donà v. Mantero* held that limiting the participation of foreigners (foreign nationals) in matches of national teams in international competitions is acceptable if it is an essential feature of the sport. However, the EU rejects the practice of limiting the number of foreigners in a team under other circumstances (e.g., the 3+2 rule). In the most famous sports law case of the CJEU, the *Bosman* case, the CJEU rejected the principle of 3+2 as inconsistent with the principle of non-discrimination. At the same time, the court refused to limit freedom of movement of a football player whose professional contract expired. Similarly, the court protected freedom of movement in the cases of *Lehtonen*, *Simutenkov, Kolpak* and *Bernard*. In the *Deliège* case, the Court also held that the nomination of athletes for an international competition is fully within the competence of the sports organizations (national associations), and thus there is no full equality of opportunity to exercise the freedom.

38. The decisions of the CJEU created a special policy in relation to this issue that could be summarized as follows. *Freedom of movement can be adequately restricted in cases of:*

(1) selection of athletes for national team;
(2) limited nomination of competing athletes;
(3) a transfer which is allowed only during transfer windows.

39. The question of selecting players to national teams was again of importance when FIFA and UEFA presented their idea of the ideal composition of national teams in their competitions. It was the 6+5 rule (FIFA has waived it in June 2010), followed by the so-called rule of domestic players (*home-grown players rule*). Both rules required clubs to employ players who may qualify to participate in a national representative team (the 6+5 rule would mean that such national players have to be at least six in number – having the nationality of the country), or who were brought up on home lawns (home-grown players rule). The home-grown player is a player who, aged between 15 and 21 years, spent at least three years in a club operating within the country. There is no condition that these players have to possess citizenship of the country. Thus, it is not a direct discrimination, as in the 3+2 or 6+5 rule. These latter two rules were rejected by the European Commission and European

Parliament as directly discriminatory and restrictive of the freedom of movement.[22] On the other hand, the *home-grown players rule* is rather indirectly discriminatory, which can be justified by the fact that it is intended to support and nurture young talents and to motivate national clubs to educate young players. In the light of the decision in the *Bernard* case, which also argues by the necessity to encourage clubs to educate young players, it seems that the CJEU would accept such indirect discrimination.

2. Restriction of Basic Rights by Contractual Agreement

40. Usual responsibilities of top athletes often include a duty to report their residence (information regarding their whereabouts) in order to submit to a doping test. There may arise a question regarding whether this is a proportionate interference with the privacy of the athletes. Under the Slovak Constitution, fundamental rights and freedoms can be limited by an act of Parliament. Article 16 section 1 of the Constitution reads as follows:

> The inviolability and privacy of a person are guaranteed. It may be restricted only in cases specified by law. (trans. T.G.)
> However, the question is how to assess such an invasion in privacy if the obligation is not imposed by the Act, as it is imposed under the WADA Code. It is thus an extra-legal obligation, acceptable only under a contractual theory of acceptance of these terms.

41. Fundamental rights and freedoms of athletes are very often limited by contractual arrangements between the sports organizations (clubs) and athletes. One can mention possible interference with the right to privacy of a player in the so-called players' contracts, restricting the freedom of speech (expression of opinion for the media) or lifestyle (diets). As a basic principle in these cases, the consent of the athlete is presumed. Given the nature of sports contracts and the dominance of the club, however, this assumption is questionable, as well as the proportionality of such restrictions with respect to the specific needs of the other party (employer, or in Slovak conditions, the contractual partner, that is, the club).

42. Proportionality of restrictions of basic rights is to be assessed through a prism of specific needs of the sports sector. This assumes importance especially when invoking a breach of a contractual term and subsequent imposing of a sanction.

22. Samuli Miettinen & Richard Parrish, *Nationality Discrimination in Community Law: An Assessment of UEFA Regulations Governing Player Eligibility for European Club Competitions (The Home-Grown Player Rule)*, 5(2) Ent. & Sports L.J. (2007).

Chapter 2. History of Sports Law

§1. History of Sport in Slovakia

43. The modern history of organized sport in the territory of what is now the SR dates back to the nineteenth century. The oldest organized sport was horse racing. In 1839, a racing association was established. In 1844, F. Martinengo founded the first gym and fencing school in the Hungarian Kingdom – in Bratislava. The first modern sports club in the territory of Slovakia was the Bratislava rowing club, founded in 1862. Slovaks even attended the first Olympic Games in Athens in 1896, where a Slovak A. Szokol won a bronze medal for the 100 metre sprint.

44. After the establishment of the Czechoslovak Republic in 1918, the pivotal sports organization was the Czechoslovak Sports Community, which in 1928 transformed into the Czechoslovak All-Sports Committee. It existed alongside the Czechoslovak Olympic Committee. With regard to individual sports and their organizations, football, the most popular sport in Slovakia, developed since the late nineteenth century. The first Slovak football club, 1. Čs. ŠK Bratislava, was founded in 1919, and in 1938, the Slovak Football Association (SFA) was established. Ice hockey, another popular sport, began to develop after World War I, particularly after the European Championship was organized in 1925 in Slovakia.

45. When the Czechoslovak Republic in 1939 temporarily split into the Protectorate of Bohemia and Moravia and the Slovak State, in the territory of Slovakia, the Slovak Central Sports Council was constituted (1939–1944), besides the Slovak Olympic Committee (SOC). The reunification of Czechoslovakia took place in 1945, and the common State persisted since then (with a conversion from a unitary State into a federation in 1969) until 1992. Since 1 January 1993, the Czech Republic and the SR became its successor states, after a peaceful disintegration. In the independent SR, the SOC was re-established.

46. Slovak athletes participate regularly in international sporting events, including the Olympic Games. The most successful Slovak Olympic sports are canoeing, shooting, wrestling, judo, snowboarding, biathlon, ice hockey and women's basketball. From among non-Olympic sports, it is mainly bodybuilding and karate.

§2. History of Legal Regulation of Sport in Slovakia

I. Period until 1945

47. The modern history of the regulation of sport in Slovakia has a tradition dating back to the origins of the Czechoslovak State. One of the first legal norms of the Czechoslovak Republic (no. 2/1918 Coll.) established the Office (Ministry) of Public Health and Physical Education. About two years later, on 30 March 1920, Act no. 228/1920 Coll. establishing an Advisory Council for Physical Education was adopted. This body was established within the Ministry of Public Health and

Physical Education, based in Prague. Its task was to examine all issues relating to physical education (the Act did not speak explicitly about 'sport'). Details of the activities of the advisory board were specified by governmental regulation no. 616/1920 Coll. The Council was to have twenty members from among the representatives of sports organizations and educational institutions and communities, such as the Sokol. The basic principle in this period was the virtual absence of legal regulation of sport. In general, sport in Czechoslovakia was considered a private matter, and the State was not supposed to interfere with sports.[23] One of the few public expressions of interest in sport was in addition to the establishment of the Advisory Council, the adoption of Act no. 73/1935 Coll. establishing the Tyrš' State physical education institute of the Czechoslovak Republic in Prague, with educational, scientific and promotional functions in physical education. The principal features of the sports movement in this period were autonomy, the inherent right to associate and the independent internal regulation of individual clubs and organizations. In 1938, in terms of the inclination to fascism in Slovakia, all physical training associations were incorporated into the paramilitary Hlinka Guard.[24]

II. Sport under the People's Democratic and Socialist Law

48. After 1945, in the field of physical culture, the plurality of sports organizations was restored. However, as soon as the Communist Party took over the power in 1948, Act no. 68/1951 Coll. again repealed all associations and replaced them with mass organizations under direct State control. The fundamentals of state management of sport were laid down by Act no. 187/1949 Coll. of 14 July 1949 on State care for physical education and sport. This Act has, in addition to physical education, also introduced the concept of sport, with the role to:

> maintain and improve the health of the people, increase their physical and military capacities and work efficiency and to educate them towards commitment and bravery in defending the homeland and its people's democratic state system. (trans. T.G.)

49. The new trend was marked by the following features:

(1) politicization and militarization of physical education – proven by the above-mentioned understanding of sport as a means of preparing for homeland defence;
(2) undermining autonomy in favour of state interventionism, which also had a positive outcome – creating an educational system in the sport, as well as social recognition of athletes' value;

23. Jan Štumbauer, '40 let zákona o státní péči o tělesnou výchovu a sport', *Teorie apraxe tělesné výchovy* 37, no. 11 (1989): 689 et seq.
24. Ján Grexa, 'Občiansky atribút v športovom hnutí na Slovensku', in *Občan aobčianstvo 2002* (Bratislava: FTVŠ, 2002), 104.

(3) centralized management of sport, through mergers of sports organizations and by creating a single system within the Czechoslovak Association of Physical Education.

50. Centralism and interventionism were also expressed in the Act no. 187/1949 Coll., which constituted the *State Committee for Physical Education and Sport,* composed of representatives of the Czechoslovak Sokol (surviving from before 1948; it took over the property of all other sports organizations as of 31 March 1948), people's organizations nationwide and outstanding workers in the fields of health, physical training and sport. In Slovakia (as a part of Czechoslovakia) the same tasks were performed by the *Slovak Committee for Physical Education and Sport.* Functions of both committees were advisory in nature.

51. In addition to the Committee as a central governmental body for physical education and sports, a *National Office for Physical Education and Sport,* and in Slovakia, the *Slovak Office for Physical Education and Sport* were established. Their task was to issue general regulations, such as, uniform guidelines for physical training and sport, the principles for training staff and a uniform set of rules for institutions of physical training and sport. The State's interest in the sport is also reflected in government regulation no. 38/1951 Coll. of 10 April 1951 on the honours connected to honorary degrees in physical education and sport, in the form of badges and diplomas, honorary wages or gifts. This arrangement was inspired by the Soviet model.

52. The terminology 'physical education and sport' was also preserved in the next act of Parliament governing this issue, Act no. 71/1952 Coll. on the organization of physical education and sport. Under the Act, the management and control of physical education and sport were still being continuously performed by the *State Committee for Physical Education and Sport* and the *Slovak Committee for Physical Education and Sport.* However, the State Committee was no longer only a major ideological authority but also a legislative body – it *united the functions of the previous Office and Committee,* and then it abolished *the National Office for Physical Education and Sport and the Slovak Office for Physical Education and Sport.* In addition, the Act stipulated that the regional and district national committees (local authorities) will set up local *committees for physical education and sport.*

53. Government regulation no. 24/1953 Coll. established an Institute of Physical Education and Sport in Prague, as a college whose graduates were to be titled 'graduate teacher of physical education'.

54. In the following physical education legislation there was a return to the terminology of the first Czechoslovak Republic, when the Act no. 68/1956 Coll. of 20 December 1956 on the organization of physical education only used the term 'physical education' and abandoned the term 'sport'. The Act transferred the management of the entire physical education movement onto the *Czechoslovak Association of Physical Education*, which put an end to inefficient direct state control through special State Committee.[25]

55. During the so-called Prague Spring in the 1960s civic associations were to be restored, but after the Soviet invasion into Czechoslovakia in August 1968, this idea was abandoned. In 1969, a *Ministry of Youth and Physical Education* was established in the Czech Republic, but soon – in 1970 it was repealed, and a new managing body of physical education was created by the resolution of the federal government no. 80/1978: governmental committees for physical education and sport within the government of Czechoslovakia (federal government), and within Czech and Slovak republican governments. These committees were repealed in 1988, when their competence was transferred to *the republican ministries of education.*

56. Particular attention was paid to young athletes – not only in addition to the school system but also within the school system, provided for by the ordinance of the Ministry of Education, Youth and Physical Education of the Slovak Socialist Republic (Member State of the Czechoslovak Federation) of 27 April 1988 on sports schools and secondary vocational schools and classes with top-sport training. However, despite the positives, it is clear that in this period, sport became an instrument of political power, and education and athletic performance were to serve as tools of confirmation of the dominance of communist ideology.

III. Modern Legal Regulation of Sport

57. After the collapse of the so-called communist regime in Czechoslovakia in 1989, a disintegrating process of decentralization and de-statization started in sport, but interference of politics into sport never really disappeared. Sport is in fact still used as a means of political struggle, for example, in the elections. A new trend was the regulation of new areas connected to sports activities – for example, entrepreneurship in the sport or organization of public sports events, and similar. The first step to set aside statism and state interventionism after 1989 was the Act no. 173/1990 Coll. of 9 May 1990, repealing the Act no. 68/1956 Coll. on the organization of physical education. This Act returned the *property rights of voluntary organizations,* which were taken from them by Act no. 187/1949 Coll., no. 71/1952 Coll. and no. 68/1956 Coll., as of 31 March 1948, to Czechoslovak Sokol and other voluntary organizations that were recreated again, as of 31 December 1991. Eligible physical education organizations, which existed as separate legal entities as of 31 March 1948, were the ones enumerated by the government regulation no. 321/1991 Coll. Organizations that were required to return property rights were successors of the Czechoslovak Association of Physical Education, namely:

25. Ján Grexa, 'Šport na Slovensku – štát versus občianske združenia', *Telesná výchova ašport* 10, no. 3 (2000): 39.

(1) Slovak Association of Physical Culture (SAPC).
(2) PEUs.

58. Slovak National Council as the legislative authority of the Slovaks within the Czechoslovak federation subsequently adopted a new framework law for the regulation of physical culture (again the concept of sport was missing, and instead the physical education and physical culture were mentioned). It was the Act no. 198/1990 Coll. of 18 May 1990 on physical culture. A new concept, physical culture, was defined in the Act as 'organized and unorganized individual, group, union and other type of activities related to physical education, sports, tourism and recreational movement activity of citizens (trans. T.G.)'. Unlike the previous period, there was a demilitarization of the initial statement on the mission of physical culture, which was to carry out more humanist targets than preparation for military service.

59. In terms of institutions involved in the organization and development of physical culture, this Act recognized an *autonomous position of sports organizations.*

60. The physical culture was performed according to the Act no. 198/1990 Coll. by the following bodies:

(1) Ministry of Education, Youth and Physical Education of the SR.
(2) Other State bodies with specific tasks.
(3) Physical education, sports and tourism associations.
(4) Other associations.
(5) State enterprises, cooperatives and other organizations.
(6) Entrepreneurs in the field of physical culture.
(7) Unorganized participants in physical activities.

61. Physical culture was to be *financed from:*

(1) revenues from Sazka and Sportka (lotteries) and other similar games;
(2) profits from business, economic, physical-educational, sports, cultural and social activities and services;
(3) the State budget;
(4) subsidies, contributions and gifts;
(5) income from advertising and sponsorship; and
(6) from other sources.

62. Although the system of financing shows partial de-statization and decentralization of sport after 1989, national interest was subsequently shown by creating a special National Fund of Physical Culture (Act no. 264/1993 Coll., abolished in the meanwhile, with attempts at restoration in 2019) for the purpose of funding physical education. The Fund was managed by the Ministry of Education and Science of the SR. According to the National Sport Development Programme of the

Ministry of Education for the years 2001–2010, the main source of funding of sport in Czechoslovakia and Slovakia have been, are and should be the revenues obtained from lotteries and similar games. The interrelation of the proceeds from lotteries with the sports subsidies is however only indirect. Extracts from the lottery are channelled to the State budget and from there subsequently allocated to the Sports Section of the Ministry of Education.

63. A governmental regulation no. 469/1991 Coll. implementing the Act of the Slovak National Council no. 198/1990 Coll. on physical culture can be considered the first legislative act responding to the commercialization of sport in Slovakia in the second half of the twentieth century, since §5 regulated *Doing Business in the field of physical culture*, with an enumeration of types of business activities.

64. Furthermore, special arrangements *for organizing public sporting events* were introduced by the Act no. 315/1992 Coll. of 7 May 1992 on public physical education, sports and tourist events. The Act governed the rights and obligations of primary stakeholders: organizers, organizing service, participants and municipality. The aim of the legislation was to ensure the safety of the participants – athletes and spectators. Therefore, the State issued detailed instructions on how to prevent violence, or how to facilitate intervention.

65. Certain expressions of modern state interventionism in sport was the adoption of Act no. 226/1994 Coll. on the use and protection of Olympic symbols and the SOC, replaced by the current Act on Sports from 2015. Three years later, in 1997, Act no. 288/1997 Coll. on physical culture was enacted. This among others deals with the education, trade and trade licenses in sport and is also still valid and effective.

66. A more detailed regulation of sport was enacted after several unsuccessful attempts only in 2008, when the National Council of the SR approved a new Act no. 300/2008 Coll. on the organization and promotion of sports, which governed the State support of sports, care about sports talents and sporting activities of children outside school hours, provides for training of athletes to represent the SR, measures to combat doping in sport and the functions of the Slovak Anti-doping Agency (SADA), the dispute settlement in sport and ultimately the establishment and management of public administration information systems for sport.

67. Many other legislations before and after 1989 were concerned and related to sports, although they did not always necessarily deal explicitly with the sport, for example, the Act on association of citizens, tax and customs acts, the Firearms and Ammunition Act, the Act on local government, school acts, ordinances and guidelines of the Ministry of Education and others. The SR at the same time joined the international and supranational organizations and gradually became a signatory of several international documents that expressed politically or legally binding *international commitments of the* SR concerning sporting activity.

68. Some *remnants of the socialist system* of sport survived, however, despite revolutionary changes after 1989. This was particularly a problem of the legal status of athletes who were considered self-employed even in team sports, while in Western Europe players are usually considered employees.[26] This had its roots in an effort to maintain the so-called amateur status of athletes, particularly due to reasons of the Olympic idea of amateurism. It was only Juan Antonio Samaranch at the head of the International Olympic Committee (IOC) who allowed the participation of professionals in the Olympics.[27] Limiting participation of the best Western athletes in the Olympic Games because of their professionalism favoured the socialist countries, which introduced a system of 'state amateurs' – athletes supported by the State. Athletes received fictitious jobs, from which they were released for sports training with pay. It was only in 1981 when the Olympic Congress in Baden-Baden adopted a new legislation that strictly prohibited receiving financial compensation without the knowledge of sports federations and National Olympic Committee. Subsequently, in 1985, it was decided that age would be the only eligibility criterion in football, ice hockey and tennis. Finally, in 1986, in Lausanne, a code was adopted, which allowed the participation of professionals in the Olympics. This substantially weakened the socialist countries. However, their internal system of state athletes was not changed.

69. In the SR, after 1989, there was a transition only in the sense that the athlete instead of a fictitious job besides the sporting activity has no other job, and in relation to a club, players were still not considered employees, but rather self-employed. Therefore, the complete professionalization of sport did not take place – in the form of an employment. Instead, professional players (athletes) concluded atypical contracts with the clubs under the Civil and Commercial Code, which saved the club the cost of contributions for social insurance of players.

70. In Western Europe, the situation was the same a few decades ago.[28] In France, according to Mouly,[29] the existence of an employment relationship between athletes and the employer (club) was confirmed as early as in 1960 in the case *Rostollan*. The *Cour de Cassation* subsequently extended the application of labour law to all athletes, whether professionals or amateurs. Since the 1980s, the employment contract has become commonplace in French sport. At that time, however, many other countries were a step ahead and introduced a special regime for sports affairs instead of applying the general employment law. An example is Portugal, where the institute of sporting employment contracts was introduced, which is defined in the

26. Cf. Ladislav Križan, 'Právne postavenie profesionálnych futbalistov pôsobiacich vo vybraných krajinách EÚ z hľadiska ich vnútroštátnej legislatívy', *Notitiae ex Academia Bratislavensi Iurisprudentiae* 4, no. 1 (2010): 61–78.
27. Brigita Stloukalová, 'Profesionalismus a amatérismus v zrcadle socialistického sportu', *Tělesná kultura* 31, no. 1 (2008): 68–84.
28. Jean-Claude Germaine, *Lesportifs et le droit* (Liége: Faculté de droit de Liége, 1975), 107–109, 116.
29. Jean Mouly, 'Sur le recours au contrat de travail à durée déterminée dans les port professionnel: Le droit commun du travail a-t-il encore un avenir dans le domaine du sport?', *Droit social* 5 (2000): 508.

sense that the athlete undertakes to perform sports activities for an individual or collective persons, for remuneration, through participation in sporting activities, under the supervision of that person(s).[30] The practice of employing sports employment contracts is also known in other even non-European countries, such as Brazil. Therefore, it is to be noted that the question of the status of players is still evolving – and the same applies to the SR. A chance for a change occurred in Slovakia in 2015, with the new Act on Sports, which regulates the status of sports people performing dependent work so as to be considered employees. Thereby, special regulation was proposed instead of the problematic rules of the Labour Code. The Act is hence to be considered a special act regulating a specific type of employment relationship, where the Labour Code applies only if the Act on Sports allows for this. This solution was accepted by all the stakeholders and the new Act no. 440/2015 Coll. on Sports entered into effect as of 1 January 2016, with the exception of provisions on social insurance which have a delayed effectiveness – as of 1 January 2022. This Act repealed all the previous Acts of the Parliament that had to do with sports, except the recently enacted Act no. 1/2014 Coll. on the organization of sports events.

30. José María Gonzalez del Rio, 'El contrato de trabajo del deportista en Portugal', *Revista española de Derecho del Trabajo* 116 (2003): 226.

Chapter 3. Sources of Sports Law

71. When discussing the sources of sports law, the latest opinion of a Czech author Michal Králík is to be noted first. He does not recognize sports law as a separate legal branch though. Its sources are therefore referred to only as the information sources, 'the sources of knowledge', while only some of them are formal sources of law:

(1) legislation: general and sportive, national and international;
(2) case law;
(3) sports rules;
(4) institutionalized reporting of information (through universities, etc.); and
(5) scholarship and literature.

72. It is quite clear that universities and science are not a formal source of law. Case law is not considered a source of law in the continental legal system either. It can however affect the decision-making activity of courts through its persuasiveness, de facto. Hereinafter, we will deal with only the formal sources of sports law. However, due to questionable character of sports rules it might be problematic to speak of sources of sports law. Maybe the term 'sporting normative system' could be used instead. We will use both these terms interchangeably.

73. The primary issue in a treatise on the sources of sports law is to clarify the concept of law as such. We stick to the classical positivist understanding of law as a body of norms in the form set or recognized by the state (public authorities) and enforceable by the state (public authorities). We are speaking of public authority besides the State due to Article 7 of the Constitution of the SR as well as due to the EU membership of Slovakia. Based on that, one cannot limit 'law' to standards set by a state – the SR. One has to also take international treaties and the EU law into account. According to Article 7 section 5:

> International treaties on human rights and fundamental freedoms, international treaties for execution of which no special law is required and international treaties which directly confer rights or obligations on natural or legal persons and which were ratified and promulgated in the manner prescribed by law shall prevail above the law. (trans. T.G.)
> In relation to the EU, a similar provision can be found in Article 7 section 2: '… *Legally binding acts of the European Communities and the European Union take precedence over the laws of the Slovak Republic.* (trans. T.G.)'
> Finally, under Article 154c section 1:
> International treaties on human rights and fundamental freedoms, which the Slovak Republic ratified and promulgated in a manner prescribed by law before the entry into force of this constitutional Act, are part of the legal system and take precedence over the law, if they provide a wider range of constitutional rights and freedoms. (trans. T.G.)

74. Based on these assumptions, the following summary of the sources of sporting normative system in Slovakia may be offered:

(1) the highest ranking legal rules:
   (a) primary, secondary and tertiary laws of the EU, which has precedence over the laws of the SR, and according to the case law of the CJEU (e.g., in the case of *Van Gend en Loos, Costa v. Enel, Internationale Handelsgesellschaft, or Simmenthal*) has precedence even over the Constitution of the SR;
   (b) Constitution of the SR;
   (c) constitutional acts;
   (d) results of the referendum with the force of constitutional act;
   (e) international treaties, by which the SR is bound, and which take precedence over the laws under the conditions laid down in Article 7 and Article 154c of the Constitution.

(2) other acts of the highest constitutional authorities:
   (a) finding of the Constitutional Court, whereas in case of an established non-compliance with the Constitution, the norm (the Act) first loses effectiveness and after a period to be amended by the National Council (six months) it loses validity;
   (b) decision of the President on amnesty.

(3) rules with the force of an act of Parliament:
   (a) act of Parliament;
   (b) results of the referendum with the force of an act of Parliament;
   (c) international treaties with the force of an act of Parliament (other than those mentioned in Article 7 of the Constitution, e.g., those referred to in Article 154c section 2); and
   (d) at the time of accession negotiations to the EU (until 2004), the governmental regulations under Article 120 section 2 of the Constitution (approximating the Slovak laws with the EU law).

(4) subordinate legislation:
   (a) governmental regulations;
   (b) generally binding norms of ministries and other central government bodies (ordinances and notices);
   (c) generally binding ordinances of local government bodies;
   (d) generally binding regulations of higher territorial units (autonomous regions) and municipalities;
   (e) internal rules, which are envisaged by law (e.g., in the case of professional chambers with mandatory membership); however, sporting rules do not fall into this category.

(5) collective agreements in employment law (the majority of athletes are not affected by these, since in practice they are usually not subject to labour law).

75. The question whether the internal rules of the sports movement should be considered a source of law is controversial and also depends on the questionable nature of sport organizations as public or private subjects. According to Prusák, sports rules are not legal norms. On the other hand, we have already pointed out the view of P. Holländer from 1989, who concluded that some rules of civic associations play a role as a source of law in the practice.[31] A similar question was also dealt with by the socialist labour law scholarship in relation to internal guidelines in the workplace, such as disciplinary code, work rules and similar things. These were generally also not considered as sources of law, but their legal significance was particularly emphasized in socialist literature as a source of Czechoslovak labour law, having the nature of both a legal act and a legislative act.[32]

76. We have already pointed to the fact that the Act no. 440/2015 Coll. on the organization and promotion of sports recognizes internal standards of the WADA, international federations, as well as national sports associations and sports clubs. On the other hand, other internal standards may also occur in sport, that is, governing matters other than as expected under Act no. 440/2015 Coll. From a formalist interpretation, it could be inferred that in this case it is a rule, which the law did not foresee, and its 'legal' character could thus be compromised. It could be argued that these 'other' rules are binding on athletes (and clubs) only on the basis of their mutual contract (explicit or tacit), or a member relationship based on the Act no. 83/1990 Coll. on association of citizens and based on the statutes of the civic association.

77. The rights and obligations are recognized by the court, even if arising from atypical contracts. They cannot be considered the sources of law, since their nature of 'law' can be doubted just like the 'legal' nature of any contract, since these are not universally binding, but rather rules which bind only the specific parties. Nevertheless, they have legal significance, just like all contractual arrangements in the traditional branches of civil or commercial law. The entire theoretical reasoning on the legal nature of the internal regulations of the sports movement is further complicated by their possible breakdown into international and national rules. In this context, one may come across expressions such as 'international sports law' or 'global sports law'.

78. Foster in this regard claims that international law is primarily concerned with the relations among states (and international organizations), thus international sports law is only an international law applicable to sport.[33] On the other hand, Nafziger speaks of a regime with its own authority and legitimacy.[34] Foster makes a distinction between international and global sports law (*lex sportiva*). The former seems to be rather the general principles of international law applied in the field of sport by the courts, and the latter is defined as an autonomous transnational legal order created by global private institutions that govern international sport (e.g., the Court of Arbitration for Sport (CAS)).[35] It should be noted that Foster does not

31. Blaho & Holländer, *Postavenie práva v systéme metód štátneho riadenia spoločnosti*, 144.
32. Jaroslav Filo et al., *Československé pracovné právo* (Bratislava: Obzor, 1981), 65.
33. Cf. Parrish & Miettinen, *The Sporting Exception in European Union Law*, 16.
34. James A.R. Nafziger, *The Court of Arbitration for Sport and the General Process of International Sports Law*, in *International Law and The Hagués 750th Anniversary* 241 (Wybo P. Heere ed., T.M.C. Asser Press 1999).
35. Ken Foster, *Is There a Global Sports Law?*, 2(1) Ent. L 1–2 (2003).

understand global sports law (*lex sportiva*), in contrast to other authors, as an analogy of international trade law *lex mercatoria* and claims that while *lex mercatoria* is based on contractual relations, global sports law has no contractual basis. He considers it an autonomous and sui generis system.

79. To summarize the views of Foster on the system of transnational sports law, one may distinguish four types of international rules:

(1) rules of the game (*lex ludica*);
(2) ethical principles of sport;
(3) international sports law (international law applied to the sport); and
(4) global sports law (i.e., the customs and practices which arise within the international sports organizations).

80. Apart from ethical principles, a major problem is seen in distinguishing between the rules of the game (*lex ludica*) and other sports rules, as also admitted by the CAS decision at the Olympic Games in Atlanta in 1996 (*Mendy v. IABA*). In this case, the boxer was disqualified for a low blow against the rules. The panel acknowledged that according to the traditional theory there is a difference between the rules of the game, which the court cannot consider (unless they are in breach of fundamental rights), and other sports rules, which the court may assess if asked to do so. The distinction between these two types of rules is unclear and may well be that the difference between them will become even more blurred because of the growing economic importance of sport.[36]

81. The whole complicated system of sources of sporting normative system (involving law applicable to sport, as well as internal sporting rules) can be simplified as follows:

(1) *Laws applicable to sport* (the norms of international law, European law and national law). From a national perspective it is the system of the sources of law described above.
(2) *Sporting rules*, which are further subdivided into:
    (a) *rules of the game* (*lex ludica*), which must respect fundamental principles of law and justice; the rules of the game will automatically include the ethics of sport and the principle of fair play (or good morals);
    (b) *sporting* rules (*lex sportiva*), namely:
        – *national* (created by national sports organizations as their internal regulations), influenced and limited by applicable law and by global *lex sportiva*; and
        – *global* (international, established by international sports organizations and transnational bodies such as FIFA, UEFA or CAS). *Lex sportiva* global rules are subject to review for compliance with international, European and national law applicable to the sport.

36. *Ibid.*, 5.

82. Finally one can conclude that in the current legal scholarship in the SR, the view that internal rules of the sports movement, whether at national or international level do not have the nature of sources of law, still dominates. In practice, the theoretical question of the legal nature of these standards does not arise because the sports organizations themselves refuse to apply the sanctions resulting from their by-laws before the courts, and rather prefer their own independent means of dispute settlement, within the sports family. In our opinion, one can recognize that although they are not a source of law, the sports by-laws are regulations with legal significance, particularly for resolving disputes – for example, in order to assess whether a general obligation to prevent damage was observed. For instance, in the event of a breach of internal rules, or more specifically rules of the game, it is considered that the person did not act bona fide, and breached the obligation of general prevention.

Part I. Organization of Sport in Slovakia

Chapter 1. General Issues

83. The nature of sports organizations may be either that of public administration or of private organizations and businesses, representing private governance. A third option would be a hybrid nature of sports organizations. This debate is present mainly in the common law countries, but efforts to include sports organizations in the public administration can also be found in the Czech and SR. This chapter therefore considers the question of whether sport is in the public interest, that is, a public matter, or represents solely a private issue. Answering this question has significance in two ways:

(1) If it is shown that sports organizations are part of public administration (representing professional autonomy, such as Bar Associations), their decisions should be issued under the Administrative Procedure Code or special legislation and should be subject to review under the so-called administrative court procedure, which is not the case nowadays.
(2) The second line is the already mentioned issue of the nature of internal regulations of sports organizations. Should sports organizations represent special interest bodies just like professional chambers with compulsory membership, their internal rules could be considered rules with the nature of the sources of law.

§1. Public Administration and Sport

84. The concept of public administration in the SR includes state administration and self-government. State administration is divided into central and local. Central comprises the ministries and other central government bodies. Local state government may be general (e.g., district office) or specialized (e.g., mining authority). The self-government is divided into territorial and self-government of interest (professional self-government). Territorial self-government comprises municipalities and higher territorial units (self-governing regions). Professional self-government is made up of professional chambers, such as the Bar Association. These are usually created by a special act of Parliament, and therefore their internal regulations have a specific nature, potentially considered a source of law.

I. Sport at the Crossroads of Public and Private Governance

85. The question regarding whether sports organizations and sporting relations have purely private law foundation or also include an element of public law was already dealt with abroad. English courts in cases of *Aga Khan* and *R v. Panel on Takeovers and Mergers ex parte Datafin* took the view that they are private contractual relations.[37] In the *Aga Khan* case (1993), a horse was disqualified from the competition because of a positive test for doping, and it was decided that the court could not review the decision in an administrative court procedure. Against this attitude, the plaintiff argued that a horse racing sports organization has a national monopoly, and in the absence of such an organization, its functions would most likely be carried out by the State. This should indicate that associations formed on a voluntary basis might in fact represent and protect the public interest, and represent a public administration. In the Australian case *Western Australian Turf Club v. Federal Commissioner of Taxation*, however, the court expressly noted that the sports organizations, although some are entrusted with public responsibilities, remain private, which is also reflected by their public functions being just additions to the primary mission of a commercial organization. Thus, in the *common law* system, the form dominates over substance, that is, the form of private organizations dominates over the possible public functions and public interest. It is difficult to accept that some decisions may be reviewed by the administrative courts and others not, just because of the formal nature of the organization itself. Exclusion of certain groups of cases from judicial review follows the goal of proper functioning of the courts, which might otherwise be overwhelmed by too many cases.[38]

86. Thus, the current predominant approach is that the sports organizations are private, not public, and therefore their decisions cannot be reviewed in the administrative court proceedings.

II. Sport Between the Public and Private in Slovakia

87. Regarding the situation in Slovakia, the basic rules (laws) governing sport and physical culture spoke candidly not only of state administration in the field of sport but also of the operation of non-State bodies. Specifically, the former Act no. 288/1997 Coll. on physical culture in its §1 stated:

> This Act regulates the care of physical culture and the role of government bodies, autonomous regions, municipalities, civic associations in the field of physical culture (hereinafter referred to as 'civic association') and the role of other legal persons and natural persons in its assurance. (trans. T.G.)

37. Michael Beloff, Tim Kerr & Marie Demetriou, *Sports Law* 229.
38. Cf. with arguments in cases *Stevenage Borough FC Limited v. The Football Limited*; *Modahl v. British Athletic Federation Limited. Ibid.*

Thus, the following bodies operated in the area of physical culture:

(1) governmental bodies;
(2) autonomous regions;
(3) municipalities;
(4) civic associations; and
(5) other legal and natural persons.

88. Government authorities and the autonomous regions and municipalities can thereby be clearly labelled as public administration, notwithstanding whether the care of physical culture was carried out as a state administration or local self-government. However, a question arises as to whether civic associations and other legal and natural persons operating in the field of physical culture represent a private administration or public administration. Albeit the Act no. 288/2007 Coll. was repealed in the meanwhile by the Act no. 440/2015 Coll., the same questions remain open without offering a specific answer – in contrast, strengthening the competences of private sports organizations with a detailed regulation laid down in the Act leads some scholars to propose that even the private sports organizations have shifted more towards being of a nature of administrative bodies, performing tasks of public administration, reviewable under the rules of administrative judiciary. The final word on this issue is not spoken yet, though.

§2. Professional Self-Government?

89. While examining the nature of sports organizations closely, professional self-government should be analysed first. A Czech author, Zdeněk Koudelka, divided this type of self-government into professional chambers with compulsory membership, chambers with non-compulsory membership and university autonomy.[39] The common features are the legal basis of constitution of these bodies, their own legal personality, ability to regulate internal relations together with the behaviour of subordinate bodies and finally a certain property basis and personal basis.

90. Professional chambers with compulsory membership may issue their internal rules, which according to Koudelka possess the nature of legislation, being generally binding upon members of the chamber. The regulations issued by the professional (vocational) chambers may impose obligations only on the basis of law and must respect the legitimate scope of the chamber, otherwise their actions may be annulled by the administrative judiciary. Should one therefore consider sports organizations to be professional chambers with compulsory membership, their decisions would have to be subject to review by administrative courts, and their regulations would be considered legislation. However, the problem is that sports organizations are not established individually by an act of Parliament. Moreover,

39. Koudelka, *Samospráva*, 339.

currently the athletes are often not formal members of sports clubs, for example, if the club has a legal form of a business company. In this case, there is a contractual relationship rather than a membership-based relationship between the athlete and the club.

91. Another group of subjects according to Koudelka is the *chambers with non-compulsory membership,* where their rules are not legislation, since they are not generally binding, and their competence can be avoided by leaving the chamber.[40]

92. In the *case of universities,* Koudelka does not accept their internal rules as legislation, because of the lack of their general application, which can be avoided by leaving the school and a transfer to another school.

93. From the above considerations, the conclusions can be drawn on similarity of sports organizations and professional chambers with compulsory membership, as outside of the national association, professional sports occupation is not possible. The principal argument against the perception of professional sports organizations as chambers with compulsory membership is however the private law character of sports organizations. This problem was also noticed by S. Sádovský in his doctoral dissertation:

> [S]tatus of professional athletes as members of the sporting corporation is the closest to a member of professional chambers with compulsory membership. If anyone wants to pursue a profession supervised by the chamber, declaration of intention (application) to become a member of this chamber is required. If an athlete wants to pursue his 'profession' he has to become a member of the sports organization. (trans. T.G.)[41]

§3. Persons of Public Law?

94. Karel Beran in his examination of the public sector uses different terminology and classification than Koudelka does. Beran distinguishes between public corporations and public institutions. Both categories represent public law persons.[42] Basic feature of a public corporation lies in the fact that it bears public authority as a kind of legislative and executive power, while other public entities (e.g., public institutions) dispose of only executive power.[43]

95. Beran distinguishes between legal persons of public law in the narrow sense (only corporations and public institutions) and all organizations which perform public duties even through private law means. It is this second category where sports

40. *Ibid.*, 361–362.
41. Stanislav Sádovský, *Boj proti dopingu aprávní garance lidských práv* (PhD Dissertation) (Bratislava: Comenius University in Bratislava, 2008), 71.
42. Karel Beran, *Právnické osoby veřejného práva* (Prague: Linde, 2006), 172–173.
43. *Ibid.*, 173–175.

organizations could fall into, if one admits that they actually carry out public functions, although they are private in nature. The concept of public tasks, however, is not considered sufficient to consider the entity as a subject of public law in the strict sense. Sports organizations would have to be a bearer of public authority and dispose of the legislative and executive power, in order to be considered real persons of public law, that is, public corporations or public institutions.

§4. Private and Public Organizations Sui Generis?

96. Beran also opened a very inspiring discussion on the nature of churches as sui generis public organizations, although the Czech Constitutional Court considers them private entities. They explicitly have the power to produce their own normative system – the canon law. It is precisely this category of sui generis public organizations, or from the opposite point of view, sui generis private organizations, that sports organizations could also fall into. It should also be noted that, according to the theory of administrative law, some private organizations might exercise public powers, albeit this will not make them public corporations. In this case, according to Průcha, activity of these entities is not a private activity, but rather public administration, performed in public interest.[44] Private sports organizations would thus be able to carry out public functions, if sporting was considered a matter of public interest pertaining primarily to the State, and the State would delegate these tasks to the private sports organizations. However, this conclusion cannot be drawn from the current law in Slovakia. It would be characteristic for the so-called interventionist policy of the State in relation to sport, which is not the case in the SR, although sport is a matter of public health.

§5. Public Administration and Public Interest in Sport

97. The competence of state administrative bodies in sport is specified in the Act no. 440/2015 Coll. They concern, in particular, the financing of sport, anti-doping and legal forms used to carry out tasks in the field of sport. In other issues (education, training, infrastructure, organization of events), the State has only coordinating and supporting functions.

98. Sport is at least in some of its aspects the object of public interest, as reflected, for example, under the directive of the European Parliament and the Council 2010/13/EU of 10 March 2010 (Directive on audiovisual media services), in its Article 14, where European legislation allows Member States to ensure public access to television broadcasts of sporting events that are considered of 'major importance for society'. Similarly, the Slovak Act no. 308/2000 Coll. on broadcasting and retransmission regulates in §31 public access to major events.

44. Petr Průcha, *Veřejná správa a samospráva* (Prague: Vysoká škola aplikovaného práva, 2004), 10–11.

99. Public interest is enforced through particular tools used by the State. Jozef Čorba distinguishes various legislative, institutional, financial, tax and competition instruments of the State in sport.[45] The sport is mostly affected by adopting specific sport legislation, as well as by the establishment of the special Ministry of Sport, which can be understood as both legislative and institutional instrument. Other instruments are closely linked with the funding of sport – namely, financial, tax and competition law, which are, inherently, also legislative instruments.

100. From among the types of direct state interventions, one can provide the following examples:

(1) The State interferes with doping prevention institutionally – through the establishment of the SADA (in the Act no. 300/2008 Coll. on the organization and promotion of sports, confirmed also in the Act no. 440/2015 Coll.), which is a contributory organization of the Ministry of Education (and Sports).
(2) Another example of public interest is the regulation of safety in the Act no. 1/2014 Coll. on the organization of public sporting events. According to its §1:

> This Act regulates the conditions for the organization of public sporting events, the privileges and responsibilities of the organizer, activities, privileges and responsibilities of a member of the organizing service, the role of the municipality and the police, obligations and prohibitions for event participants, arrangements to ensure security at the event, and liability and sanctions for breach of the obligations established by this Act. (trans. T.G.)

101. Thus, the State intervenes directly in the sport and protects the fundamental ideas of fair and safe competition, but at the same time appropriates the sporting results of athletes as 'representation' of the SR. It also provides financial subsidies, which can be considered another way of direct interference in sporting activities in Slovakia. The extent to which the State intervenes in activities of sports organizations depends on national traditions and national policy in relation to sport. Two types of approaches can be discerned: interventionist model and non-interventionist model.[46] This can be ascertained according to whether any reference to sport exists in the Constitution of the country, as to whether there are specific provisions on sport in valid law, such as specific contract types, special treatment of criminal liability for sports injuries and so on.

102. The relationship between the State and sport in Slovakia at the beginning of the third millennium was accurately described by *the Legislative Intent of the Sports Act from 2004.* According to this Intent:

45. Jozef Čorba, *Obchodnoprávne vzťahy v oblasti športu* (PhD Dissertation) (Košice: UPJŠ, 2008),49 et seq.
46. André-Noel Chaker, *Study on National Sports Legislation in Europe* (Council of Europe Publishing 1999).

> The current rules of sport in the Slovak Republic live up to the expectations of the state relationship to the sport from the beginning of the second half of the 20th Century … With the exception of sports clubs of the armed forces, sport was not only separate from government but also from the business entities and sports activity was based on sports organizations operating on a voluntary basis … The autonomy of sport therefore did not require state intervention and in fact, this was limited to questions of material support of some sporting activities.

103. The Legislative Intent considered that an ambivalent relationship between the State and the sport still prevailed, with the State supporting sport financially, while, respecting its autonomy. However, many laws governing the sport activity in the SR were enacted since the times of the Legislative Intent. However, one cannot claim that there was also a change in the relationship between the State and the sport. The Act no. 300/2008 Coll. as the main source of 'sports law' was very brief and essentially only a kind of framework. It was only the regulation on doping, which could seem interventionist, albeit only in cases of the absence of autonomous international regulation. Autonomy of sport was thus formally recognized even in matters of doping. In this respect, the SR was to be considered only a moderate model of an interventionist country. However, the new Act on Sports no. 440/2015 Coll. is more intervening in this respect. As already pointed out, it even seems that the sports organizations could newly be considered as performing public administration in sports, and their decisions could be considered administrative decisions, reviewable by courts. This is nevertheless something that is not explicitly invoked in the wording of the Act on Sports, but is rather only an interpretation of the Act proposed by some of the prominent legal experts in Slovakia. The final word on whether Slovakia will shift from a moderate model to a more interventionist model is thus to be spoken yet.

§6. Public Legal Framework of the Sports Movement

104. The State, in addition to creating a legislative framework, leaves to the sports movement a relatively large degree of autonomy under the heading of internal activities of a civic association or a business company (or other legal forms). The Slovak Act on Sports no. 440/2015 Coll., e.g., leaves it fully for the sports organizations to regulate the disciplinary sanctions, including sanctions in case of doping rules violation.

105. The following types of non-public administration sports organizations were recognized by the Act no. 300/2008 Coll. and basically preserved also under the new Act no. 440/2015 Coll.:

(1) the SOC;
(2) the Slovak Paralympic Committee (SPC);

(3) national sports associations (being a specific form of a sports organization under the new Act no. 4402015 Coll.); and
(4) sports clubs (also being a specific form of a sports organization under the new Act no. 4402015 Coll.).

106. The framework regulation of the Olympic movement in Slovakia was originally contained in the Act no. 226/1994 Coll. on the use and protection of Olympic symbols and the SOC. Under this Act, the SOC was a civic association which managed the Olympic movement in the SR, and had the status and entitlements of a National Olympic Committee under the Olympic Charter, and in accordance with §6 subsection 4, it had the power to permit the use of Olympic symbols, which were protected by the law. This Act was subsequently repealed and replaced by the new Act no. 440/2015 Coll. on Sports, having preserved the same principles of the SOC regulation (in 2019, SOC changed its name to the Slovak Olympic and Sports Committee (SOSC), requiring now a change in the Act on Sports). National sports associations and sports clubs are also governed in detail by the Act no. 440/2015 Coll., which also provides for their funding, the legal form and obligation to provide information to public administration information system, which could indicate again a certain public interest in sport.

107. According to the Act no. 400/2015 Coll., sports associations have a legal form of civic associations and sports clubs have a legal form of business companies, civic associations, or budgetary or contributory organizations. These are fundamentally private entities, which is also the view of J. Čorba, who points to a similar debate highlighted in connection with the *Piau* case of the CJEU.[47] The budgetary and contributory companies however lack a strictly private law character, since they are created by the State or public authority (municipality, higher territorial unit), and are not created by the sports movement itself, or individuals on the basis of the right of association. Still, they enter into private law relationships.

108. Should one consider all-sports organizations as public corporations, it would be necessary to allow for examination of all decisions of the sports organizations in administrative court proceedings and to consider their decisions as issued in administrative proceedings. This is however in conflict with the current legal practice. Fear of a high number of lawsuits in the event that any decision taken by sports organizations could be examined in the administrative judiciary will continue to be the main argument of opponents of such a solution. Moreover, it cannot be assumed that the sports organizations themselves would be willing to recognize their character of public administration and allow for review of their decisions within administrative courts. The conclusion may therefore be that, in the case of sports organizations, these are mostly private entities that perform certain tasks of public interest. The fact that public interest exists (particularly in terms of

47. Čorba, *Obchodnoprávne vzt'ahy v oblasti športu*, 49 ff.

organizational, financial aspects, safety, security and integrity of the competition) does not in itself turn a private administration into a public administration. Depending on a multitude of public elements, one could at most talk about hybrid entities, but this would only be a theoretical conclusion without practical consequences.

Chapter 2. Public Regulation

§1. Freedom of Association and Sport

109. Private legal entities of various legal forms dominate the area of sports. They have a legal form of civic associations, business companies and in some cases, also forms of interest associations of legal persons, or associations of civic associations and others.

I. Civic (Private) Associations

110. The primary legal basis of sports organizations in Slovakia is Act no. 83/1990 Coll. of 27 March 1990 on association of citizens as amended. It further elaborates on the international and constitutional basic right to associate and provides that citizens have the right to associate freely, whereby it is not necessary for a state body to authorize the exercise of this right. Therefore, the principle of registration applies, rather than of authorization.

111. Individual manifestations of association right are in practice, under §2, unions, societies, associations, movements, clubs and other civic associations, as well as trade unions. The Act confers on them the status of legal persons. They are registered with the Ministry of Interior. Special arrangements apply to trade unions – they become legal persons on the day following the date on which the Ministry receives a proposal for registration. The Act however does not apply to an association of citizens:

(1) within political parties and political movements;
(2) for business aims or to ensure a proper practice of certain professions;
(3) in churches and religious societies; and
(4) to exercise the right to hunt.

112. It may be questionable as to what extent the association of athletes is or is not an association for exercising a profession, particularly if the sports federation or club has a monopolistic power to allow or deny exercise of a professional sporting activity.

113. According to Z. Magurová, the prohibitions to follow business aims in the Act no. 83/1990 Coll. did not intend to restrict the business activity of civic associations completely. It is clear from the explanatory memorandum to the Act. Nevertheless, in practice there are cases when the Ministry of Interior did not register a civic association, which had a business activity in its scope of activities. On the other hand, Trade Offices routinely allow civic associations to obtain trade licences.[48]

114. Another problematic issue is the membership in legal entities. Pursuant to §2 subsection 2 of the Act no. 83/1990 Coll., members of civic associations may *also* be legal persons. However, if there were only members in the nature of legal persons, it would be more appropriate to use an 'interest association of legal persons' institute under §§20f et seq. Civil Code (this is the legal form of the Union of League Clubs (ULC) within the SFA), in place of an institute of civic association, established pursuant to Act no. 83/1990 Coll. Act no. 83/1990 Coll. does not, however, discern a specific reason for the extinction of a civic association due to membership consisting solely of legal persons. Thus, it must be established that the current practice also accepts civic associations whose members are solely legal entities.

115. Another controversial issue is the *positive and negative association freedom.* According to §3 of the Act, no one may be compelled to associate, to join an association or to participate in their activities, and everyone can freely withdraw from the association. Some provisions of the internal regulations of sports clubs, however, stipulate that an athlete cannot be registered by a different sports club, and that he/she still be registered as a member of the former club, after the abandonment of that club, for a given period (e.g., one year), as a member of the former club, apparently, in order to avoid registration with another club.[49] In case of a dispute in front of a court, sports organizations would probably have to look for serious arguments that would justify such treatment. They could, for example, rely on the argument that the statutes of sports clubs possess the nature of contract that the parties agreed to. However, in our opinion, the court should hold that the registration maintained even after the manifestation of will to withdraw from the association (and from the 'contract') limits the right of the association (in the negative meaning of association freedom) because the goals are likely to be achieved in other ways – for example, instead of keeping the player as a member after leaving the club, by introducing a ban on the registration of a new player by a club if he/she was previously registered in another club.

116. Finally, another problem is the legal issue of *competence* of sports organizations in relation to individual athletes, depending on the legal form of a sports organization. Essentially, in *civic associations,* their internal rules are binding upon members, but not upon public authorities, and they also may not impose duties on citizens who are not members of the association. Thus, if the individual athletes are not regarded as members of sports organizations (e.g., of national associations), they

48. Zuzana Magurová, 'Legislatíva tretieho (neziskového) sektora na Slovensku', *Právny obzor* 79, no. 3 (1996): 198–223, 206.

49. Registration Rules of the Slovak Football Association (Art. 14), of the Slovak Ice Hockey Federation (SIHF) (Art. 6), and Transfer Rules of the Slovak Federation of Karate and Martial Arts (Art. II).

could not be forced to any obligations. The only way is through a contractual submission to the competence of these associations. The regulation of membership in civic associations is thereby a responsibility of the association. The law does not require an explicit list of members, only the determination of rules of membership. In the case of civic associations – sports *clubs* – the issue of membership can be solved by stipulating that members of civic associations are always the current registered players for this club. In most of the internal regulations of the national sports *associations*, the issue is solved by making the membership of athletes indirect – through their membership in sports clubs that are direct members of the association. The athletes' membership is thus only *mediated.* The Act does not preclude this. On the contrary, one could again speak of a contractual relationship, or fictitious contractual relationship, creating the competence of a sports organization in relation to the athlete. Proof of this concept could be the wording of the former Act no. 300/2008 Coll. on the organization and promotion of sport, which, in §25, referred to the athlete or sports expert who 'is a member or in a contractual relationship to the sports club' (trans. T.G.). From grammatical interpretation it appears that even an athlete, and not only a sports specialist, could be in a contractual relationship with the sports club. If, however, the person does not feel subject to the discretion of an association, he/she may object and invoke the provision of the Act, which prohibits the imposition of obligations on a person who is not a member of the association.

117. In another case, namely, when the sport organization (club) is *a business company*, there is only a possibility of a non-member, private contractual relationship between the organization and athletes. 'Membership' in this club and also in the national association, recognizing individuals as mediated members through their membership in clubs, is more or less fictitious, based not on law but rather on the internal sports rules governing registration (or licensing) of athletes, and on a voluntary submission to the authority of sports organizations in a contract. This submission as a separate contractual relationship can thus take the form of:

(1) an explicit players' contract (in writing), which confers competence to the sports organization and the obligation of the player to comply with internal rules and decisions of the organization; or
(2) a tacit contract, that is, a fictitious contract – if the relationship between athletes and the organization (e.g., club as a business company) stems from the fact that the athlete is 'registered' in an organization.

118. Relationship between the club and the athlete may therefore take the form of:

(1) membership (in case of civic associations, whose members are directly athletes themselves);
(2) contractual relationship (contract players);
(3) quasi-contractual or tacitly contractual relationship (based on registration).

One could also speak of 'true membership' and 'quasi-membership'. This was also confirmed by the law regulating the sport – namely, the Act no. 300/2008 Coll.

on the organization and promotion of sport. In the definition of sports associations, it explicitly used the phrase that the association 'has the athletes' (§8 subsection 1 letter c). Apparently, the legislator was aware of the problematic legal aspects of the relationship between athletes and sports organizations. Finally, the new Act no. 440/ 2015 Coll. solved this issue by introducing the concept of 'jurisdiction' of sports organization with respect to any persons taking part in the activities of the sports organization, notwithstanding their membership or any other legal basis of their relationship with the organization.

119. It should also be pointed out that *coercion* of 'members' of sports organizations is usually not implemented in practice through the law (contract) and legal proceedings, but mostly only on the basis of the authority of a monopolistic sports organization – in particular, the national association. Therefore, the legal nuances of the relationship between the athlete and the organization do not really play a role in practice.

II. Association of Civic (Private) Associations

120. Association of civic associations can be created pursuant to §16 of the Act no. 83/1990 Coll. on the association of citizens. It is a form that allows only for the association of legal entities – civic associations – on the basis of contract on collaboration. The legal regulation is only brief in the Act. Under section 1, associations may enter into mutual contracts to co-operate to achieve certain goals or in order to achieve some common interest. The validity of such a contract requires a written form. The contract on collaboration shall specify in particular:

(1) the purpose of the collaboration;
(2) the way of its implementation;
(3) the rights and obligations of the participating associations; and
(4) the means to contribute to any collaboration.

The contract on collaboration may provide that the contract expires, by agreement of the participating associations, upon the achievement of the goal for which it was concluded or by any other event mentioned in the contract. For these associations, *mutatis mutandis*, the provisions of the Act relating to civic associations will apply. An example of such a legal form is the Slovak Basketball Association (SBA) – the national sports association of basketball.

III. Interest Association of Legal Entities

121. Interest association of legal entities has a legal basis in §§20f et seq. of the Civil Code (Act no. 40/1964 Coll.). They represent one of the basic types of legal entities in the SR. According to §18 subsection 2 of the Civil Code, legal persons are:

(1) associations of natural or legal persons (i.e., civic associations, interest associations of legal entities);
(2) association of property (i.e., foundations);
(3) territorial self-government units; and
(4) other entities, if regulated by law (e.g., non-profit organization, business companies).

122. Interest associations under §20f can be created to protect the interests of legal persons or to achieve another purpose. To establish an association a written founding contract is required or an approval of the establishment at the constituent meeting of members. The contract or record of a general meeting must be accompanied by the articles of association, and persons authorized to act on behalf of the association have to be identified. The association obtains legal personality upon an entry in the register of associations kept at the district office in the seat of the region, depending on the registered seat of the association.

IV. Business Company

123. The various types of business companies in Slovakia are discerned in the Commercial Code no. 513/1991 Coll. A company is formed by registration with the Commercial Register, kept by the district courts in the seat of the regional court. Under §56 of the Commercial Code, commercial companies are legal entities established primarily for business purposes. The Code distinguishes between commercial companies and cooperatives. The individual types of business companies are the following: general partnership, limited partnership, limited liability company (with basic capital of at least EUR 5,000) and joint-stock company (with basic share capital of at least EUR 25,000). Legal entities established under the EU law have a position analogous to the business companies.

124. Companies with limited liability and joint-stock companies may also be established for purposes other than business. The Act on the organization and promotion of sport no. 300/2008 Coll. expressly required that sports clubs with a legal form of business company are set up for non-business purposes. In practice, however, the non-business purpose could hardly be discerned in the content of most of the clubs' articles of association. Therefore, the new Act on Sports no. 440/2015 Coll. left this principle behind and sports organizations can now freely perform business and for-profit activities with no limitation.

125. According to §§21 and 22 of the Commercial Code, foreign persons may conduct business in the SR under the same conditions and in the same scope as Slovak persons, unless the law stipulates otherwise. The legal capacity of a foreign person is governed by the law under which it is created. The law under which it was established also governs its internal legal relations and the liability of members or partners for its obligations. In sports, the presence of foreign entities comes into consideration especially in the form of owners (shareholders, partners) of Slovakian sports organizations.

V. Non-profit Organization

126. Another form in which it is possible to develop sport and physical culture is a non-profit organization.

127. Non-profit organizations are governed by Act no. 213/1997 Coll. of 2 July 1997 on non-profit organizations providing public benefit services. A non-profit organization is a legal person constituted under this Act, which provides public benefit services under pre-established conditions which are the same for all users, and whose profit may not be used for the benefit of its founders, board members or employees, but must be used entirely for procurement of public benefit services. These services comprise, *inter alia*, teaching, education, and development of physical culture. A non-profit organization may be established by a natural person, legal entity or state. It is created on the basis of a founding charter signed by all founders. Written application for registration of a non-profit organization must be filed by a founder or a person authorized by the founder in writing, within sixty days from the establishment of a non-profit organization.

VI. Foundation

128. Foundations unlike civic associations are only associations of property, not of persons. They are governed by the Act no. 34/2002 Coll. on foundations. According to §1, the foundation is a block of assets, which serves the public benefit purpose. It is a legal person listed in the register of foundations, which is kept by the Ministry of Interior of the SR. Public benefit purpose for the sake of this Act means, in particular, the development and protection of spiritual and cultural values, implementation and protection of human rights or other humanitarian objectives, protection and development of the environment, preservation of natural values, protection of health, protection of rights of children and youth, the development of science, education, *sports education* and implementation of individually directed humanitarian aid for individuals or groups who have found themselves in jeopardy of life or need urgent help as a result of a natural disaster.

129. A foundation may be established by a natural or legal person and is based on the foundation charter, signed by all founders. It arises upon the registration in the register of foundations.

VII. Non-investment Fund

130. A non-investment fund is a rare legal form, which does not appear regularly in the field of physical culture and sport in Slovakia. It can be established under the Act no. 147/1997 Coll. on non-investment funds. Under its §2, the fund is a non-profit legal person, which represents funds for the implementation of public benefit purposes or individually directed humanitarian aid for an individual or group of persons, the lives of whom are endangered or need urgent assistance in case of a natural disaster. Among the demonstratively calculated public benefit purposes, neither sport nor physical culture are mentioned, but their subordination under the broader concept of cultural values is not excluded. A fund is established by a foundation charter or a foundation contract, and it may be established by a natural and legal person. The fund arises on the date on which it is enlisted in the register kept by the district office in the seat of the region.

§2. Governmental Conditions and Permits

131. Besides private entities, bodies and organizations of the State and public administration are also active in the field of sport, in the broadest sense. They carry out public policy in relation to sport.

I. Public Policy in Relation to Sport

132. In view of the particular State policy in sport, it is necessary to refer first to the National Sport Development Programme for the period 2001–2010, implemented as a joint programme of all subjects participating in physical education and in sports movement, central government bodies, non-governmental organizations, sporting civic associations, local administration and self-governing entities. This material was prepared by the Ministry of Education of the SR in accordance with the conclusions and resolutions adopted at the Ninth Conference of Ministers responsible for sport, held on 30 and 31 May 2000 in Bratislava, with the title 'Clean and Healthy Sport for the Third Millennium'. The programme was approved by governmental Resolution no. 838/2001. This programme expired without any evaluation being prepared. A new concept of national programmes on sport was to be ready by the end of 2011, which would focus only on areas that fall within the competence of the Ministry of Education and Sport, based on the government programme of 2010. The sport was mentioned in the previous programme statements of Slovak governments as well, but mostly in vague terms. The Governmental Programme from 2010 is also relatively brief: 'The Government will place emphasis on the aim that sports activities and competitions financed by public funds are intended not only for talented, but create the appropriate framework for all … ' (trans. T.G.). The emphasis on funding was reflected in 2010 in the adoption of an amendment to the Act on the organization and promotion of sport no. 300/2008 Coll., dealing, in particular, with the revised procedure for awarding subsidies to sports organizations. A new national programme, labelled as concept of state policy in the area of sports, 'Slovakia 2020', was approved by the government of Slovakia in 2012. One of its major aims was to prepare a new act on sports, which could bring the long-awaited breakthrough in the relationship between the State and sport in Slovakia, and remedy the failure and imperfection of the current Act no. 300/2008 Coll. This has materialized in the new Slovak Act on Sports no. 440/2015 Coll.

II. The Basic Legislation Governing Sports Activities in Slovakia

133. Regulation of sport in Slovakia can be found mainly in the acts of Parliament and in norms of lower legal force. From another perspective – of the object, one can discern: (1) *basic sources* designed primarily for sport and physical culture; (2) *ancillary sources* that contain the regulation of sport and physical culture as an incidental element; and (3) *the remaining general sources* not aimed to regulate issues of sport and physical culture at all.

134. (1) *The basic sources* are two types of laws. The first is general *organizational framework laws*:

(1) Act no. 440/2015 Coll. on Sports.
(2) Act no. 1/2014 Coll. on the organization of public sporting events.

135. (2) *Ancillary sources* are the legal norms in which the position of sports organizations and sports activity is an incidental matter. These are provisions from various branches of law. For example, the Act no. 278/1993 Coll. on the administration of State property has abolished (in §18) the institute of the right of permanent use of property by sports organizations, which was established under the previous laws. Since the entry into force of this Act, PEUs have to pay for the use of the property. This Act also amended the Act on municipal property no. 138/1991 Coll. as amended, under §2 of which:

> Immovable property of the state, to which the right of permanent use by physical education units extinguished under a special regulation, shall be vested on the date of its entry into force to the ownership of the municipality on whose territory these are situated. The municipality is obliged to maintain the intended purpose of such property. (trans. T.G.)

From among other laws one can mention the Offences Act no. 372/1990 Coll. which ruled that in relation to sport it is not considered an offence against public order to carry bladed weapons in public, if they are designed for sporting activities (§47 subsection 1 letter h). Act no. 543/2002 Coll. on nature and landscape protection in its §§13 et seq. stated that the territory in which a certain level of protection applies requires the consent of authority of nature protection to organize and perform public physical education, sports and tourist events, as well as other publicly accessible social events. Of the many other regulations, one could also mention the Trade Act no. 455/1991 Coll., which provides for a number of trades closely associated with sporting activity.

136. (3) Finally, the last category of legislation with relevance for sports is generally binding legal regulations, in which the concept of sport or physical education may not be mentioned at all, but still these are rules that are also binding on subjects of the sports movement, due to the general jurisdiction of these Acts. These are, for example, the Constitution, Civil Code, Commercial Code or the Criminal Code and others.

A. Genesis of the Current Legislation on Sports

137. The system of current legislation, fragmented into a number of acts governing the physical culture, sport, the Olympic movement, safety at sports events, etc., has undoubtedly failed in meeting the requirements for a modern regulation of the relationship between law and sport. The original intention from 2004, when the first project of an act on sports was prepared, was to combine all these issues together in a single act of Parliament. The Act was to solve matters of institutional and organizational structure of sports organizations, matters of public interest in sports, including health and safety, and legal status of athletes. The Legislative Intent also contained a proposal of *the definition of sport, definition of collective sport and of professional sportsmen*. The intent predicted enrichment of the organizational structure of sport with a special chamber for sport, the list of sporting subjects comprising:

(1) Sports club.
(2) Sports association.
(3) *Chamber for sport.*
(4) SOC.
(5) SPC.
(6) Government bodies and local self-government (Ministry of Education of the SR, Ministry of Defence, Ministry of Interior, higher territorial units, municipalities).

138. The need for the establishment of the Chamber for sport as a voluntary professional association was based on governmental Resolution no. 830/2003, resulting from an analysis according to which, in 2004, there were fifty-six sports associations grouped in the Confederation of Slovak Sports Federations (CSSF) (twenty-seven sports associations were not grouped in the Confederation, however), seven associations were united in the Association of Sports for All, forty-one associations in the Association of PEUs and clubs, six in the SFA, eighteen in the Association of sporting and technical activities of the SR, seven in the Slovak non-traditional sports club and two in Christian Sports Union. Despite the great project, the finally prepared draft from 2006 was submitted neither to the government nor to the parliament.

139. Next in line was a draft bill on sport as *an initiative of parliamentary group of Members of Parliament from 2007,*[50] which in some parts was almost identical, in some other aspects reviewed and amended (e.g., in the regulation of the legal status of a professional sportsman, dispute settlement in sport and others). In its explanatory memorandum, the system of funding of sport was openly criticized, claiming that subjects were financed instead of financing activities. At the end of

50. *See* www.nrsr.sk/Default.aspx?sid=zakony/cpt&ZakZborID=13&CisObdobia=4&ID=335, 30 Dec. 2010.

the day, however, this proposal from 2007 did not become valid law, and the new leftist government subsequently submitted a new proposal, which was largely different from the previous ones.

140. The government bill on the organization and promotion of sports from 2008,[51] unlike previous proposals, dealt expressly with the issue of doping, which was planned by the previous proposals to be regulated separately in a special act. On the other hand, the general part of the explanatory memorandum suggested the omission of some other partial matters and rather to include them in a revised Act on physical culture (Act no. 288/1997 Coll. on physical culture). Specifically, the creation of a national sports tribunal (court of arbitration) within the SOC, and the issue of the accreditation committee, which would examine the level of education in sport, were to be added to the Act on physical culture.

141. Even this very restricted bill was, however, after presentation in the Parliament, significantly amended, and the idea of a uniform national Supreme Arbitration Tribunal for sport has never materialized at all. The definition of sport, collective sports and the idea of division of clubs and competitions into professional and others were abandoned as well. Only the proposed breakdown of the legal forms of sport clubs, which could be established either as a civic association or as a business company not following a business aim pursuant to §56 subsection 1 of the Commercial Code was preserved. The reason for this breakdown was, according to the explanatory memorandum, that under the rules of some international sports federations, participants of top national sporting competitions must have a form of business company, particularly the form of joint-stock companies. Finally, in 2015, a new, revolutionary Act on Sports no. 440/2015 Coll. was adopted, which entered into force as of 1 January 2016, repealing all the previous framework acts that had to do with sports, except the recent Act no. 1/2014 Coll. on the organization of public sporting events.

B. Organization of Sport

1. Act on Physical Culture

142. From among the Acts repealed and replaced by the new Act on Sports no. 440/2015 Coll., the Act no. 288/1997 Coll. of 3 October 1997 on physical culture basically only enumerated the entities operating in the field of physical culture, which were already mentioned above. Closer attention was paid to the state administration in the sporting field. Individual bodies of state administration in the area of care for physical culture were (and still are) in particular:

(1) Ministry of Education of the SR;
(2) Ministry of Defence of the SR;

51. *See* www.nrsr.sk/Default.aspx?sid=zakony/cpt&ZakZborID=13&CisObdobia=4&ID=588, 30 Dec. 2010.

(3) Ministry of Interior of the SR;
(4) Ministry of Health of the SR; and
(5) Ministry of Economy of the SR.

143. The most important ministry in the field of sport is thereby still the *Ministry of Education* (and Sports). Ministries of Interior and Defence perform administrative tasks only in relation to sports organizations, which fall within their competence.

2. Act on the Organization and Promotion of Sports

144. The previous Sports Act, the Act no. 300/2008 Coll. of 2 July 2008 on the organization and promotion of sports and amending certain acts further developed the provisions of the Act on physical culture, which was a *lex generalis* in relation to the Act on the organization and promotion of sports. The Act no. 300/2008 Coll. specifically regulated:

(1) State support of sports, care for sporting talents and sporting activities of children, pupils and students.
(2) Training of athletes to represent the SR.
(3) Measures in the fight against doping in sport and the position of the SADA.
(4) Dispute resolution in sport.
(5) Establishment and management of public administration information system for sport.

145. Unlike the Act on physical culture, the tasks in the field of sport were to be performed under Act no. 300/2008 Coll. only by the Government and three ministries:

(1) Government of the SR;
(2) Ministry of Education of the SR;
(3) Ministry of Defence of the SR; and
(4) Ministry of Interior of the SR.

3. Government and Central Governmental Authorities

146. The *Government* creates conditions for sports representation, for the preparation of sporting talents, sporting outside of school and for the construction of sports facilities of special importance. *The Ministry of Education* was according to the Act no. 300/2008 Coll. (and even under the Act no. 440/2015 Coll. still is) the most important governmental body for the sport. Its role in this area is performed by a special *section of State care for sports.* In particular, it has a role in the following areas:

(1) state administration in sport;
(2) coordination of actors in the field of sport; and
(3) financing of sport.

147. Under the new Act no. 440/2015 Coll., the Government (under §55) is responsible for approving the general concept of development of sports, provides guarantees for major events of international dimension, decides on major construction of sports infrastructure and provides for special support in sports. It can also attribute honorary titles to respectable sportsperson and sports experts. Ministry of Education (and Sports) further (under §58) develops the concept of development of sports in Slovakia, provides for financing and coordination in sports, draws a list of recognized sports, provides for training of best sportsperson selected to represent the country and training of promising sportsperson, runs the electronic information system of sports and supports the construction of infrastructure as well as organization of major sporting events. Additionally, in the premises of Ministry, an office of Main Controller in Sports was established, to perform supervision of all the sports organizations in Slovakia. The controller is appointed by the Government of the SR for a period of five years.

148. The *Ministry of Defence and Ministry of Interior* in conjunction with national sports associations ensure the development of sport, training of sports talents and sports representatives in ministerial sports centres, which are their budgetary organizations.

4. State Budgetary and Subsidized (Contributory) Sports Organizations

a. Military Sports Centre Dukla Banská Bystrica

149. On 1 January 2006, the merger of two existing Army Sports Clubs (ASC) Dukla Banská Bystrica and ASC Dukla Trenčín took place, creating a new *budgetary organization* of the Ministry of Defence – Military Sports Centre Dukla Banská Bystrica, which originally until 31 December 2009 consisted of two clubs: Military Sports Club (MSC) Dukla Banská Bystrica and MSC Dukla Trenčín. After the reorganization on 1 January 2010, the two clubs disappeared, and all the sports sections operate under the auspices of the Military Sports Centre Dukla Banská Bystrica. It is headed by *a Director.*

150. The athletes of the Military Sports Centre Dukla Banská Bystrica have an employee status under the Act no. 552/2003 Coll. on the work in the public interest, and if they are professional soldiers, under provisions of Act no. 281/2015 Coll. on state service of professional soldiers of the SR. A special group of talented young people are active within the Centre upon an agreement on the performance of sports activities concluded on the basis of §51 of the Civil Code.

b. Centre of National Sports Representation of the Ministry of Interior

151. The Centre of National Sports Representation of the Ministry of Interior of the SR was established by the governmental Resolution no. 197/1993 of 1 July 1993. It is a *budgetary organization* with an independent legal personality. It is headed by a *Director.* The main task of the Centre is to provide for the preparation of athletes to represent the SR and especially the athletes of the police sports clubs. Athletes may have a status of 'top' or 'supported' athlete. In the first case, the athlete becomes an employee of the Centre on the basis of a standard contract of employment under the Labour Code. In addition to employees under the Labour Code, the Centre employs athletes and coaches, who are police officers, and their status is governed by Act no. 73/1998 Coll. on civil service of the police forces. Supported athletes are provided only with sporting material, based on a contract under §51 of the Civil Code.

c. National Sports Centre

152. The National Sports Centre (NSC) is a *budgetary organization* directly responsible to the Ministry of Education of the SR, established on 1 January 2004 for an indefinite period. It is headed by a *Director.* It was an outcome of a merger of the Academic Sport Centre of the Ministry of Education and National Sports Institute. Its mission is to provide all-round care for selected sports representatives of the SR and selected talented athletes. By 2010, the NSC employed approximately fourteen athletes in the position of employees. Fifty-four additional athletes were supported by contracts on being provided financial support, depending on their achieved performance. Another 156 athletes were monitored as talents, which means that they are diagnosed by the NSC, and if an association is interested, based on a contract on joint implementation of tasks under §51 of the Civil Code, monitoring of changes in fitness of these athletes can be performed.

d. The SADA

153. The SADA is *a State-subsidized contributory organization* with a separate legal personality, headed by a *Director.* Its foundation charter and statute was issued by the Ministry of Education of the SR on 19 December 2008, with effect from 1 January 2009. Relations between SADA and the Ministry of Education as the founder are arranged through a special 'contract' which is not a classical contract in the meaning of law of obligations, but rather a planning and organizational act defining content and various financial relations between a central government authority and a centrally administered organization. The contract determines mandatory tasks arising for the duration of this contract.

154. The basic purpose of the activities of SADA is to fight against doping in sport in the SR. Albeit a new legal basis of SADA was introduced under the Act on Sports no. 440/2015 Coll. as of 1 January 2016, in general all the previous principles of its organization and competences were preserved.

155. As part of its activities, SADA provides consultation and advice. For example, in 2009, SADA had provided consultation to a total of 308 subjects and in 2010, to 419 subjects, concerning banned substances, interpretation of the rules governing the performance of doping controls and whereabouts information. As of 31 December 2009, SADA worked with twenty-six commissioners and other four candidates, covering the territory of Slovakia. In the year 2010, 629 doping controls were performed with nine identified transgressions (six positive findings and three other transgressions). In the same year, under the national monitoring of whereabouts information, 1,279 athletes were monitored – 777 in individual sports and 502 in collective sports. Under monitoring by international federations, 145 athletes were monitored, with future efforts to reduce this number. In 2010, twenty-two athletes violated the obligation of reporting their whereabouts information. They have subsequently been warned by the first of three possible warnings.

156. Due to the absence of any WADA accredited analytical facility in Slovakia, it is necessary to co-operate with accredited doping laboratories abroad, to ensure analysis of samples in doping control under the WADA International Standard for sample analysis. Samples were hence usually sent to specialized laboratories abroad: Institut für Biochemie DSH Cologne (Germany), Institut für und Dopinganalytik Sportbiochemie Kreischa (Germany), Doping Control Department of General Faculty Hospital in Prague (Czech Republic) and, in particular, the Austrian Laboratories GmbH, WADA Dopingkontrol Labor Seibersdorf (Austria).

157. From the SADA programme for the future one may mention, for example, efforts to expand education and awareness campaigns in the fight against doping in sport, creating high quality information service for athletes and their support staff to obtain information about suitability of various medicines, as well as to initiate a creation of an information system on food supplements and their nutritional composition.

158. Finally, one can mention *other state organizations* in sports, for example, *the Institute of Information and Prognoses of Education*, which carries out an analysis of selected indicators in the physical culture of children and youth, and *the State Pedagogical Institute* every year.

5. Self-Government and Its Budgetary and Contributory Sports Organizations

159. At the level of non-state, local public administration, *autonomous regions* as well as *municipalities* focus on organizing sporting events, construction of sporting facilities and care for physical culture in schools.

160. Act no. 523/2004 Coll. on budgetary rules of public administration in its §21 subsections 1 and 2 first defines the state budgetary and state contributory organizations and then *budgetary and contributory organizations of a municipality or higher territorial unit.* At the municipality level and the level of a higher territorial unit, sporting needs of the population are mainly provided by contributory – subsidized – organizations. A contributory organization is a legal entity, where less than 50% of the cost is covered by business profit, and which is dependent on the municipal budget or the budget of the higher territorial unit through a contribution. Examples include Administration of Sports and Recreation Facilities of the capital city of Bratislava, which is a city contributory organization since 2007. Until 2007, it was a city budgetary organization.

6. Other Entities Regulated in Sports Legislation

161. Other legal persons mentioned in the Act on Sports are foremost the following legal persons.

a. The Olympic Movement

162. The SOSC and the SPC perform tasks associated with ensuring the participation of Slovak sports representation at the Olympic Games and Paralympic Games. According to Act no. 226/1994 Coll. of 18 August 1994 on the use and protection of Olympic symbols and the SOC, the SOC originally was, and under the new Act no. 440/2015 Coll. it still is, a *civic association* (since 2019, renamed to SOSC, with the ambition to become a roof or umbrella sports organization in Slovakia). Its mission is to manage the Olympic movement in Slovakia, whereby it has the status and powers of the national Olympic Committee under the Olympic Charter.

163. The State also specifically protects *Olympic symbols.* Protected Olympic symbols of the IOC comprise the Olympic symbol, the Olympic flag, Olympic motto, Olympic Flame, Olympic Torch, Olympic anthem, Olympic emblem and the words ‘Olympic’ and ‘Olympics’. Special Olympic symbols of the SOSC comprise the emblem (badge), flag and other symbols approved by the IOC.

164. Olympic symbols of the SOSC and of the Organizing Committee of Olympic Games may be used by natural and legal persons and foreign persons in the SR *for commercial or other purposes only in harmony with the Olympic Charter and with the consent of the Olympic Committee,* which is the IOC or the SOSC. Consent of the Olympic committee is not necessary if the Olympic symbols are used to disseminate the ideas of the Olympics.

165. Disputes in matters concerning the protection of Olympic symbols are decided by the courts, and the breach of obligations established by this Act is an offence or criminal act in the area of infringement of copyright, trademark rights, trade names and protected designations of origin.

b. National Sports Associations

166. Under the Act no. 440/2015 Coll., *national sports association* is a *sports organization*, which is:

(1) a member of an international sports federation active worldwide;
(2) performs exclusive jurisdiction for the respective sports in Slovakia;
(3) has at least five clubs and 100 sportsperson registered in the information system of sports;
(4) organizes a Slovak-wide competition for adults and juniors at least for two years consecutively;
(5) selects and trains sportsperson to represent the country in international competitions; and
(6) provides for training of talented sportsperson.

167. The wording '*has at least 100 sportsperson* does not mean that athletes need to be members of the association in the legal sense'.

168. The national sports association finances its tasks specified under the Act on Sports (in §16) as well as all its activities from its own resources and from a subsidy from the State. The Act moreover provides for specific rules for the internal structure, democracy and transparency within the National Sports Associations – e.g., providing for the right to vote to the members, regular meetings of the supreme bodies, drafting minutes from the meetings, providing for quorums to pass changes to the statutes, providing for representation of sportsperson in the structures of the associations, as well as preventing potential conflicts of interest.

169. The national sports association may also establish a business company. For business purposes *in sports representation*, a business company may be established only if the association is the sole shareholder (or shareholder together with the State or a public administrative body) and the company's profit may be used only to fulfil sporting tasks and activities of the association.

c. Sports Clubs

170. Sports club, according to §15 of the Act no. 440/2015 Coll., is a legal entity established for the performance of sport, organization of sports competitions, and for preparation and participation of individuals or teams in competitions. Sports club can in general be established as a *civic association, as a business company*, a *budgetary organization or as a subsidized (contributory) organization.* The latter is the case of ministerial sports clubs and municipality sports organizations.

171. Sports clubs finance their activities from their own resources. These mostly come from:

(1) member contributions;
(2) profit from management of their own property;
(3) revenue from marketing activities and sales of souvenirs (*merchandising*);

(4) revenue from television and radio broadcasting rights to sports competitions and sporting events;
(5) proceeds from the sale of tickets of sporting events;
(6) income from transfers of athletes;
(7) income from international sports federations for participation in international sports competitions and international sporting events;
(8) subsidies from the public administration budgets and grants;
(9) donations and contributions;
(10) other income.

172. A sports club may, just like the national association, establish a business company. The law contains no restriction that the club has to be the only shareholder and that company profits can be used only for sports tasks and club activities.

d. PEUs

173. Another subject of sports movement, which is not *expressly* mentioned in the Act on the organization and promotion of sports, is the PEU. It is a term for sports units of the period before 1989. Currently, they are transformed into civic associations with their own legal personality. By its very nature the unit is not different from the clubs, except perhaps that, unlike most of the clubs, units are usually further broken down to sections, departments, associations, or clubs, while these usually do not have their own legal personality. The question whether the officials of sections or departments within the unit may perform certain acts with legal consequences depends on internal adjustments in the statutes or internal directives. If such an official exceeds his/her competence arising from internal regulation, the acts will bind the organization only if the other party with whom the official acted, could not have known that the official exceeded his/her powers.

C. Funding of Sport in Slovakia

174. According to the Act on physical culture no. 288/1997 Coll., sources of funding physical education were originally in particular:

(1) the State budget sources of at least 0.5% of its annual volume or the sources from the State budget provided for by a special law for the promotion of sport by the State;
(2) proceeds from lotteries and other similar games;
(3) the means of civic associations operating in the field of physical culture;
(4) revenue from the ads;
(5) funds from donations;
(6) funds from corporate loans;
(7) funds from self-governing regions and municipalities.

175. The last amendment to Act no. 300/2008 Coll. on the organization and promotion of sports, i.e., the Act no. 528/2010 Coll., newly modified sources of funding sport. Under this revision, the sources of financing sport included:

(1) the State budget within the budget of the Ministry of Education;
(2) means of the Ministry of Defence and Ministry of Interior within their budgetary chapters;
(3) funds from municipal budgets;
(4) funds from the budgets of higher territorial units;
(5) donations and contributions from legal entities and individuals;
(6) income from business;
(7) sources from the EU;
(8) own funds of entities and individuals engaged in sporting activities;
(9) other sources.

The new Act on Sports no. 440/2015 Coll. aimed at raising the level of State funding of sports. Hence, §77 of the Act presupposes not only financing of sports from the State budget, but additionally specified, that out of gambling, in 2016 25%, in 2017 50%, in 2018 75% and in 2019 100% of the income flowing to the State budget should be redirected to finance the sports. The State funds should be redistributed to sports associations in the form of: (a) obligatory State subsidies; (b) facultative subsidies; (c) contributions to sports projects; and finally (d) contributions to fund sporting of children.

1. Funding Sport and Physical Culture from Gambling

176. Like in other countries, in the SR also the financing of sport, to some extent, is based on gambling, even though it is an indirect relationship in Slovakia – through the State budget. The Act no. 30/2019 Coll. on gambling in its §§70 and 71 imposes upon the operator of gambling a mandatory premium to be paid to the State (or the municipality) budget, the amount of which is mainly determined by a percentage of the gross amount in the individual types of games. The payment is due for most games as an advance payment payable each month. The revenue from the levy under the Act on gambling should be used for the implementation of public benefit services, which comprise, in addition to *the development of sport*, in particular, the provision of health care, provision of social care and humanitarian assistance and care, design, development, protection and restoration of cultural values, support for art and cultural activities, education, development and environmental protection and protection of public health. However, a mechanism that would ensure that a specific portion of the levy is actually used for the development of sport, did not exist until the Act no. 440/2015 Coll. introduced the above-mentioned rule in §77 under which from among the State income out of gambling, in 2016 25%, in 2017 50%, in 2018 75% and in 2019 100% should be used to finance sports.

177. In relation to gambling, it is necessary to mention another aspect of its connection to sport. The sports scores are clearly an object of gambling. The Act no.

30/2019 Coll. on gambling regulates in §8 'betting' as gambling including betting on sports events, that is, 'a sports competition, even virtual one, including horse racing'. In order to operate gambling, a licence is required. Pursuant to §35 and following of the Act, an application for a licence to operate gambling requires specific information and attachments, including a *declaration of the applicant that he/she is not through property, person or otherwise related to sports organizations and clubs operating in the SR, the results of which will be subject to a stake* (§51 subsection 3), and also requiring an *approval of the Ministry of Agriculture of the SR in case of operation of betting on horseracing* (§45).

2. Funding Sport Through Subsidies from the State Budget

178. From the total State budget, traditionally about 0.43% was spent on sports. In 2010, EUR 84,712,046 was available for sports.[52] The Act no. 440/2015 Coll. in its §65 and following states that funding sport from the State budget is implemented through a budgetary chapter of the Ministry of Education by providing subsidies assigned for sport. There is a legal entitlement to provision of the subsidy for each national sports association meeting the set criteria.

179. Additionally, facultative subsidy may be provided on the basis of a contract concluded between the Ministry of Education and the applicant. The Act specifies precisely its essential elements.

a. Funding of Olympic and Non-Olympic Sports

180. Until 2010, principles, conditions and criteria for funding from the State budget were used to ensure the proper allocation of funds, which ensured that the total subsidy for the operation of sports representation is distributed as follows:

(1) Olympic and non-Olympic sports – 97.5%.
(2) Sports of athletes with disabilities – 2.5%.

181. The first category was further divided as follows:

(1) Olympic sports – 85%, from which the team sports received 50%, and individual sports 50%.
(2) Non-Olympic sports – 15%, whereby the team sports received 10%, and individual sports 90%.

From the total subsidy for the *collective Olympic sports*, 20% was shared based on the number of national teams and athletes enrolled among them who in that year took part in major international events, including qualifying matches, and the

52. 'Peniaze zo štátneho rozpočtu na šport', *Športinform* 20, no. 7 (2010): 22, http://www.sportcenter.sk/userfiles/file/Studovna/Sportinform/07_2010.pdf, 30 Dec. 2010.

remaining 80% was shared as per the points that were allocated for placements at major international events and for the results of all games played at these events, including qualifications. Calculation was further multiplied by a *coefficient* of *popularity and coefficient of international competition*. For *individual Olympic sports and non-Olympic sports*, the total subsidy was shared similarly.

182. Albeit these principles were valid only for the period of 2006–2010, they were used further with minor changes – in 2011, sportsperson with disabilities received 3% and the Olympic sports altogether 90%. By the Act no. 440/2015 Coll., a complex system of redistribution was introduced, based on a specific formula to calculate the subsidies, taking into account the achievements of the various fields of sports, and their popularity both in Slovakia and abroad.

b. Financing Sports of Athletes with Disabilities

183. Sports of athletes with disabilities as a second category were funded on the basis of division of sports into specific groups, for example, Paralympic sports and others. Currently, subsidies are also calculated based on the formula given by the Act no. 440/2015 Coll.

184. In other sectors, special regulation on providing funds to promote the sport exists in the form of the Act no. 526/2010 Coll. on granting of subsidies by the Ministry of Interior of the SR. The *Ministry of Defence* provides subsidies to promote the sport on the basis of Act no. 435/2010 Coll. on granting of subsidies by the Ministry of Defence.

3. Funding Sport by the Self-Government

185. In addition to funding from the State budget, sport is also funded by self-governing regions and municipalities. Following examples show the support for sport in three *regions* in 2010:[53] Bratislava region spent only EUR 58,734 of standard expenses and EUR 66,080 of investment expenditures in 2010, thus in total EUR 124,814. The most generous Trnava region spent EUR 223,362. Žilina region on the other hand spent only EUR 24,910 on sport subsidies. Within *municipality* subsidies, one can use an example of the city Stará Ľubovňa (approx. 16,500 inhabitants), which in 2010 contributed to sports clubs in the city the total of EUR 120,850. Another way of funding sports by self-government is an example of the Municipal Assembly of the Slovak capital Bratislava, which by Resolution no. 1184/2006 of 26 October 2006, established as of 30 November 2006 a fund to support the development of physical culture in the capital of the SR, Bratislava.

---

53. 'Podpora športu z rozpočtov českých a slovenských krajov v roku 2009', *Športinform* 20, no. 6 (2010): 5, http://www.sportcenter.sk/userfiles/file/Studovna/Sportinform/06_2010.pdf, 30 Dec. 2010.

D. *Information System*

186. The repealed Act on the organization and promotion of sports from 2008 required the Ministry of Education to perform a newly created task of keeping an information system, which was to contain a register of data from individual sports sectors. The sports register data was to be divided into:

(1) register of national sports associations;
(2) register of sports clubs;
(3) register of sportsmen;
(4) register of sports experts and sports agents;
(5) register of accredited educational institutions under a special regulation;
(6) register of subsidies from the State budget.

This provision of Act no. 300/2008 Coll. did not become a reality before the Act was replaced by the new Act on Sports no. 440/2015 Coll. The new Act has introduced a detailed regulation of the information system in sports, which has still not become a reality in full extent. The new system under §79 and following consists of four modules: (1) register of natural persons in sports; (2) register of legal entities in sports; (3) public portal; and (4) sports experts training module.

E. *Sports Education*

1. Accreditation

187. Another area where the State plays a role and creates a legal framework in sports is the promotion of sports education. Legislation specifically governs the issue of qualification requirements for execution of specialized activities in sports, including education, which used to be State-controlled and accredited before the new Act no. 440/2015 Coll. was introduced. Educational facilities were namely subject to accreditation, carried out by the Accreditation Commission established by the Decree of the Ministry of Education of the SR no. 444/2008 Coll. of 27 October 2008 on the accreditation committee for the area of physical culture and on a single education system for experts in sports of the SR.

188. The certificate of accreditation in sport was attributed to around 140 subjects. Their list was published on the website of the Ministry of Education. Educational facilities then issued to the participants an evidence of proficiency. National sports associations subsequently allowed for carrying out specialized sports activities by issuing and updating licences to sports specialists pursuant to Act no. 300/2008 Coll., §8 subsection 2 letter f. The aim of the Ministry in this area was to ensure that individual facilities provide accredited training in sports in degrees specified in the so-called *uniform education system,* concerning the education for the coaches, referees and other experts. Special requirements for education of organizers of sporting events were specified in the Directive no. 10/2010-R of 20 April

2010 on the education of organizers of sporting events. However, the new Act on Sports no. 440/2015 Coll. has made these rules more flexible and abolished the process of accreditation. Any national sports association can now provide the relevant training and education in cooperation with a university.

2. Sport Schools

189. Guidelines of the Ministry of Education of the SR of 1 February 2002 no. 151/2002-71 on care for sports-talented youth governed the:

(1) sports classes and sports schools;
(2) talented youth centres; and
(3) association youth training centres.

190. Sport classes in schools are established by the principal of the school upon prior approval by the founder, in agreement with the PEU within which they are established, and after inclusion into the network by the Ministry of Education. *Sports schools* are included into the network of schools by the Ministry of Education of the SR on a proposal by the founder. Some schools may have a nature of *centres of Olympic training,* regulated by Methodological guideline no. 17/2009-R of 20 October 2009 on the organization and operation of Olympic training centres. A *Centre for talented youth* serves for sports training of talented youth controlled by the sports association and the CSSF in cooperation with the Ministry of Education. *Association youth training centres* are destined for long-term concentrated sports training of the most talented athletes and of the junior category (under 23 years) in the sports sector. It is established by sports association or upon agreement with the Ministry of Education. Overall, these various forms register 34,204 young athletes, representing 3.5% of the population attending primary and secondary schools (in total 980,114 pupils and students) and 20.5% of the total active sporting youth (167,470 youth athletes registered by sports associations). Additionally, in 2015, a concept of development of movement activities of children and youth was approved by the government of Slovakia.

3. Sports Competitions of Pupils

191. Ministry of Education in cooperation with civic associations in the field of physical culture and other subjects promulgates sports competitions for elementary and secondary schools. The basic document governing a competition is the organizational rules, approved and registered by the Ministry. Current organizational rules have been set by the Ministry under Directive no. 23/2017. It discerns between A, B and C category of competitions. A is organized by the Ministry, B is organized by other legal entities, but subsidized by the Ministry, and C is only registered by the Ministry.

192. With the aim of unification, in February 2010, the Minister appointed a nationwide committee for sports competitions for elementary and secondary school pupils. The Commission has a status of advisory body to the Ministry of Education of the SR.

F. Status of Foreign Athletes in Slovakia

193. Residence of foreigners in the SR is regulated by the Act no. 404/2011 Coll. on the residence of foreigners. The police department may expel foreigners and determine bans of residence for specified reasons (e.g., if the foreigner endangers national security, public order, health or the rights and freedoms of others, or the environment).

194. In relation to *nationals of countries of the European Economic Area* and their families, they may be refused entry to the SR only if:

(1) the foreigner is an undesirable person;
(2) reasonable suspicion exists that the foreigner threatens national security, public order or it is necessary to protect public health; or
(3) the foreigner cannot show a valid travel document or visa, if required.

195. To permit access of *persons outside of the European Economic Area*, the requirement to demonstrate a sufficient amount of funds is imposed in order to prevent the foreigner from becoming a burden for the social system of the State. The Ministry of Interior of the SR shall determine the amount of funds required.

196. For *underage* (minor) athletes an important restriction is that the entry of a foreigner younger than 16 years, who is not a travel document holder, is possible only with a person in whose travel document the person is registered.

197. Foreigner (regardless of nationality) may be granted a temporary residence permit or permanent residence permit. The police department issues the relevant residence document. A temporary residence permit may be granted to a foreigner expressly *for the purpose of a sporting activity.*

198. The foreigners must submit evidence proving to the police an existing health insurance during their stay in the SR and a document certifying that they do not have a disease that threatens public health.

199. The police department may renew a temporary residence permit, otherwise, the permit may expire or be cancelled.

200. The second type of residence permit is *permanent residence.* The permit is first granted for five years. After five years, the police department, on the basis of another application, grants permanent residence for an unlimited time, should all the conditions set by law be fulfilled.

§3. PUBLIC SAFETY

I. Safety at Sports Events

201. Safety of spectators, athletes and other stakeholders is an issue at the international as well as national level. SR is bound by *the European Convention of the Council of Europe on Spectator Violence and Misbehaviour at Sports Events and, in particular, at Football Matches,* which was concluded on 19 August 1985 in Strasbourg. It has been in force since 1 November 1985 and for the SR, it came into force on 1 July 1993. Violence at sporting events is an area that was also identified as critical by the EU and was mentioned in the EU Action Plan Pierre de Coubertin, accompanying the White Paper on Sport. It is also referenced in several documents of the EU Council: Council Recommendation of 22 April 1996, three resolutions of the Council – of 9 June 1997, 21 June 1999 and 6 December 2001 (the latter two relating to police cooperation), and finally, also in a binding Decision 2002/348/JHA (amended by Decision 2007/412/SVV) on safety at the football matches with international aspects, which bound Member States to establish national police files with information that is relevant to football events. Other documents in this area are mainly the Council Resolution of 17 November 2003 on the prohibition of access to sporting events, and the latest Council Resolution of 4 December 2006 concerning a Handbook for police and security authorities concerning cooperation at major events with an international dimension.[54]

202. In this context it is widely discussed whether the ban on attendance at sporting events imposed in a particular city or state can have an effect on other Member States. As counter-arguments, in particular, violation of the principle of proportionality is mentioned, as well as punishing only on suspicion. Similarly, the need for privacy protection of participants in the events is stressed. The result of this controversy is the missing single EU policy. Nonetheless, some convergence took place under the above-mentioned decisions and resolutions promoting police cooperation between the EU Member States.

A. *Act No. 1/2014 Coll. on the Organization of Public Sporting Events*

203. At the national level, issues of health and safety at sporting events are dealt with in the Slovak Act no. 1/2014 Coll. on the organization of public sporting events. This issue of violence at sporting events as well as the safety of participants (athletes, spectators and others) was originally regulated by the Act no. 315/1992 Coll. and then under the Act no. 479/2008 Coll. A comparison of the two regulations was offered by Ž. Surmajová,[55] and it shows that the latter Act has been extended mainly concerning preventive and repressive measures by the organizer. The latter Act also introduced an information system containing personal data and

54. Cf. Žaneta Surmajová, 'Právna úprava eliminácie násilia na športových podujatiach v Slovenskej republike', *Notitiae ex Academia Bratislavensi Iurisprudentiae* 3, no. 1 (2009): 84–85.
55. *Ibid.*

photographs of individuals who were to be prevented from entering sporting events. In fact, however, there remained a problem with obtaining such data and personal portraits. In practice, courts did not provide the organizers of sporting events with portraits of the people who were prohibited to enter by a court decision, and the organizers had no way of identifying these persons.

204. The new Act was drafted in accordance with the concept on combating spectator violence for the years 2013–2016 approved by the Slovak Government Resolution no. 44/2013. The Act is also based on the Council of Europe European Convention on Spectator Violence and Misbehaviour at Sports Events and in particular at football matches, and on the recommendations of the Council of Europe Standing Committee to the Convention.

205. The Act imposes a minimum burden on small sports events (up to 300 spectators), closed community events (organized by school, business company, etc.), as well as events with no recorded previous acts of violence. Small and community sporting events have in fact been exempted from the scope of the Act. Their organization is to be governed only by the general laws and internal regulations of sports federations and national associations. On the other hand, the Act brings stricter rules in the case of sporting events with the special regime, which is where a security risk is present either due to the presence of a greater number of persons at the place of the event, or due to a higher occurrence of security incidents (in case of football or ice hockey) or due to the nature of the event participants. Events of the special regime comprise:

- risk events (of any sports discipline);
- football game or ice hockey matches in two top national competitions for adults, or the last four rounds of cup competitions in football and ice hockey in the adult category;
- event, which foresees the participation of 4,000 or more spectators; or
- event, which foresees more than 90% occupancy of sports facilities with a capacity of at least 2,000 spectators.[56]

206. The Act emphasizes the measures of preventive nature (such as the ban on participation in public events). The law allows for minor offences to impose only reprimand or admonition by the police, if it can be assumed that such measure is sufficient. Other alternatives sanctions are fines (in case of risk events it is up to EUR 1,000), forfeiture and protective measures – such as prohibition of participation in sporting events for up to five years. The Act additionally tightens penalties for violence and misdemeanour recidivism, which may result in criminal liability instead of liability for offences. Within criminal sanctions, the Act provides for a new alternative punishment – punishment of prohibition of participation in public events. It includes the obligation of the accused/convicted person to appear at a

56. Peter Sepeši, *Návrh zákona o organizovaní športových podujatí v medzirezortnom pripomienkovom konaní*, http://www.ucps.sk/Navrh_zakona_o_organizovani_sportovych_podujati_v_medzirezortnom_pripomienkovom_konani, 30 Aug. 2014.

specified time (at the time of the event to which the prohibition applies) at the relevant police station in the place of person's habitual residence.[57]

207. In case of risk events, organizers are required to ensure that all tickets to sectors for fans of guests are sold with the names of ticket holders printed on the tickets. Additionally, a security manager is to be determined by the organizer mandatorily. A new system of training, education and examination of the organizers and security managers was also introduced, whereby the national sports associations will provide respective education by professionally qualified persons.

208. The Act also redefines the role and tasks of persons delegated by sports associations. The delegate is charged with a professional surveillance and with drawing up a report on the events, to which the delegate attaches photos or short videos demonstrating the shortcomings identified in the organization of the sports event.

209. The agenda of hearing respective administrative offences, which was previously in the competence of the municipality, has been moved to the police force of the SR because of a potential conflict of interest, since municipalities are in many cases co-owners (shareholders) or major sponsors of the organizer (club).[58]

210. The Act regulates in greater detail the information system to ensure security at sporting events, containing individual registers and specifying the persons authorized to use the data from the records.

211. The issue of violence and misbehaviour by spectators (fan violence) is closely related to the issues of racism, discrimination, intolerance and other symptoms of extremism. In this respect, the new Act responds to previous legal loopholes consisting of the fact that Slovak law did not know any offences of extremism, resulting in some less serious forms of misconduct either being considered as criminal deeds which were perceived as excessively strict, or they were not sanctioned at all, which was perceived unacceptable.[59]

212. Finally, the police force is now able – in the case of a necessary police intervention in the sports facilities on the grounds of the gross neglect of the duty organizer – to apply for compensation of all reasonably incurred costs of such a police action. The same will apply to the intervention of the municipal police. The Act also provides for the possibility that the police force or the municipal police will provide stewarding services at sports stadiums under contract for consideration, especially at international events and other risk events.[60]

---

57. *Ibid.*
58. *Ibid.*
59. *Ibid.*
60. *Ibid.*

B. Related Criminal Acts and Offences

213. Elements of criminal acts, which may be committed at the stadium, are mostly the standard elements of criminal acts against life, limb and property. Sport is explicitly mentioned only within the *disorderly conduct* offence under §364 of the Criminal Code no. 300/2005 Coll. as an act by which a person verbally or physically, publicly or in a place open to the public commits a gross indecency or riots, in particular, that the person in a rude way *disturbs* a meeting of people or *the due course of sporting or cultural events.* Other criminal acts that can take place in a stadium are mainly the injury to health (§§155–157 Criminal Code), extremist behaviour (§§421–424a Criminal Code) and alcoholism (§363 Criminal Code). Special relationship with the sport can be identified in the measures provided for in §51 of the Criminal Code. Under this regulation, the court may impose on the offender, besides a conditional prison sentence on probation, also a *restriction consisting in the prohibition to visit sporting or other mass events* (§51 subsections 1–3). Additionally, the amendment to the Criminal Code by the Act no. 1/2014 Coll. on the organization of public sporting events has introduced a new type of criminal sanction – prohibition of attendance at sporting events (§§62a and 112a).

214. In case of a milder form of illegal conduct, the rioters may be punished for *an offence* under the Offences Act no. 372/1990 Coll. or for an offence or other administrative delict under the Act no. 1/2014 Coll. on organization of public sporting events. According to §1 of the Offences Act, an offence is a wrongful conduct which violates or threatens the interests of society and is expressly designated as an offence in this or another Act, unless it is other administrative offence punishable under special laws, or a crime. The Act no. 1/2014 Coll. on the organization of public sporting events has amended the Offences Act and introduced a new offence into the Offences Act – the offence of extremism, which is specifically aimed at hooligans, albeit sporting events are not mentioned in this respect in the wording of the offence itself. In addition, with respect to sporting events, the *offence* generally formulated in the Offences Act as offence *in the field of protection against alcoholism and other addictions* (§30), restricting the serving of alcoholic beverages to persons specified by the law, and the drinking of alcohol or ingesting other addictive substances, if the transgressor knows that he/she will perform work or other activities in which he/she could endanger public health or damage the property (e.g., drive a vehicle from the stadium) also come into account.

215. Another possible category of offences to be invoked are *offences against public order* under §47 of the Offences Act, which cover a failure to comply with an order of a public official, stirring up public outrage, breach of conditions designed to protect public order in cultural events or in places of recreation or tourism, damage or wrongful occupation of a public place, making publicly accessible a facility or a public benefit facility, carrying in places accessible to the public cold weapons and other objects that may cause harm, if it is possible from the circumstances of the case to presume that they are to be used for violence or threat of violence, using pyrotechnics in violation of the generally binding legal regulations or instructions for their use. According to §48, offences against public order also comprise a breach of obligations other than those specified in §47, if they are regulated in generally applicable legislation, including the generally binding municipal regulations and generally binding ordinances of local governments, if such conduct harms or disturbs public order. All these violations are sanctioned by a fine.

216. Finally, a battery in the stadium may well lead to a small personal injury, which is punishable as *an offence against civic cohabitation* under §49 of the Act. When intentionally causing damage to foreign property – for example, stadium facilities, this may be an *offence against property* under §50.

217. A perpetrator of an offence in the field of protection against alcoholism and other addictions (§30), offence against public order (§§47 and 48) and the violation of civic cohabitation (§49) may be under §17 of the Act sanctioned by *a restrictive measure* which consists *of the prohibition to visit* publicly accessible areas and rooms where alcoholic beverages are served or where *sporting or cultural events* are taking place. Such a restrictive measure may be imposed only with another penalty and its duration is limited to one year.

C. *Mobile Courts*

218. Introduction of the camera system and the usefulness of recordings as evidence resulted in changes in criminal procedure, when in order to speed up and make it more effective, the amendment to the Criminal Procedure Code introduced the possibility of a court hearing to take place directly and immediately on the spot where the criminal act was committed. This is the institute of so-called *mobile courts* in a new version of §248 subsection 1 of the Criminal Procedure Code:

> Where appropriate and practical, the main hearing may be held directly and immediately on the spot where the offence was committed, with the application of expedited investigation (§203, §204 of this Act) … (trans. T.G.)

This option was introduced by Act no. 93/2010 Coll. as an amendment to the Criminal Procedure Code no. 301/2005 Coll. The project of the mobile courts has previously been applied in the Czech Republic on the basis of an agreement between the Police and the Public Prosecutor, by which a provisional court was created in Prague with the seat at stadium of Sparta Prague. Such an option was possible as the Czech Criminal Procedure Code in §199 allowed to act directly where there had been an infringement, just as it was in Slovakia until 2005, when the old Czechoslovak Criminal Procedure Code no. 141/1961 Coll. was still applicable. The new Slovak Criminal Procedure Code no. 301/2005 Coll. left this option out, to be reintroduced in 2010 by the Act no. 93/2010 Coll.

II. Health Protection in Sports Facilities

219. Issues of safety and health, from a slightly different point of view, were first dealt with in the governmental regulation no. 313/2006 Coll. of 10 May 2006, on details of the requirements for *physical training facilities* and on particulars of their operational policy, and subsequently by the ordinance of the Ministry of Health of the SR no. 525/2007 Coll. of 16 August 2007, on details of the requirements for physical training and sporting facilities. Examples include fitness centres, which must have issued their operating rules in harmony with this ordinance. Operating rules must be located in an appropriate and visible place.

220. The minor restrictions relating to participation in sports and sporting events are also mentioned in the provisions of Act no. 377/2004 Coll. on the protection of non-smokers, prohibiting smoking in sports venues.

III. Private Law Liability in Sport

221. Questions of liability for unlawful conduct in sport are governed by civil (rarely commercial) and criminal law. A classic example is the civil liability of players (athletes), which may arise as a result of an accident. This issue is not specifically regulated in Slovakia. The general rule of civil law, that is, a general preventive obligation enshrined in §415 of the Civil Code applies: 'Everyone is obliged to behave so as to avoid damage to health, property, nature and the environment.' (trans. T.G.)

A. *Sportsman's Liability for Injuries*

222. According to M. Králík, the Slovak author, P. Gališin in 1980s offered a survey of more than forty theories that justify the exclusion or vice versa admit the civil liability for sports injuries.[61] Králík offers an overview of the most important of these theories,[62] and points to a steady Czechoslovak and Czech case laws, which would also probably be followed in similar cases in Slovakia since the legislative basis is still the common former Czechoslovak Civil Code of 1964.

223. The original concept of the Czechoslovak civil liability requires violation of a duty (in case of sports injury it is violation of the general obligation to prevent damage), the damage, causal link between the breach and the occurrence of damage and fault. The most problematic here is the determination of the general obligation of prevention in sport and setting standards of fault.

---

61. Peter Gališin, *Šport a právoIII* (Bratislava: ŠVOČ), 1986. Cf. Michal Králík, 'Civilněprávní odpovědnost sportovců za sportovní úrazy ve světle evropské a světové judikatury 20. a 21. století', *Soudní rozhledy* 12, no. 8 (2006): 285–295.
62. Michal Králík, 'Několik poznámek k právní odpovědnosti sportovců za sportovní úrazy', *Právní rozhledy* 14, no. 15 (2006): 539–548.

224. *Standards of fault* in the case of sporting injuries were already questioned earlier by Czechoslovak courts, namely, in the decision of the Supreme Court of 26 January 1954, Cz 486/53, published in the Collection of Supreme Court, 1954, no. 5, p. under no. 44:

> negligence would be possible to invoke only if the player is moving excessively fast, where he is in danger not arising from the nature of the game. It cannot be considered negligence, when a player does not expect a teammate intentionally violating rules of the game. But it would be negligence if a player saw that his teammate set him a foot, and still he would run to it rapidly. (trans. T.G.)

225. In principle, therefore, danger of the game is usual, and negligence is present only in the event of the failure to take into account imminent danger arising from any other sources than present in the nature of the game. This source may be any behaviour that is not a normal part of the game.

226. Another decision prior to the adoption of the Civil Code of 1964, the Supreme Court decision of 29 October 1962, Cz 38/1962, published in the *Collection of Judgments and Opinions* in 1963 under serial no. 15 further specifies how to evaluate the specific limits of liability, be it intentional or negligent. In principle, it should be evaluated subject to the player's experience, adequacy of the operation and also with regard to whether it was a lawful or unlawful intervention. In practice, therefore, the question of assessing the liability must be determined ad hoc, on a case-by-case basis.

227. The clarification of issues concerning *the prevention obligation* was at the centre of a decision of the Municipal Court in Prague in case of 17 May 1978, 10 Co 190/76, published in the *Collection of Judgments and Opinions* of 1980, under no. 16. From this, it follows that a breach of statutory obligations of prevention certainly is present in the case of non-compliance with the rules of the game:

> non-compliance with rules of the game in sports games (e.g. football), consisting in playing in breach of rules is to be assessed as an act contrary to the obligation to act so to avoid damage to health (§415 Civil Code). Consequently, it is a breach of legal obligation, which establishes liability for damage (§420 subsection 1 Civil Code). (trans. T.G.)

228. In the latest Czech case law from 2003, the Supreme Court of the Czech Republic in a decision of 17 December 2003, 25 Cdo 1960/2002, continues the similar trend of decision-making from 1978 and considers violation of the rules of game as a violation of general prevention obligation: 'A punch by an opponent which is inconsistent with the rules of karate, in which the victim suffered damage to health, is punishable not only under the rules of karate match, but at the same time is a breach of prevention duties … .' (trans. T. G.)' From this argument, it thus

appears that the courts in the Czech Republic and Slovakia currently accept the civil liability of an athlete for injury caused to another athlete, if there is a proven breach of the rules of the game. Liability depends on the evidence of infringement of sporting rules, as a condition to establish an infringement of the general prevention obligation: 'Everyone is obliged to behave so as to avoid damage to health, property, nature and the environment.' (trans. T. G.)'[63]

229. Duty to respect sporting rules (including rules of the game) essentially arise from the rules of the organization of which the athlete becomes a member, namely, the organization in which he/she is registered. This commitment may be expressly stated in the contract with the club. If the contract has no reference to internal regulations to make them binding, Králík argues that the obligation to respect these rules does not arise from the contract.[64] This is, however, in our opinion questionable since it is obvious that the athlete (player), who registered in the sports club, did so in order to pursue sporting activities accepting the conditions of the club. It is therefore certainly at least a tacit agreement.

B. Liability Between the Spectator and the Organizing Service/Organizer

230. Liability for injury caused by athletes to another athlete in the course of the game is only one aspect of civil liability in sport. An athlete may *be also responsible for damage caused to the spectator*, either in connection with the violation of sporting rules or not. Often, however, *the responsibility is taken over by the organizer or organizing service,* which should ensure the safety of spectators. One cannot exclude a shared responsibility of the athlete and the organizer/organizing service. Arguments in assessing the liability are the same as in the case of the athlete's responsibility for an injury caused to another athlete – prevention duty, violation of the duty, damage, causal link and fault. The spectator is not expected to count with excesses, namely, with regard to the violation of the rules of sport (of game). In such a case of excess, only the organizer/organizing service or athlete (or both) bears the responsibility.

231. A similar case was dealt with by the Czechoslovak Supreme Court in the case of a spectator hit by puck in 1981 – Case *1 Cz 37/81*, where the court found that:

> non-compliance and failure to implement measures that are binding on the organizers of sports games (e.g., ice hockey) due to Competition Rules issued by the competent authority of the Czechoslovak Physical Training Association and the directives of this authority for operation and use of equipment in the administration of sports organizations, should be taken into account when assessing the liability for damage caused to spectators at sporting matches,

63. Michal Králík, 'Právní odpovědnost za sportovní úrazy', in *Otázky sportovního práva* (Plzeň: Aleš Čeněk, 2008), 55.
64. *Ibid.*, 62.

> because of the obligation of organizations to behave so as to avoid damage to health (§415 CC), and therefore also because of the breach of legal obligations under §421 subsection 1 CC. (trans. T.G.)

232. However, the mere violation of the rules of sports (not just the rules of the game) in itself does not give rise to civil liability. It is necessary to also prove a breach of the general preventive obligations under the Civil Code.

233. Responsibility between the spectators and organizing service also takes the opposite form – the form of *liability of spectators for the damage they cause in the stadium*, or civil *liability* of *the spectator for a fine* imposed on a club by a sports association or international federation. The inspiration could be a decision of the Higher Regional Court in Rostock (Germany) of 28 April 2006 – Case *3 U 106/05*, which held the spectator responsible for a fine imposed by the football association on the club.

C. Liability between an Athlete and Organizer/Organizing Service

234. Liability *of the athletes to organizers and organizing service and vice versa* arises from specific contractual relations between them, and from the fundamental principles of civil liability (breach of duty, damage, causal link and the fault). The responsibility of the organizing service, that is, the organizer towards the athlete (amateur, in the case of recreational sport) was already dealt with by the court in a case from 1939, where the court considered it the responsibility of the promoter of an ice-rink to consider the safety of visitors. The legal sentence of this decision I Rv 468/39 states:

> Entrepreneur administering the rink assumes by acceptance of fee from the paying visitors a contractual obligation to provide them the opportunity for safe skating and also is responsible for the fault of his employees under §1313 a) of the Civil Code. (trans. T.G.)
> The essence was that the '*entrepreneur is responsible for damage suffered by the visitor upon his/her fall, the cause of which was the poor condition of the ice.*' (trans. T.G.)

D. Liability Between a Coach and Athlete

235. Another possible form of accountability is the *liability of the coach towards the athletes, often minors.* The doctrine of civil liability under the Civil Code and the Family Act makes the parent the first and foremost responsible for a child. Entrusting the care to another person is possible only with the consent of the legal guardian or by a court decision. The question of liability of 'others', for example, coach, is then dependent on the civil liability provisions in the Civil Code. Again, it would be necessary to prove that the coach violated his/her duty, which resulted in a damage (injury), then to prove causation, and a fault of the coach. On the other hand, responsibility for damage caused by a minor athlete is regulated by the Civil Code in §422 and §423 as liability for damage caused by those who cannot assess the consequences of their actions:

> a minor or a person, who is suffering from a mental disorder, is responsible for damage caused by them if they can control their behaviour and assess the consequences; jointly and severally responsible with them is a person, who is obliged to exercise supervision over them. If the person who causes damage, is due to minor age or mental disability, unable to control the conduct or to assess the consequences, the person who is obliged to exercise supervision over them is solely responsible for the damage. Who is obliged to supervise, may relieve himself from liability if he proves that proper oversight was not neglected. (trans. T.G.)

236. Thus, in principle the trainer (coach) is responsible for damage caused by the minor athlete, if he/she neglected surveillance, which is a question of evidence. If the child is unable to assess the consequences of their actions, the coach is liable on his/her own – unless he/she proves that proper oversight was not neglected.

E. Liability of a Club for Injury Caused to an Athlete

237. According to J. Čorba, in sport there also exists a possibility of *commercial law liability.* The club may claim compensation for an injured player from another club whose player caused the injury. This liability relationship arises from the breach of rules laid down by the internal regulations of sports organizations, which both clubs accepted by their membership in a sports association.[65] This case of commercial law liability would be relevant if the two clubs had the legal form of business companies.

IV. Criminal Liability in Sport

238. Until 2005, there existed in the Slovak Criminal Code no. 140/1961 Coll. a material understanding of a criminal act (meaning a real danger to society was to be present), which could lead to staying criminal proceedings due to the lack of the danger for society. This would not influence in any way, criminal liability in cases of corruption or current liability for doping in sports, however, it had a major impact in cases of injury caused while doing sports. This was not considered a socially dangerous act. In contrast, current formalism of criminal law requires, on the other hand, only fulfilment of the constitutive elements of a criminal deed, if circumstances precluding unlawfulness are not present. Minor criminal offences (misdemeanours) are the exception, where still the gravity of the act is taken into account

65. Čorba, *Obchodnoprávne vzt'ahy v oblasti športu*, 157.

as the so-called material corrective. That means that currently even the injuries caused while playing sports could potentially be considered criminal deeds.

239. The question of criminal liability in sporting activities in connection with sporting injuries was at the centre of attention of Czechoslovak lawyers already at the end of the 1970s, although during this period no clear concept of the legal approach to this issue was formulated.[66] Czechoslovak solution was the use of the materialist understanding of the criminal act – if the act was not dangerous to society, the offender was not prosecuted. It was a sort of de facto immunity of sport.

240. After a theoretical examination of this issue by J. Prusák in the 1980s, this issue, like the whole issue of sports law, had to wait for further scientific research until the turn of the twentieth and twenty-first centuries. Its modern-day pioneer in the Czech Republic, and thus, also close to Slovakia, is M. Králík.[67] According to him, the theory of criminal liability of athletes distinguishes three possible approaches:[68]

(1) athletes should be punished for a crime committed within sports always; or
(2) never; or
(3) should not be punished under specific conditions that must be met.

241. These special conditions are explained by various theories, for example:

(1) theory of tolerable risk that the athlete accepts;
(2) the consent of the victim theory (but the problem is that one cannot accept any intervention in health and physical integrity);
(3) theory of customary law;
(4) State permit, expressed by the consent to organize sports events;
(5) theory of unfortunate coincidence, that is, the theory of lack of fault (when even negligence is not found).

242. There are also theories that rely on the specificity – the specific nature of sport, which in itself should enjoy immunity, without any need for regulation, or government recognition. It is a so-called theory of sporting immunity, as long as the behaviour complies with the rules of sport.

A. Czechoslovak and Czech Case Law

243. The beginnings of Czechoslovak criminal law doctrine in relation to sport can be identified already in the inter-war period, under the Criminal Codes of the

66. Jiří Hora, 'K otázce trestní odpovědnosti hráčů při sportovních úrazech', *Acta Universitatis Carolinae Gymnica* 15, no. 1 (1979): 15–24.
67. Michal Králík, 'Trestněprávní odpovědnost sportovců za sportovní úrazy ve světle evropské a světové judikatury 20. a 21. století', *Soudní rozhledy* 12, no. 10 (2006): 365–373.
68. Králík, *Právní odpovědnost za sportovní úrazy*, 38.

Austro-Hungarian Empire, which were still valid in Czechoslovakia until 1950.[69] In the oldest identified Czechoslovak court decision concerning the criminal aspects of sports injuries – Zm II 14/25 – the Supreme Court held that:

> *There is no criminal culpability (§431 Criminal Code), if, prior to boxing, the wrestling arena floor was not covered with a soft blanket and the wrestlers were not examined by a doctor.* (trans. T.G.)
> This was claimed to be an obligation of the organizer. The question of soft blanket was not considered significant by the court, it rather focused on the question of compulsory medical examination. The organizer is, according to the court, not obliged to provide medical examination of athletes, it is the responsibility of athletes to consider their own health: 'diminished prospect of success naturally leads the wrestler, feeling somewhat more seriously indisposed, to withdraw from the match ... ' (trans. T.G.) The court in this case also generally held that in assessing fault in sport 'it remains ... to adjudge risks by their natural consequences and according to the special conditions of employment or of the person of accused'. (trans. T.G.)

244. Issue of risk assessment and the need to take into account the circumstances and conditions of the offender, was dealt with by the court in the award no. Zm II 453/26. It was a case of a street fight, in which the defendant was a boxer. The court, however, rejected the contention that based on experience from the box, it can be automatically assumed that the offender was able to assess the danger of punches in a street brawl. According to the court, the box clearly has an entirely different purpose from a fight in the street. Standards of risk in the box are therefore not comparable with the standards of a street fight, that is, in the fight, it is necessary to consider all the circumstances of the case, and the state of mind, while in sport, the purpose of punches is clear. In this case, therefore, the court focused on the issues of injury caused outside sport field, not injuries caused within sport. The court thereby pointed out that the punches in a battle have a completely different purpose than punches in boxing, a fact that acknowledges the special nature of sport.

245. From the later period, a case from 1985 was a case of injury caused on the field, but outside of the game. An ice hockey player was punished by a sentence of imprisonment for attacking another player on the field, when the puck was already taken over by other players, causing him injuries outside of the game. It is thus clear that this behaviour had not much to do with an accidental injury caused within a game. A defence of any kind of sporting exemption could thus not be invoked.[70] Besides this case, we are not aware of any other cases in which courts would comment on the issue of assessing criminal liability for injuries caused in the sport. This may reflect the above-outlined trends related to the material understanding of the

69. Jozef Kolárik, 'Trestnoprávne predpisy v prvých rokoch existencie Československej republiky', in *Acta Iuridica Sladkoviciensia I* (Sládkovičovo: Vysoká škola v Sládkovičove, 2010), 63–75.
70. Cf. Stanislav Sádovský, *Právní aspekty násilí ve sportu* (Prague: Karolinum, 2010), 74–75.

offence due to which sports injuries were not considered an act dangerous to society, and therefore were not prosecuted before the Czechoslovak courts.

246. From the last years, Králík calls attention to two Czech cases. The first is the resolution of the Supreme Court of the Czech Republic of 11 December 2002, no. 5 Tdo 997/2002, the legal sentence of which states:

> The criminal liability of offenders in sports arises after overstepping the risk arising from the game that every athlete is undergoing, whereby the specific circumstances under which the act occurred are crucial to the finding of fault. (trans. T.G.)
>
> The essence of this approach can be summarized in a sense that the athlete is responsible for injury only if he/she exceeded the risk arising out of the game, and the situation is to be considered on a case-by-case basis. The same is the opinion of the Czech Supreme Court expressed in Resolution 3 Tdo 1355/2006 from 21 March 2007, according to which:
>
> it is strictly necessary to individually assess the injuries suffered by players not only in various types of sport, but also the degree of violation of the rules governing the sports industry. Only on the basis of such assessments it can be concluded that the injuries incurred by an opponent can be sanctioned within the sporting rules, or whether criminal law is applicable … (trans. T.G.)

247. The court specified that the risk arising out of the game should be judged according to 'sports rules', apparently understood as representing the 'rules of the game'. The gravity of an act depends on the degree of violation of sporting rules. The Court thereby understands criminal law as a last resort (*ultima ratio*):

> the Supreme Court in these cases accepts the principle of subsidiarity of criminal law (in addition to subsidiarity of civil law in terms of possible damage caused) and is of the opinion that the standards of criminal law must be applied where the conduct is considered culpable excess from the relevant provisions of the rules of sport in the sense that it is a practice that is not permitted by these rules and is not sanctioned by these rules as regards the effect on health caused by the act. (trans. T.G.)

248. Criminal law is therefore, in the opinion of the court, limited to cases of culpable breach of the rules, which lack (adequate) sporting sanctions. This approach of Czech courts could be summarized in a way that *the criminal act arises under the following conditions:*

(1) serious breach of the rules of sport;
(2) causing the result fulfilling the elements of a criminal act;
(3) causal link;
(4) lack of proportionate penalty imposed by a sports organization; and
(5) fault of the defendant having regard to all circumstances of the act.

249. In this case, it appeared that all the aspects have been met, the crucial aspect was the question of fault. The court finally classified the fault instead of indirect intent only as a gross negligence. Ultimately, having regard to all circumstances, and particularly to the fact that it was a sporting injury, while recognizing criminal liability, the court decided not to impose any criminal sanction.

B. The Current Regulation of Criminal Liability in Sport in Slovakia

250. After an excursion into the Czechoslovak and Czech contemporary case law on sports injuries (possibly even fatal injuries, manslaughter or killing), from a criminal law perspective, we can proceed to consider the possible Slovak solutions when dealing with similar cases. It should be noted that in 2005, the SR adopted a new Criminal Code and Criminal Procedure Code. The material understanding of criminal acts was abandoned and largely replaced by the formal concept. The current Slovak criminal law theory, therefore, does not allow arguing by a lack of social danger anymore. The so-called material corrective may be reflected only in case of criminal offences (misdemeanours).

251. Fundamental *prerequisites of criminal liability* under the criminal law of the SR are the following:

(1) criminally liable entity (natural person aged at least 14 years and one day, sane);
(2) fault (intention or negligence);
(3) act fulfilling elements of a crime listed in the Criminal Code, while in the case of criminal offences (committed through negligence, or intentionally if punishable by imprisonment of less than five years) under §10 subsection 2 it is not an offence, if given the manner of the act and its consequences, and the circumstances under which the act was committed, the degree of fault and motive of the offender is negligible. Similarly, according to §95 subsection 2 'an offence, the features of which are mentioned in this act, is not a criminal offence if committed by a juvenile and its gravity is low'. (trans. T. G.)

252. Theory of criminal law operates within the issue of criminal liability with the so-called *circumstances precluding unlawfulness.* Slovak criminal law distinguishes various such circumstances out of which one is, in particular, applicable to sports. It is the *exercise of rights and obligations* (§28 Criminal Code), which means that:

> an act which is otherwise criminal, is not a criminal deed, if it represents the exercise of rights or obligations arising from generally binding legal regulation, decision of a court or other public authority, performance of work or other tasks or contract, which does not breach generally binding legal regulation or circumvent it, as far as the way the rights and duties are performed does not contradict generally binding legal regulation. (trans. T.G.)

253. Exercise of rights and duties therefore does not need to result from a generally binding regulation, but also from the work tasks or other tasks under a contract.[71] This, however, does not exclude the unlawfulness of every injury. Acting beyond the rules of the game when exercising the duties of a player would still be criminal, 'circumstance precluding unlawfulness is present only if it is performed within established rules ... otherwise criminal liability is not excluded.' (trans. T. G.)'.[72] *Criminal liability is thus applicable only in case of excess from rights and duties, thus from the rules of the game.* However, this does not mean that any breach of the rules of the game should have criminal consequences. The Czech route outlined above speaks in this context of:

(1) serious breach of the rules, meeting the constituent elements of the criminal deed; while
(2) violation is not sufficiently sanctioned by rules of the sports organization; and
(3) fault of the offender is present.

254. Such a definition of the conditions of criminal responsibility would limit the criminal liability only to cases of obvious excesses, which would otherwise go unpunished or unduly punished, making criminal law truly an *ultima ratio*.

255. Finally, as already indicated, the criminal responsibility in sport is connected not only to causing injuries, that is, *bodily harm*, but may also meet elements of other criminal acts. These include, for example, a deed of *killing* pursuant to §147 of the Criminal Code. This lies in the fact that someone 'in the intent to cause grievous bodily harm to another causes death through negligence'. (trans. T.G.) Similarly, the intent may lead *to harm the health of the other.*

256. Negligently caused death is also covered by §149 – the criminal act *of manslaughter*: 'who negligently causes the death of another person, shall be punished by imprisonment of up to three years'. (trans. T.G.)

257. At the very end, it is necessary to draw attention to *another kind of criminal liability in sport – corruption.* Previously, the criminal deed of *bribery* was applicable to sports corruption, as regulated in §332 of the Criminal Code (direct corruption) and in §336 subsection 2 of the Criminal Code (*indirect corruption*).

258. However, the new Act on Sports no. 440/2015 Coll. introduced a new delict of sports corruption in §336b of the Criminal Code, under which (in section 1):

> Whoever, directly or through intermediary promises, offers or bribes another to act or to abstain from acting in order to affect the course or outcome of a sports competition, shall be punished by imprisonment of one to five years.

71. Jaroslav Ivor et al., *Trestné právo hmotné 1* (Bratislava: Iura Edition, 2010), 194.
72. *Ibid.*, 203.

Similarly, whoever, directly or through intermediary, accepts, requires or accepts an offer of a bribe for himself or another to act or to abstain from acting in order to affect the course or outcome of a sports competition shall be punished in the same way as under subsection 1. (trans. T.G.)

§4. TAX

259. Since the sport has an economic effect it necessarily brings certain tax consequences. *Tax system* of the SR consists of direct and indirect taxes.

260. Direct taxes in Slovakia include:

(1) income tax (a tax from income of natural persons and legal persons);
(2) property tax (land tax, tax on buildings, tax on flats);
(3) tax on a dog;
(4) tax on use of public space;
(5) accommodation tax;
(6) tax on vending machines;
(7) tax on non-winning game machines;
(8) tax on entry and parking of motor vehicles in the historic city centre;
(9) nuclear facility tax;
(10) motor vehicle tax.

261. Indirect taxes are the following:

(1) Value Added Tax (VAT); and
(2) excise duties (excise duty on wine, beer, alcohol, tobacco products, mineral oil, electricity, coal and natural gas).

262. From another perspective *income tax and property tax* can be distinguished.[73] For the sport, VAT, income tax and property tax are of particular relevance. Other taxes are too specific and not directly connected to any sporting activity.

I. VAT

263. The VAT is regulated in the SR by the Act no. 222/2004 Coll. of 6 April 2004 on VAT. This tax is imposed on:

(1) supply for consideration within the country;
(2) service (delivery of service) for consideration within the country;

73. Ladislav Balko et al., *Finančné právo*, 2nd ed. (Bratislava: Bratislavská vysoká škola práva, 2009), 192.

(3) acquisition of goods for consideration in the country from another Member State of the EU; and
(4) import of goods into the country.

264. The tax *base* for the supply of goods or services is *everything which constitutes a consideration* that the supplier received or is to receive from the recipient of the transaction or any other person for the supply of goods or services, *minus tax.* The place of taxable transaction in the case of *supply of goods* is the place of delivery of goods or in the case of transport the place of departure (but in the case of catalogue shopping, it is the place of delivery), otherwise the installation site, or the place where the personal transport services start. In the case of *delivery of services,* it is the principal place of business/establishment; in the case of *import from another Member State,* it is the place of delivery, or the place of first entry into the EU Member State.

265. The *basic tax rate* is 20% (for some products it is 10%, or 6% respectively) from 1 January 2011 to the last day of the calendar year in which the European Commission (Eurostat) publishes data on the actual general government deficit of the SR, being less than 3%. Then the rate drops to 19%, that is, the previous rate.

266. Taxable person is any person who independently carries out any economic activity, whatever is the purpose or result of this activity, and even though the person has not been established for business purposes.[74] Economic activity means any activity from which income arises, and that includes:

(1) activities of producers, traders and service providers, including mining, construction and agricultural activities;
(2) activity undertaken as a profession, according to special regulations;
(3) intellectual creative activity; and
(4) *sporting activity.*

267. This means that sports clubs and athletes, as self-employed persons, are taxable persons for the sake of VAT. Sporting activity is explicitly deemed as a supply of services. According to §16 subsection 3:

> The place of supply of cultural, artistic, *sporting*, scientific, educational, entertainment and similar services, such as services at exhibitions and fairs, including their organization and related ancillary services and entry to these events, if those services are delivered by a person other than taxable person, is the place where the services are physically carried out. The place of supply of services in connection with admission to cultural, artistic, sporting, scientific, educational, entertainment and other similar events such as exhibitions and fairs,

74. *Ibid.*, 206.

and ancillary services associated with this entry, if the services are supplied by a taxable person, is the place where these events actually take place. (trans. T.G.)

268. Entities with a turnover of EUR 49,790 or more in the previous twelve calendar months, are required to lodge an application to the tax authorities *for tax registration.*

II. Income Tax

269. Direct taxes in sport are imposed on formal property (income) and material assets (material property – real estate). The most relevant is *income tax.* Income tax is governed by the Act no. 595/2003 Coll. of 4 December 2003 on income tax as amended. This is a flat rate tax, meaning its *rate* is currently fixed at 19%.

270. In the case of *natural persons,* subject to tax is the following income representing a *tax base:*

(1) income from employment (§5);
(2) income *from activity of a sportsperson or of a sports expert* (§6 subsection 2 letter e);
(3) capital income (§7);
(4) *other income* (§8).

271. As far as the *taxable person* is concerned, a distinction is made between *residents* (who spend at least 183 days a year in Slovakia, but not as a student, or patient in medical treatment), whose worldwide income is taxed in Slovakia, and *non-residents* who are taxed only on income with a source in Slovakia.

272. Whereas in the SR, a majority of athletes did not have the status of an employee previously (except for employees of the state budgetary and contributory organizations), they were taxed as self-employed persons and their income came 'from other self-employment'. Since the coming into force of the Act no. 440/2015 Coll., the inclusion under income from dependent work under §5 of the Act on income tax took place, which speaks in letter m of revenue 'from the activity of a sportsperson based on the contract on professional performance of sport under special law'. In case of self-employed sportsperson, their income is to be newly considered under §6 subsection 2 letter e as coming 'from activity of a sportsperson or of a sports expert'.

273. In the case of *corporate tax*, similar to natural persons, one can distinguish between legal person with unlimited tax liability and person with limited tax liability to be taxed only on income from Slovakia. Details on taxation of civic associations and business companies established for purposes other than for business purposes will be mentioned in the Part 2 of this work.

III. International Taxation of Income

274. If a taxpayer with unlimited tax liability receives revenue from a country with which Slovakia has entered into an agreement on avoidance of double taxation, the procedure for the avoidance of double taxation under this agreement will be used. Where under the agreement a *tax credit method* is applicable, the tax paid in the other contracting state shall be set off against the payment of tax under Act no. 595/2003 Coll. up to a maximum amount that may be levied by the other contracting state in accordance with this agreement. The tax credit shall be given up to the amount of tax attributable to income from foreign sources. Where under the agreement an *exemption method* applies, tax base from income subject to taxation abroad for the purposes of exemption is the tax base as quantified under §5 subsection 8 of the Act or the difference between taxable income from foreign sources and tax expenditures. The exemption method will also be applied if the taxpayer with unlimited tax liability derives income from dependent work abroad, from a country with which the SR has not concluded an agreement, if these revenues were provably taxed abroad. The exemption method would thus also be applied in cases of income derived from foreign sources in a country with which the SR has concluded an agreement, and these revenues have probably been taxed abroad, if this procedure is more advantageous for the taxpayer.

IV. Real Estate Tax

275. Clubs and associations are subject to *local taxes* – specifically, the taxes levied by the municipality, mainly the *real estate tax* (on land and buildings, or dwellings) based on the Act no. 582/2004 Coll., whereby under §17 subsection 2 the tax authority can provide by a generally binding regulation a tax reduction or exemption from land tax on parks open to the public and from tax on sports facilities (letter e).

§5. Dispute Settlement

I. Right to a Fair Trial

276. The right to a fair trial is a fundamental constitutional principle (Article 46 section 1 of the Constitution of SR), but also international legal principle enshrined in all the conventions on human rights and fundamental freedoms.[75] The Constitution specifically provides for:

(1) right to claim the rights at independent and impartial court (Article 46 section 1);

75. Marek Števček, *Right to a Fair Trial in Relation to Judiciary System of the Slovak Republic*, in *Prawa czlowieka* 128–137 (Oficyna Wydawnicza Waclaw Walasek, 2008).

(2) right to go to court to review the decision of a public authority (Article 46 section 2);
(3) right to public hearing without undue delay (Article 48 section 2); and
(4) presumption of innocence (Article 50 section 2).

277. The Universal Declaration of Human Rights of 1948 guaranteed the right to an effective protection by relevant national courts against acts violating the fundamental rights granted by constitution or by law (Article 8). Article 10 fully guarantees the right to a fair and public hearing by an independent and impartial tribunal, deciding on rights and obligations and on any criminal charge. The European Convention (of Council of Europe) for the Protection of Human Rights and Fundamental Freedoms from 1950 in its Article 6 also guarantees the right to a fair trial. Moreover, Article 13 of the Convention guarantees the right to an effective remedy. Finally, Articles 47 and 48 of the Charter of Fundamental Rights of EU as a legally binding document (by reference in the Lisbon Treaty from 2009) enshrines the right to a fair trial as a procedural guarantee of rights and freedoms.

278. In terms of sport, these provisions are important in the context of whether the right to a fair trial includes *arbitration and disciplinary proceedings within the sports organizations,* which may lead to a restriction of sporting activity, that is, basically, of an occupation of the player. The right to a fair trial means that when a sports organization by its decision (or act or omission) interferes with the rights and freedoms of an athlete, the athlete should always have the opportunity to have this decision (act, omission) reviewed by the court. In practice, however, internal rules of sporting organizations explicitly prohibit athletes to turn to civil courts. Such provisions are entirely void for inconsistency with the fundamental rights of athletes. Any interference with the rights and freedoms is reviewable by ordinary courts or arbitration courts to which the parties submit their case.

279. Review process by courts was governed by the Slovak Civil Procedure Code no. 99/1963 Coll. until 1 July 2016, replaced since then by three new codes – for litigious, non-litigious and administrative procedures, no. 160–162/2015 Coll.,[76] specifying standards for protection and enforcement of the substantive law and rights guaranteed at all three levels of the judicial proceedings in Slovakia – district, regional and Supreme Court. Exceptional decision-making by the Constitutional Court is governed by Act no. 38/1993 Coll. The administrative judiciary is represented by specialized judges and panels within the general system of courts, mainly on the second – regional – level of courts.

---

76. Marek Števček et al., *Občiansky súdny poriadok: Komentár* (Prague: C.H.Beck, 2009).

II. Arbitration

280. In addition to the system of national and international courts, the right to a fair trial also includes the protection of litigants in an arbitration.[77] Alternative dispute resolution in Slovakia is governed by a special Act no. 244/2002 Coll. of 3 April 2002 Arbitration Act that governs:

(1) deciding property disputes arising from domestic and international, commercial, and civil relations (but not, for example, labour disputes), if the place of arbitration is in the SR; and
(2) recognition and enforcement of domestic and foreign arbitration awards in the SR.

281. According to the Arbitration Act, within arbitration procedure, only those disputes may be decided, which the parties can conclude by settlement. It is expressly prohibited to decide disputes:

(1) concerning the establishment, modification or termination of ownership rights and other rights to immovable property;
(2) concerning personal status;
(3) associated with enforcement of a decision;
(4) incurred during the bankruptcy and restructuring proceedings.

282. The same limits apply to use of the arbitration method in sports. The use of arbitration services in sport should therefore be allowed only when dealing with certain issues. If an athlete were in a regular employment relationship with a sports organization, the settlement of labour disputes would be excluded from the scope of any arbitration. Still, it may be questionable whether the disputes between sports organizations and sportsperson under the Act no. 440/2015 Coll. on Sports are arbitrable. It is namely only the Labour Code that precludes employment disputes from being arbitrable, and the Labour Code is not applicable to sportsperson unless the Act on Sports provides otherwise. Still, the majority opinion in Slovakia currently is that despite the fact that Labour Code does not apply to sportsperson, their disputes with sports organizations are not arbitrable. This approach, however, makes the whole system of judicial dispute resolution in sporting employment dependent on regular courts, where the procedure can take years.

283. The Arbitration Act allows parties to agree on a person of arbitrator (arbitrators) or on a procedure for appointment of the arbitrator. This agreement should have a form of a written contract or of a contract clause. Only specific legal persons such as sporting associations, professional chambers or associations of legal persons may establish and maintain *an arbitration court.* Its establishment is notified in the Business Journal. A register is kept by the Ministry of Justice, and it is also

77. Marek Števček, 'Základné teoretické problémy a východiská rozhodcovského konania v Slovenskej republike', in *Aktuálne problémy vovývoji právaSR a ČR* (Bratislava: VO PraF UK, 2008), 114–121.

published on its website.[78] Each arbitration court must have its own statute and rules of procedure. Every arbitration court also maintains a list of arbitrators, although the parties to the arbitration may also appoint an unregistered person as an arbitrator.

284. At present, there are only two sporting arbitration courts in Slovakia – *Arbitration Court of the Slovak Curling Association* and the *Slovak Mediation and Arbitration Centre of the Slovak Squash Association.* With regard to the former Arbitration Court of the SFA, in 2016, its competences were transferred to the SFA Dispute Resolution Chamber. Thereby, neither the Dispute Resolution Chamber nor any other body of sports associations in Slovakia has an official character of an arbitration court.

285. An application to the arbitration court has thereby the same legal effect as if the action was brought to a regular court. After the initiation of arbitration, no longer can the same thing be presented to a court or before any other arbitration court. The arbitral tribunal may like any formal court grant an interim relief if it deems it necessary, upon an application by the party. The enforcement of an interim measure may be performed by the ordinary court, upon request. Similarly, if the tribunal cannot ensure the production of evidence on its own, it may ask the regular court for intervention.

286. A very important issue, particularly in cross-border disputes, is the question of applicable law. The arbitral tribunal shall decide according to the law upon which the parties agree. If the parties fail to agree on applicable law, the court decides according to the law determined by domestic conflict rules, in case of the SR contained in the Act on International Private and Procedural Law no. 97/1963 Coll. In domestic disputes, the court shall proceed under the Slovak law. The court also takes into account the provisions of the contract concluded between the parties, commercial practices, fair trade principles and good morals. The arbitral tribunal may also decide commercial disputes solely on the basis of principles of equity (*ex aequo et bono*) notwithstanding the existence of legal norms. It is permissible only if the parties to arbitration explicitly authorize the arbitration tribunal to do so.

287. According to the Act, an arbitration award, which cannot be examined by any other arbitrator on the basis of a prior agreement between the parties, has the same effect as a final court decision. After the decision, the annulment of the arbitration award may be requested by an action filed with the competent court within sixty days from receipt of the award, but only upon conditions which became very strictly formulated through an amendment effective as of 1 January 2015.

288. After bringing an action to the court, the arbitration award remains valid. The court, ruling on an appeal, may, upon application, postpone the enforceability of the arbitration award.

---

78. *See* https://www.justice.gov.sk/Stranky/Registre/Dalsie-uzitocne-zoznamy-a-registre/Rozhodcovske-sudy/Zoznam-rozhodcovskych-sudov.aspx, 6 Jan. 2011.

289. A party seeking recognition and enforcement of a foreign arbitration award is required to submit a written *application for recognition and enforcement of* foreign arbitration award to the court and attach an original of the foreign arbitration award or a certified copy and the original arbitration agreement or a certified copy, along with an official translation into Slovak language. It is however important to note that the effects can be granted only to an arbitration decision which is not beyond the arbitration jurisdiction under Slovak law – the Act on Arbitration. We have already explicitly pointed out that the Slovak law does not allow arbitration in labour matters and many other issues. In the event that the foreign decision meets the requirements of the Slovak arbitration, recognition of foreign arbitration award does not require a specific judicial decision. A foreign decision is recognized by the court by considering it as if it were a domestic arbitration award. Recognition and enforcement of foreign arbitration *award may be denied by the court upon proposal* from a party, only if that party can show to the court that there were procedural errors in the process of awarding the arbitral award. The *Court refuses* recognition and enforcement of foreign arbitration *award even without a motion by a party* if it finds that under the law of the SR, the matter cannot be resolved in arbitration or if the recognition and enforcement would be contrary to public policy. Denial must always be justified.

Chapter 3. Private Regulation

290. The autonomous sports movement in Slovakia comprises at the regional and local level some 7,000 sports clubs and organizations. There are a few superior (roof, umbrella) sports organizations, which are in different mutual relationships:[79]

(1) SOSC.
(2) SPC.
(3) SAPC.
(4) CSSF.
(5) Slovak Sport for all Association.
(6) Association of Sports Clubs of the SR.
(7) Association of Technical and Sporting Activities of the SR.
(8) Association of Technical and Sporting Activities of Regions of the SR.
(9) Slovak Schoolsport Association.
(10) Slovak University Sports Association.
(11) Special Olympics Slovakia.
(12) Christian Sport Union.
(13) Slovak Orol.
(14) Slovak Sokol.
(15) Slovak University Federation of Technical Sports.
(16) Slovak Federation of Technical Sports.
(17) Slovak Federation for Physical Testing.
(18) Police Sport Clubs Union.
(19) Zálesák – Slovak Branch of Hiking.
(20) Association of Children and Youth Sport.
(21) Slovak Union of Physical Education, Sport and Recreation.

291. Other organizations associated with sporting activities and athletes are mainly:

(1) The Slovak Pierre de Coubertin Committee.
(2) Sport Journalist Association of Slovakia.
(3) Physical Culture Museum in the SR.
(4) Slovak Society of Olympic and Sports Philately.
(5) The Society of Sport Psychology.
(6) Slovak Society of Sport Medicine.
(7) Slovak Scientific Society for Physical Education and Sport.
(8) Slovak Society of Olympic and Sport Symbolics.

292. In general, it is possible to split the sports movement in Slovakia into:

(1) umbrella organizations, bringing together a variety of sports organizations, especially national sports associations;

79. *See* www.adapt-europe.org/slovakia/sport.htm, 28 Dec. 2010.

(2) national sports associations; and
(3) clubs.

293. Basic principles of their operation show the following features:

(1) In terms of *legal status*, the umbrella organizations of national associations are civic associations founded under the Act no. 83/1990 Coll. on association of citizens, or associations formed under a contract of association according to §16 of Act no. 83/1990 Coll. (e.g., SBA). A form of interest association of legal persons pursuant to Civil Code §20f may also be used (e.g., the ULC within the SFA). Clubs take usually the form of civic associations (called club or PEU, while both types may contain more sections without legal personality, covering a variety of sports) or business companies. A rare form is that of contributory or budgetary organizations connected to the national budget, that is, the budget of central government authorities, higher territorial units or municipality budget.
(2) In view of their *organization*, umbrella organizations are made up of several types of sports organizations – not only national associations mainly, but also other umbrella organizations. National associations do not comprise only clubs but also various provincial or regional associations. Clubs and PEUs, in turn, may consist of the already mentioned different units known as divisions, associations, sections or clubs, which usually lack separate legal personality.
(3) In terms *of membership*, one can distinguish between organizations that bring together only legal persons and associations of legal and natural persons. When uniting individuals (from 7 years of age, for example, in the case of the Slovak Ski Association), these may be in some cases individual members, in other cases, however, they have only indirect membership through the club, that is, organizations of which they are members. In most cases, sports civic associations also allow membership of individuals, at least in the form of honorary membership.
(4) In view of the *bodies*, all the organizations have a broad membership meeting (general assembly, congress, conference), which may meet at a lower frequency. Moreover, a permanent body (Board, Executive Committee), and usually also a control body (Supervisory Board, the Audit Commission) and a President or also a Secretary General at the head of the Secretariat are established.
(5) In terms of *assets* and management, the organizations typically manage their own assets and received subsidies, as well as their income from their own activities. Civic associations may in fact be carriers of business licences, although their goal is not (should not be) primarily the distribution of profit, but only to use the business profit for the purpose of fulfilling their primary mission – the promotion and implementation of sporting activities.

§1. UMBRELLA SPORTS ORGANIZATIONS IN THE SR

I. The SOSC

294. The SOC was founded in 1992 and was recognized as a National Olympic Committee of the SR on 24 September 1993, at the 101st meeting of the IOC. Previously, in the territory of the SR, the Czechoslovak Olympic Committee in Prague had this competence.

295. The SOC (renamed in 2019 to SOSC) mission is to disseminate and popularize the fundamental principles of Olympics, and thereby contribute to the harmonious development of human beings and mutual understanding and friendship among nations and for the deepening of peaceful coexistence. The Olympic movement in Slovakia comprises the national sports associations representing sports that are included in the Olympic Games and Winter Olympic Games, and further athletes, referees, coaches and others. The Olympic movement also includes other sports associations, organizations and institutions recognized and authorized by the SOC. The SOSC is composed of members and honorary members.

296. The SOSC bodies are:

(1) General Assembly.
(2) Executive Committee.
(3) President elected by the General Assembly.
(4) Secretary General.
(5) Supervisory Board.

297. The President and the Secretary General are statutory bodies of the SOSC.

298. The SOSC budget is approved each calendar year by the General Assembly of SOSC. The SOSC can also set up business companies or join a business company.

II. The SPC

299. The SPC was created on 31 January 1995 upon the initiative of associations of disabled athletes (the Slovak Federation of Sportsmen with Physical Disabilities, Association of the Blind and Poor Eye-sighted Slovak Sportsmen, the Slovak Federation of Sportsmen with Mental Disabilities and the Slovak Federation of Deaf Sportsmen, whereby the last one has left SPC in 2005 to establish its own Slovak Deaflympic Committee). The SPC is a member of the International Paralympic Committee and the European Paralympic Committee. Its member organizations are:

(1) Slovak Federation of Sportsmen with Physical Disabilities.
(2) Association of the Blind and Poor Eye-sighted Slovak Sportsmen.

(3) Slovak Federation of Sportsmen with Mental Disabilities.

III. The SAPC

300. The SAPC is a civic association, comprising legal entities of physical culture with nationwide coverage, based on the Act no. 83/1990 Coll. It is the legal successor of the Czechoslovak Association of Physical Education. The SAPC bodies are:

(1) General Assembly.
(2) Executive Committee.
(3) Audit Commission.

301. The SAPC is a civic association made up of only legal persons with no individuals as members. More appropriate solution would therefore be an association of legal persons pursuant to Civil Code §20f. An alternative solution would be to use §16 of Act no. 83/1990 Coll. on association of citizens.

302. The ordinary SAPC members are:

(1) Association of Sports Clubs of the SR.
(2) CSSF.
(3) Slovak Sport for all Association.
(4) SFA.

303. From among the four members, closer attention will be paid here to the CSSF and the SFA; the latter will be explored when discussing national sports associations.

IV. The CSSF

304. According to its statutes, the CSSF as the legal successor of the Association of Sports Federations of the SR is a civic association of sporting organizations and has a separate legal personality.

305. Members are only sports associations (i.e., only legal persons). Every sports sector can be represented by no more than one association. An organization representing non-member associations can become an associate member of the CSSF.

306. The CSSF bodies are:

(1) General Assembly.
(2) Executive Committee.

(3) Control Commission.
(4) President.
(5) General Secretary.

V. Slovak University Sport Association (SUSA)

307. The SUSA is a special type of umbrella organization, because it is oriented neither generally nor based on a sector of sports, but rather organized by object – focusing on university sports. The SUSA is explicitly a civic association of natural and legal persons involved in university and college sports in Slovakia.

308. The bodies of SUSA are:

(1) Council.
(2) Executive Committee.
(3) Regional Councils.
(4) Supervisory Board.

§2. National Sports Associations

309. The legal status, legal form, rights and obligations of the national sports associations are governed by the Act no. 440/2015 Coll. on Sports. From the large number of associations, the most popular sports associations in Slovakia take the legal form of civic associations and of an association of civic associations.

I. The SFA

310. The SFA, founded in 1938, is the largest sports organization in Slovakia, claiming to have 427,102 members. It has a status of a *civic association.* SFA is a member of the FIFA and UEFA.

311. It is made up of:

(1) ordinary members (football clubs, the regional football associations, provincial football associations, the ULC, union of football coaches, Association of Professional Footballers of Slovakia (APFS), association of referees and others);
(2) associates (e.g., women's football); and
(3) honorary members.

312. According to the statutes of the SFA, the regional and provincial football associations are responsible for the development of amateur football within their territorial jurisdiction. Establishment or abolishment of a regional or provincial football association must be approved by the conference of the SFA. Statutes and other standards of provincial and regional football associations must not contravene the statutes of SFA. Statutes of provincial football associations must not contravene the statutes of the regional associations either.

313. The SFA's bodies are:

(1) Conference.
(2) Executive Committee.
(3) President.
(4) General Secretary.
(5) Audit Commission.
(6) Electoral Commission.
(7) Expert Commissions.
(8) Dispute resolution and conciliation bodies – Disciplinary Commission (DC), dispute resolution chamber, appeals commission and licensing bodies.
(9) Administrative panels and working groups.

314. From among the individual members of the SFA attention will be paid to the ULC and the APFS.

A. The ULC

315. The ULC is the governing body of the highest competitions, the so-called Fortuna League and of the I. league. It possesses the form of *an interest association of legal persons* established under the provisions of §§20f et seq. Act no. 40/1964 Coll. Civil Code, as amended.

316. Members of the association may be legal entities with separate legal personalities, namely, football clubs. Membership is a requirement for admission to the two top football competitions. On the other hand, participation in the two highest competitions is at the same time a condition of membership in the ULC. The functioning of this system can be enforced only under monopoly of the ULC as the governing body of the two competitions. A change in membership occurs automatically after each year of the highly ranked football competitions, so that:

(1) *membership in the association rises to a football club*, the team of which met the conditions of binding application and managed to proceed from the lower level of competition into one of the top two football competitions, unless the football club already has another team in the top two football competitions;

(2) *membership in the association expires to a football club*, the team of which has been relegated from the top two football competitions into the lower level competitions, unless the football club has another team in the top two football competitions.

317. The ULC implements its mission through the bodies, which are:

(1) Presidium.
(2) President.
(3) Executive Committee.

B. Union of Football Professionals (UFP)

318. The UFP is a civic association formed pursuant to Act no. 83/1990 Coll. in order to be a professional organization of professional football players, to enter into partnership with the ULC, the Association of Referees, as well as other similar professional organizations and associations, and to become a member of the FIFPro.

319. The bodies of the UFP are:

(1) General Assembly.
(2) Presidency.
(3) President.
(4) Supervisory Board.

II. Slovak Ice Hockey Federation (SIHF)

320. The SIHF is registered as a *civic association.* Its members are divided into ordinary and honorary members. Ordinary members are clubs that can take the form of:

(1) civic associations, created under Act no. 83/1990 Coll.;
(2) business companies formed under the Commercial Code;
(3) contributory organizations established in accordance with the Act no. 523/2004 Coll. on budgetary rules; or
(4) non-profit organizations under the provisions of the Act. no. 213/1997 Coll. on non-profit organizations providing public benefit services, as amended.

321. Ordinary members may also be other legal entities with nationwide coverage, the object of which is focused on hockey. The basic organizational units of SIHF are sections – ice hockey clubs. These may set up their regional associations, and create and manage competitions in all categories. Efforts to safeguard the principle of hierarchy and monopoly in ice hockey are expressed in the statutes through the requirement for harmony between the statutes of the SIHF and its members.

Another provision with a similar goal is that which provides that final resolutions and decisions of SIHF are binding and final for the members of SIHF.

322. The SIHF bodies are:

(1) Congress.
(2) President.
(3) Executive Committee.
(4) Supervisory Board.
(5) DC.
(6) Other commissions.

III. The SBA

323. The SBA is a sports association originally formed in accordance with §16 of Act no. 83/1990 Coll. on the association of citizens, as an *association of associations, created under a contract on collaboration.* Paragraph 16 of Act no. 83/1990 Coll. provides that such associations should be regarded as an ordinary association. The SBA is therefore registered in the Register of civic associations.

324. Despite being an association of associations, even under the new statutes from 2016, there are three different types of members of the SBA:

(1) individual membership, that is, membership of an individual natural person;
(2) membership of a legal person in accordance with the Act no. 83/1990 Coll. as a collective membership;
(3) membership of interest groups and unions without legal personality, as a collective membership.

325. In case an individual is not a member of any sports club or professional association, he/she may become an individual member of the SBA based on the SBA Executive Committee decision. Evidence of membership of an individual is a licence or a member card of the SBA.

326. The SBA collective entities with legal personality are mainly basketball clubs and their associations:

(1) Association of men's basketball clubs.
(2) Association of women's basketball clubs.
(3) Regional basketball associations.
(4) Coaches' Association.
(5) Players' Association.
(6) Centre of Olympic hopes of the SBA.

327. Expert bodies within the SBA are the following:

(1) Arbitration Commission.
(2) Anti-doping Commission.
(3) Other commissions.

328. The supreme SBA bodies are:

(1) Conference.
(2) President.
(3) Executive Committee.
(4) Controller.

329. Within the SBA, as in the case of football and tennis, provincial and regional associations are created.

§3. Clubs

I. Club as a Civic Association

A. One-Sport Club

330. Civic associations – clubs or PEUs – usually have a standard structure of bodies as envisaged by the Act no. 83/1990 Coll. on association of citizens. An example is the statutes of the football club KFC Komárno.[80]

331. According to Articles 4 and 5 of the Statutes, the club has ordinary members and honorary members. A member may be every citizen, regardless of nationality, political and religious affiliations. The ordinary membership starts with the registration and payment of a basic membership fee, which is determined by the Executive Committee at the beginning of each calendar year. *Ordinary members are also players of legal age, who are duly registered* and involved in the squad of men, or juniors in the current competition year, until the end of their football activities at the club.

332. The bodies of the club are:

(1) Members' Assembly.
(2) President.
(3) Executive Committee.
(4) Commission.

80. *See* www.kfckomarno.sk/svk/pages/stanovy/, 31 Dec. 2010.

B. Club of a Number of Sports

333. Sports club, as well as an PEU, may not only focus on one particular sport. The proof is the statutes of the Sports Club Miloslavov, which is a civic association in terms of the Act no. 83/1990 Coll. on the association of citizens. Sporting interests and needs that the club meets, are, in particular, tennis, table tennis, football, ice hockey, cycling, hiking, dancing school, chess, etc.

334. An interesting feature is the regulation of business activity of this club – in this case, the Ministry of Interior registered an association, the statutes of which involved carrying out the business – but with the rule that the proceeds may be used only for the primary mission of the club (Article 2 section 2, letter g).

335. According to Articles 4 and 5 of the statutes of the Sports Club Miloslavov, in terms of internal organization, the sports club is made up of:

(1) individual members;
(2) sports association as an organizational unit acting on its own behalf, if there are more than three members;
(3) other organizational units (clubs, divisions, teams, etc.).

336. According to Article 3, minors and incapacitated persons may become members of sports club only upon the consent of their guardian.

337. The bodies of the sports club are:

(1) Members' Assembly and Extraordinary Members' Assembly.
(2) Executive Committee.
(3) Control Board.
(4) Other bodies created by a resolution of the Executive Committee.

C. PEU

338. An PEU is discerned from a club comprising several sports discipline only by its name. An example from recent is the statutes of PEU Oravan Námestovo.[81]

339. The PEU includes several subsections:

> PEU is as of the date of approval of statutes composed of the following components: basketball section, hockeyball – hockey section, table tennis section, volleyball section and cycling club. (trans. T.G.)

81. *See* www.tjoravanno.orava.sk/Stanovy%20TJ.doc, 30 Dec. 2010.

340. Although the basic elements – sections – do not have a legal personality, autonomous components are entrusted with movable and immovable property, special-purpose property and property acquired by the unit, which can be managed by the sections themselves, within existing rules. There is no concept of superiority and subordination between the PEU and sections; the interrelation between the individual components is based on equal terms.

341. Under Article 3 of the statutes of PEU Oravan Námestovo, a member is a person older than 6 years with the nationality of the SR, notwithstanding the political belief and affiliation, religion, sex and age, as well as if he/she is a foreign national if he/she resides in the SR and agrees with the Statutes. Children below the age of 6 years may participate under the supervision of their parents or other guardians (teachers, etc.).

342. The PEU bodies are the following:

(1) General Assembly of Delegates.
(2) Committee.
(3) President.
(4) Audit Committee.

343. The *supreme body of each component* of the unit is a *members' assembly.* In order to manage their own activities, the sections elect their *committee, a chairman* and other officials.

II. Club as a Business Company

344. ŠK Slovan Bratislava futbal a.s. is an example of a sports club in the form of a joint-stock company.

345. The object of its activities, according to the statutes of ŠK Slovan Bratislava futbal a.s. was:

(1) operation of sports facilities;
(2) organization of sporting events, seminars and training;
(3) advertising;
(4) market research – marketing;
(5) rental of residential and office spaces with the provision of activities other than basic services related to renting;
(6) purchase of goods for sale to final consumer (retail) or for selling to other operators (wholesale);
(7) intermediary activity in commerce, services and manufacturing;
(8) publishing non-periodicals.

The enumeration shows that the exercise of a sporting activity alone is not an object of this corporation.

346. The bodies of the joint-stock company do not differ from an ordinary joint-stock company:

(1) General Assembly.
(2) Board of Directors.
(3) Supervisory Board.
(4) CEO, President and Vice President.

III. Club as a Contributory Organization

347. Examples of a club being a contributory organization include subsidized organizations in the capital of Slovakia – Bratislava. According to a foundation charter of Dúbravský Sports Club, club's mission is to foster all-round physical training and sports in the city district, assist individuals, organized or unorganized clubs in organizing sports activities and to ensure the utilization of sports facilities in order to strengthen the physical and mental health of the people of the city district.

348. The sports club consists of separate organizational units – divisions that may or may not have separate legal personality. At the head of the sports club is *the Chief,* who is a statutory body of the sports club, and is appointed by the local council of the district of Bratislava – Dúbravka – on a proposal from the Mayor. His/her main tasks are to speak and act for the club, lead and organize its activities, including management of funds and property of the club. He/she is materially responsible for managing the assets, enters into contracts, and within his/her performance he/she is responsible to the Mayor and local council. *The Council* is a collective body of the club. Its task is to decide on the budget and major issues of club activities. The budget is approved by a *meeting of delegates* of the divisions within the club, being considered an advisory body to the Chief of the club and to the Council of the club.

IV. Club as a Budgetary Organization

349. In the past, until the merger of ASC Dukla Banská Bystrica and ASC Dukla Trenčín into the Military Sports Centre Dukla Banská Bystrica, its legal predecessors were sports clubs with a legal form of a budgetary organization of the Ministry of Defence. At the head of the organization was a *commander* and *members of the command.*

Part II. Sport and Status

Chapter 1. General Issues

350. Legal status of athletes was not clearly defined in Slovakia until 2016. Basically there were two possibilities – that the athletes were either employees or self-employed. The status of sportsmen and sports organizations thereby plays an important role in the field of labour law, social security and tax law.

351. The Slovak Labour Code contains, since 2007, in its first paragraph, an enumeration of the features of dependent work, which is an essential component of the employment relationship. According to §1 subsection 2 of the Labour Code (Act no. 311/2001 Coll.):

> Dependent work is work performed in a relationship of the employer superiority and subordination of employees, personally by an employee for the employer, under guidance of the employer, in his name, in the working time designated by the employer. (trans. T.G.)

352. Dependent work can generally be carried out only within the employment and rarely in other legal relationship, governed by special legislation (e.g., civil service).[82] However, until 2016, athletes in Slovakia usually signed a player's contract under the Civil or Commercial Code, which seemed unsustainable at least since the 2007 amendment to the Labour Code, introducing the concept of dependent work. However, even before being regulated in the Code, the definition of dependent work was known in the Slovak theory of labour law.

353. The practice of using Civil and Commercial Code contracts in sport was to be firmly rejected, with reference to §3 subsection 2 of the Labour Code as effective up to 2016:

> Labour relations of … professional athletes are governed by this Act, unless stipulated otherwise. (trans. T.G.)
> At present, the Act no. 440/2015 Coll. stipulates otherwise. It has introduced a detailed regulation of the employment within professional sports, as well as a

82. Helena Barancová, 'K vymedzeniu pojmu pracovného pomeru: Pracovný pomer alebo obchodno-právny vzt'ah?', *Právny obzor* 87, no. 1 (2004): 28–44.

detailed regulation of contracts for performing amateur sports. The Act has also introduced some amendments to the Labour Code, such as explicitly stating in §2 subsection 3 that professional sportsperson's employment is regulated by a separate Act, and the Labour Code applies only if provided by that special Act (Act on Sports no. 440/2015 Coll.).

354. Accurate classification of athletes as employees or self-employed was problematic at the European level as well. In the case *Walrave and Koch* (C-36/74), the CJEU stated that the Article 39 or 49 EC Treaty should be used (now since the Treaty of Lisbon the EC Treaty was renumbered and renamed into TFEU; the relevant Articles are now 45 and 56 TFEU). From the aforementioned two Articles, the former is concerned with the free movement of workers, and the latter with the free provision of services (through self-employment). The Court has thus not delivered a clear opinion on whether the athletes were employees or self-employed. Similarly, the Court also left the question open in the *Donà v. Mantero* case (C-13/76), despite the fact that a clear distinction is important, for example, for the sake of Regulation 1612/68 on the tax and social benefits, which only applies to employees. A change in the arguments of the Court occurred with the *Bosman* case, when the Court spoke only of Article 39 (on the free movement of workers), and said that this Article applies to rules of the organizations such as Belgian Football Association, FIFA or UEFA. This means that a permanent relationship between athletes and the club (it was a case of a football player) is to be considered an employment relationship. In another case, *Deliège* (C-51/96), which concerned an individual sport, judo, the Court declared that Article 49 should be used. In the case of basketball – *Lehtonen* (C-176/96) – the Court used the Article 39 again. Analysing these cases, Stefaan van den Bogaert[83] notes that professional footballers and players of team sports in general, show the essential features of employment as laid down in decisions such as *Lawrie Blum* and many others. In contrast, individual athletes such as skiers do not satisfy the condition of subordination, therefore the Court invokes self-employment in their case.

355. In each specific case, an athlete in Slovakia should therefore up to 2016 have been assessed either as engaged in dependent work, and therefore subject to the Labour Code and its protection, or as self-employed. This indeed was the intention of promoters of the original proposal of the former Slovak Sports Act from 2008. However, the project failed, and the 2008 Sports Act did not devote any attention to the status of sportsperson. The Slovak courts did not exert any authority to remedy the status of athletes, either. Even while deciding on the claims of players arising from a player's contract, courts did not dispute the nature of the contracts concluded as atypical contracts under §51 of the Civil Code or §269 subsection 2 of the Commercial Code. The fictitious status of these athletes as self-employed apparently did not bother any of the parties in the relationship.

---

83. Stefaan van den Bogaert, *Practical Regulation of the Mobility of Sportsmen in the EU Post Bosman*, 52–67 (The Hague: Kluwer Law International, 2005).

356. Clubs and the players thus intentionally circumvented the provisions of the Labour Code, which was understandable with reference to the rigid, predominantly mandatory nature of labour law in Slovakia. For example, repeated concluding of fixed-term contracts is restricted by both national and European labour law, whereby such employment is usually accepted only for two years, while in the sport, five-year contracts are usual. Therefore, a simple application of the Labour Code is not possible. Similarly, in case of regulation on the termination of employment, this cannot be applied in a sports relationship, in order to prevent potential termination of relationship during the season. Slovak labour law, moreover, does not accept fines or arbitration in labour disputes, which would make the application of labour law to professional sports difficult in Slovakia. Furthermore, arguments could have also been found proclaiming that even in the case of team sports, players exert a somewhat independent activity, rather than dependent work. Similarly, company managers and executives, as well as those whose work requires creativity, namely receive only framework tasks – just like footballers, having flexibility in fulfilling the tasks, it was claimed. Finally, the special status of superstars creates a better negotiating position for these athletes, who become business partners of the clubs, rather than employees.[84] All these arguments made a straightforward applicability of labour law to sports doubtful. Due to these facts, a new solution was found in the introduction of a specific regulation of sporting contracts, both for professionals, being considered employees under the special rules of the Act on Sports (with only some of the Labour Code provisions being applicable), or as self-employed, in cases where the features of dependent work are not present or in cases where the amateur sportsperson perform sports to a minor extent (of maximum eight hours per week, five days in a month or thirty days in a year).

---

84. Tomáš Sluka, *Profesionální sportovec (právní aekonomické aspekty)* (Prague: Havlíček Brain Team, 2007), 140–142.

Chapter 2. Public Regulation

§1. Qualification of Legal Status

I. Legal Status of Sport Organizations

357. Act no. 300/2008 Coll. permitted in §§8 and 9, in the case of national sports associations, only the legal form of a civic association, and in the case of clubs, allowed a civic association form, business company form or the form of a budgetary or contributory organization. Other legal persons engaged in sport may have taken other legal forms – for example, associations of civic associations, interest associations of legal persons, foundation or non-profit organizations. The new Act on Sports no. 440/2015 Coll. regulates only the legal form of national associations (and of the Olympic and Paralympic committees), which are supposed to be private (civic) associations. Legal forms of other types of entities active in sports are not specified in the new Act.

358. Sports organizations are mostly *civic associations* in practice, and their legal relationships are governed by the Civil Code. However, under the licensing system of the SFA, all football clubs applying for a licence to compete in the top Slovakian football competition (Fortuna League) need to have a legal form of a *business company* – namely, a joint-stock company (Article 22.1 of the SFA Licensing Directive).[85]

359. The 2008 Act required that sporting business companies be created for a non-business purpose. Consequences of such a distinction were not clear, though. In fact, nothing prevented clubs from indulging in business activities. *Even the sports organizations, which are constituted as civic associations, can namely pursue business activities on the basis of a trade licence.* According to J. Čorba, who has addressed this issue in Slovakia, sport organizations with a legal form of business companies were subject to the Commercial Code, although they do not operate for business purposes – because of protecting the expectations of the other contracting (business) party.[86] Likewise, a civic association with a trade licence, exercising business activities should also be subject to the Commercial Code in relation to the business activities performed.

360. Substantial legal issue here was the question of the actual *content of business* activity of the sports organizations. In fact, the 'sporting activity' is not recognized as a particular trade activity, since the trade licensing offices do not consider this activity sufficiently specific.[87] As an example, statutes of the football club in the form of a business company – ŠK Slovan Bratislava fubal a.s., did not contain sporting activity as an object of the activity of the football club. Only the activities

85. Cf. Jozef Čorba, 'Športové kluby a ich právny život', in *Otázky sportovního práva*, 80.
86. *Ibid.*, 83–84.
87. Cf. Ladislav Kopál, 'K problematike športovej činnosti v podmienkach živnostenského podnikania', *Obchodné právo* 12 (2002): 25.

are enumerated, which are recognized as trading activities by a trade office. A civic association, should it wish to do business under a trade licence, should similarly specify the scope of its activities so as to include activities that trade offices are willing to grant licences for. Besides these, the main aim of the civic association can be specified as well, but this may not be recognized as a specific trade.

361. The second problem was the *issue of profit,* since, in the case of companies that do not pursue the business purpose and also in the case of civic associations, under §1 subsection 3 letter b of Act no. 83/1990 Coll., these should not serve as a source of income for members. Therefore, Article 16 of Statutes of the football club KFC Komárno, with a legal form of a civic association, contained the sentence: 'Earned resources are used exclusively to ensure the operation of the club.' (trans. T.G.) This was to avoid any suspicion of conflict with the purpose of civic association. However, the new Act on Sports from 2015 completely abandoned any limitations as to the business activities of sports organizations. It is hence not required any longer that in case of a business entity in sports this has to perform only non-business activities and to be created for non-business purposes.

II. Legal Status of Athletes

362. As already indicated, it used to be a common practice in Slovakia to use the provisions of §51 Civil Code, or §269 subsection 2 of the Commercial Code on atypical contracts,[88] instead of subordinating the relationship between the athlete and the club under the Labour Code provisions. Employment was an exceptional situation in case of athletes of the NSC, and employees in service of the Military Sport Centre Dukla Banská Bystrica and in the Centre of National Sports Representation of the Ministry of Interior.

363. The NSC thereby employed in 2011 only fourteen athletes in the position of employees under the Labour Code. In the Military Sport Centre Dukla Banská Bystrica, athletes are public employees whose employment relationship is governed by Act no. 552/2003 Coll. on the work in the public interest and Act no. 553/2003 Coll. on the remuneration of certain employees for work in the public interest. A special group are professional soldiers, governed by the provisions of Act on civil service of professional soldiers of the SR. The Centre of National Sports Representation of the Ministry of Interior employed in 2011 thirty-four athletes under contract of employment under the Labour Code and three other employees (two athletes and a coach) under Act no. 73/1998 Coll. on civil service of the police force. Coaches who were not police officers were employed under Act no. 552/2003 Coll. on the work in the public interest.

364. Still, in the private sports sector, the use of civil and commercial contracts dominated absolutely. This phenomenon had its historical roots, as already pointed

88. Ladislav Križan, 'Mal by mať profesionálny futbalista na Slovensku postavenie zamestnanca?', *Bulletinslovenskej advokácie* XV, no. 3 (2009): 28–34.

out above in connection with the socialist ideal of amateur athletes. It was a specificity of Czechoslovak sports prior to 1989 that the athletes were, in addition to performance of a sport, officially employed by government-owned enterprises, and their sporting activity thus did not constitute an object of their contracted work.

365. Courts in Slovakia generally accepted atypical players' contracts, even in case of team sports such as football or ice hockey. Therefore, up to 2016, the practice prevailed that athletes were mostly self-employed, and only exceptionally they were considered employees.

366. Thereby, if an athlete is a self-employed person, in principle he/she should have a sporting trade licence. However, trade offices in Slovakia do not recognize sporting activity as a specific object of trading. This problem could have been solved by a draft Act on Sport prepared as a parliamentary proposal in 2007,[89] which implied that the Trade Act should be amended so as to add a point which would determine whether the occupation of a professional sportsman is considered a liberal profession and Trade Act should not apply at all. As this did not happen, sporting activity of self-employed athletes is neither conceived as a trade nor as a liberal profession. Only performance of other activities than sporting may be considered a trade performed by an athlete, for example, advertising and marketing activities. Nevertheless, their income from sporting activities is characterized for tax purposes as an income from 'activity of a sportsperson or of a sports expert' or 'other income' (§6 subsection 2 letter e and §8 subsection 1 letter j of Act no. 595/2003 Coll. on income tax).

367. In contrast, since 2016, sportsperson, whose sporting activity shows features of dependent work, are newly considered employees under the special rules on sporting employment in the Act on Sports no. 440/2015 Coll.

368. Regulations of social security law and tax law consider such athletes as employees (however, within a transitory period until 31 December 2021, professional sportsperson performing dependent work are still considered self-employed persons for social insurance purposes).

369. Hence, despite the fact that all projects addressing the status of athletes were unsuccessful previously, a major breakthrough was achieved as of 2016, introducing finally a specific regulation of sporting employment. Thereby, it was already a project from 2004 that first proposed essential elements of the sporting employment contract and enumerated provisions of Labour Code the applicability of which needed to be excluded, or needed to be adjusted. A specific sports employment contract was also proposed in the draft Act on Sport from 2007. However, the bill, which was finally presented to the parliament in 2008, did not contain any regulation on the status of athletes. During hearings in the National Council, a Member of the Parliament had tried to propose an amendment, but this proposal was rejected.

89. *See* www.nrsr.sk/Default.aspx?sid=zakony/cpt&ZakZborID=13&CisObdobia=4&ID=335, 5 Jan. 2011.

The final Act on the organization and promotion of sports no. 300/2008 Coll. thus did not regulate this issue at all. It was finally the new Act on Sports of 2015 that managed to introduce a special employment status of professional sportsperson outside of Labour Code, with special rules reflecting the specificities of sports.

§2. Basic Rights and Obligations

I. Fundamental Rights and Freedoms of Athletes as Human Beings and Citizens

370. Athletes, whether professional or amateur, regardless of whether they pursue collective or individual sport, are primarily human beings and citizens. Therefore, the Slovak athletes are subject to all international standards of human rights and fundamental freedoms, whether adopted by the UN, Council of Europe, or at the EU level.

371. *At the global level,* basic human rights and freedoms are enshrined mainly in the Universal Declaration of Human Rights from 1948, adopted by the United Nations Organization. In 1966 the International Covenant on Civil and Political Rights and the International Covenant on Economic, Social and Cultural Rights (signed by Czechoslovakia in 1968, but ratified only in 1975) followed. The other UN conventions are, for example, the Convention on the Elimination of All Forms of Racial Discrimination, the Convention on the Elimination of All Forms of Discrimination against Women and the Convention on the Rights of the Child and many others.

372. The most important convention *at the regional level* is the one adopted *by the Council of Europe*: the European Convention for Protection of Human Rights and Fundamental Freedoms (1950). Finally, the fundamental rights and freedoms at *the EU* level, such as free movement of workers, are enshrined in the TFEU (e.g., Article 45), but also in the specific EU Charter of Fundamental Rights of 2000, which follows the older and non-binding Charter of Fundamental Social Rights of 1989. The Charter of Fundamental Rights (2000, with certain amendments from 2007) became legally binding upon entry into force of the Treaty of Lisbon on 1 December 2009.

373. In the SR, the fundamental rights and freedoms are guaranteed under Title II of the Constitution. They can be broken down into:

(1) Fundamental human rights and freedoms (Articles 14–25).
(2) Political rights (Articles 26–32).
(3) Rights of national minorities and ethnic groups (Articles 33–34).
(4) Economic, social and cultural rights (Articles 35–43).
(5) Right to environmental protection and cultural heritage (Articles 44–45).
(6) Right to judicial and other legal protection (Articles 46–50).
(7) Right to asylum (Articles 53).

II. Fundamental Rights and Freedoms of Athletes as Workers

374. Basic rights of workers as a special category of humans and citizens are guaranteed worldwide mainly by the instruments of the International Labour Organization (ILO). ILO formulates international labour standards in the form of conventions to be applied to workers/employees in countries that have ratified these conventions. Note, however, that in terms of national regulation in the SR, athletes were previously not considered employees.[90] Nevertheless, we believe that in case of an international dispute, given the generally accepted nature of sporting activities as employment, as well as national legislation in the Labour Code of the SR (§3) the international standards applicable to employees should have also applied to Slovak athletes, at least in team sports, even before the introduction of sporting employment in 2016.

III. Selected Rights and Freedoms

A. *Freedom of Movement*

375. Already the Universal Declaration of Human Rights of 1948 has guaranteed in its Article 13 the fundamental freedom of movement in general. A few decades later the Protocol from 1963 to the Council of Europe, the Convention for the Protection of Human Rights and Fundamental Freedom, established the freedom of movement. In the EU, the freedom of movement for employees and self-employed is guaranteed within the TFEU (Articles 45 and 56), as well as in the Charter of Fundamental Rights (Articles 15 and 45). The Constitution of the SR guarantees this freedom in Article 23. The issue of freedom of movement also has its purely employment context in the ILO Conventions. For example, the Convention no. 97/1949 guarantees the protection of migrant workers, and should also protect the migrant athletes.

376. In this context, it might be wondered whether the transfer fees and so-called training compensation in sports are in harmony with the freedom of movement of an athlete. Requiring any charge enables restriction of the freedom of movement for lack of funds or unwillingness to pay them. The most famous sports law case of the CJEU was dealing exactly with this matter – the *Bosman* case (C-415/93). There is also a recent case from the same area, concerning training compensation – *Olivier Bernard v. Olympique Lyonnaise* (C-325/08).

377. In the *Bosman* ruling,[91] the Court recognized the right of a player (after expiry of his professional contract) to free movement. Bosman wanted a transfer to a French club U.S. Dunkerque, after his contractual relationship with the Belgian RFC Liège was over. Dunkerque was unable to pay for the transfer since the fee was set disproportionately high. Bosman thus lost any opportunity to earn his living

90. Cf. Marcel Dolobáč, 'Právne postavenie športovcov', *Justičná revue* 62, no. 6–7 (2010): 796–801.
91. Hamerník, *Sportovní právo s mezinárodním prvkem*, 39 et seq.

as a professional football player. The CJEU finally declared that the requirement for a transfer fee after the contractual relationship with the original club is over represents an unjustifiable restriction on the freedom of movement.

378. In the more recent case of *Olivier Bernard,*[92] from 16 March 2010, the CJEU ruled on the training compensation, which should not be quantified disproportionately. If a young player wants to leave the club where he/she was brought up, he/she (or the new club offering him/her his/her first professional contract) is obliged to pay a compensation, which constitutes an obstacle to free movement. Bernard left Olympique Lyonnaise and signed his first professional contract with Newcastle United. Olympique subsequently asked for the compensation. The CJEU held that the amount of compensation must reflect actual costs. Only under this condition is the training compensation not an unjustified restriction of movement within the EU.

379. In both cases – *Bosman* and *Bernard* – strictly speaking, the CJEU decision should apply only to relations with a European dimension, but not in cases of national or non-European – international background. Clearly, however, in such a situation, there would be an unequal treatment of athletes. The European standards should thus also be applied at the national level.

380. The freedom of movement for the purpose of work is closely related to the freedom of movement to provide services (Article 56 TFEU). Such a dispute was dealt with by the CJEU in a case concerning judoka *Deliège.* It was held that the freedom to provide services (freedom of movement of the self-employed) in sport is not unlimited, and depends on the nomination into the national team, which is fully within the competence of the national sports association.

B. Protection of Liberty, Personality, Speech and Privacy

1. Personal Liberty and Forced Labour

381. The Universal Declaration of Human Rights of 1948 guarantees the prohibition of slavery and forced labour in its Article 4. Similarly, the European Convention for Protection of Human Rights and Fundamental Freedoms protects against slavery, servitude and forced labour in its Article 4. The ILO standards prohibiting forced labour are Convention nos 29/1930 and 105/1957. The Charter of Fundamental Rights of the EU regulates this issue in Article 5. In the Constitution of the SR, Articles 17 on personal freedom and 18 on the prohibition of forced labour deal with these issues.

382. Regarding the sport, it might seem that sports cannot be regarded as forced labour at all. Nevertheless, it is sometimes possible to encounter views considering

92. Cf. Andrej Poruban, 'K otázke náhrady za výchovu mladých hráčov futbalovým klubom', *Justičná revue* 62, no. 5 (2010): 691–694.

a sporting activity forced labour, given the limited possibilities of termination of contract.[93] In the 1980s, Arnold Mühren approached the European Commission to assess the transfer rules in football as forced labour. However, in 1984, such a characteristic of sport was rejected by the Commission,[94] arguing that the athlete (player) became a sports employee based on his/her own will, he/she does not do anything against his/her will and is limited only to some extent.[95] Nevertheless it is clear that freedom of the player is not exactly the same freedom as that of any other employee, given the so-called contractual stability, which does not allow a player to terminate a contract with a club during the season (this issue is governed by FIFA Regulations on the status and transfer of players in Article 16). The situation of young African and Latin American players resembles forced labour even more.[96] In their case, often the problem of child labour arises in addition.

2. Privacy and Freedom of Speech

383. The Universal Declaration of Human Rights from 1948 in Article 12 guarantees the right to privacy and in Article 19 the freedom of opinion and expression. The European Convention on Human Rights and Fundamental Freedoms mentions the right to privacy in Article 8 and freedom of expression in Article 10. These rights are also guaranteed by the Charter of Fundamental Rights of the EU in Articles 7 and 11, as well as in the Constitution of the SR in Article 16 on the protection of privacy, and Article 26 on the freedom of expression.

384. These provisions in relation to sport open a debate on the players' contracts extending into the private lives of athletes (such as regulating the diets, ban on smoking and drinking or a ban on visiting bars and pubs) and prohibiting comments for the media. The same questions may arise in relation to limiting the right to privacy within the doping controls,[97] especially in connection with reporting the whereabouts information.[98]

385. Limiting the privacy of athletes and their freedom of expression usually takes the form of a contractual clause governing the conduct of an athlete. In practice, it is asserted that a contractual agreement leading to a restriction of some fundamental rights is acceptable, as long as this restriction is voluntary and does not go beyond what is necessary for the needs of the other contracting party. Nevertheless,

---

93. Cf. Roger Blanpain, *Lesgladiateurs du sport* (Brussels: La Charte, 1993).
94. Steven F.H. Jellinghaus, 'Een kennismaking met het sport(en)recht', in *Sport en Recht: Buiten Rechte of Buiten Spel?*, ed. S.F.H. Jellinghaus (Zutphen: Paris, 2008), 14.
95. Parrish & Miettinen, *The Sporting Exception in European Union Law* 172.
96. Thomas Olukayode, 'Les nouveaux esclaves du sport business', *Courrier International* 543 (2001): 46–48. Cf. The European Parliament Resolution from 8 May 2008 on White Paper on Sports, para. 104.
97. Ian Smith, *Why WADA Should Not Ban Athletes for Recreational Drug Use*, 1(2) The Intl. Sports L.J. 119 (2007).
98. Janwillem Soek, *Is the Professional Athlete's Right to Privacy Being Tacitly Ignored?*, 1(2) The Intl. Sports L.J. 100 (2008), www.asser.nl/upload/documents/1182010_43802ISLJ%202008_1-2.pdf, 11 Feb. 2011.

the boundary between permissible interference with the fundamental right to privacy and freedom of expression on one side, and disproportionate restriction of these rights on the other, remains very unclear. It becomes of importance when a sports organization applies very generally formulated rules from the contract in a specific situation – for example, when sanctioning an athlete for swearing on-field. In such a case, it is very problematic to strike a balance between fundamental freedom of expression and the interests of the employer (the club). Moreover, even some of the sanctions which may be imposed in such a case by the club, for example, a ban on competition participation could be in conflict with fundamental rights (e.g., the right to work). It is therefore necessary that the type of sanction and also the degree of restriction of a fundamental right (e.g., how long a penalty will take) are adequate. The Dispute Resolution Chamber of FIFA and the CAS in their case law offer a view of their understanding of the adequacy of penalties.

3. Personality Rights

386. Article 19 of the Slovak Constitution guarantees the right to human dignity, honour, reputation, protection of the name, protection against unauthorized intrusion into family and private life, and protection against unauthorized collection, disclosure or other misuse of personal data to a greater detail than the Universal Declaration of Human Rights (in Articles 6 and 12), the European Convention on Human Rights and Fundamental Freedoms (in Article 8) and the Charter of Fundamental Rights of the EU (Article 8).

387. This Article represents the general framework of the so-called personality rights, which are more in detail regulated by the Civil Code. Their treatment is therefore not purely declaratory as in the case of some other fundamental rights and freedoms. The personality rights are characterized as absolute, personal, non-transferable, perpetual and imprescriptible. They are protected even after the death of their holder – the Civil Code explicitly entitles husband and children, or parents to exercise these rights.

388. *General personality rights* are regulated in the Civil Code (Act no. 40/1964 Coll.) in §§11 et seq. A natural person under this scheme has the right to protection of personality, particularly its life and health, civic and human dignity, privacy, name and expressions of personal character. The systematization and terminology of general personal rights is however inconsistent among the authors.[99]

389. The individual personality rights *are the following:*

(1) the right to dignity and honour;
(2) the right to a name (also a pseudonym);

99. Ján Švidroň, 'Veda a prax pri ochrane osobnosti', *Právny obzor* 86, no. 6 (2003): 631.

(3) the right to expressions of personal character (right to a personal document, the right to a sound recording, the right of portrait, caricature, right to visual images);
(4) the right to physical integrity;
(5) the right to personal privacy;
(6) the right to personal liberty (this is not explicitly mentioned in the Civil Code).[100]

390. As regards the treatment of personality rights of athletes in the SR, *there is* currently *no specific contractual type* that would allow for disposal of these rights. A draft bill on sport from 2005 tried to introduce a specific contractual type into the Civil Code – a *contract* defined as 'contract by which a natural or legal person grants permission to use its name, emblem, likeness, picture for compensation, in particular, on objects and spaces for advertising'. (trans. T.G.) This attempt however failed.

391. The current *contractual practice* uses in the contracts between players and clubs certain clauses addressing these matters, which usually read as follows:

(1) the player agrees that the club exploits the rights of their personality, particularly the club exercises or allows dissemination of images of the player, individually or in teams, capturing game situations or the whole matches, by public or private television and film companies or other audiovisual means (*broadcasting rights*);
(2) the player allows the club to process his/her original signature as facsimile or printed for promotional purposes, or for the reproduction on the club souvenirs and products, as well as with third-party ads *(merchandising)*;
(3) the player agrees that the revenue from ads and promotional activities mentioned in subparagraphs (1) and (2) belongs to the club.[101]

392. Personality rights enjoy protection that lies in the fact that documents of a personal nature, portraits, images and video and sound recordings related to personal characteristics may be *made or used only with the consent of the athlete.* Exceptions are cases of administrative, scientific, artistic and intelligence service licence. However, even such use may not be in conflict with the legitimate interests of the individual.

393. As the *tools of protection,* the individual has, in particular, the right to request the offender to refrain from unjustified interference with the right to his/her personality, to eliminate the consequences of these interventions, and that appropriate satisfaction is provided. Satisfaction does not have a primary form of money; right to compensation in pecuniary form belongs to the individual in the event that standard satisfaction does not seem sufficient, and if the dignity of an individual or company has been considerably diminished. Amount of compensation in this case

100. Cirák et al., *Občianske právo: Všeobecná čas'*, 294 et seq.
101. Sluka, *Profesionální sportovec (právní a ekonomické aspekty)*, 125.

is determined by the court, taking into account the seriousness of the injury and the circumstances under which the right was violated.

394. These instruments of the Civil Code provide protection only to *a natural person.* Comparable protection of legal entities is laid down in §19b of the Civil Code (protection of name and reputation of a *legal person*, including the ability to claim appropriate satisfaction, even in money) and §12 of the Commercial Code (protection of trade names including the ability to claim appropriate satisfaction, even in money).

395. Protection of personality rights is not only subject to the few sections of the Civil Code, though. In addition to the general civil system of protection of personality, there is a possibility of *criminal protection as well* (§§281 and 377 of the Criminal Code protecting trademarks and private correspondence). Finally, protection of personal rights can also take the form of registering *trademarks* (name, number of the athlete). Trademarks Act no. 506/2009 Coll. governs this issue. Trademarks are registered in the register kept by the Industrial Property Office. Use of these trademarks may be allowed by the athletes to their business partners through specific contracts – in the Act no. 506/2009 Coll. on trademarks, §20 provides for the institute called *licence agreement,* which is in detail governed by §508–§515 of the Commercial Code. The contract is also entered into the register maintained by the Industrial Property Office.

396. In some cases, there may be a conflict where the club has an exclusive sponsor whose interests may be in collision with interests of the player's contractual partners. The player's contract in such cases requires that the player will not use his/her rights in conflict with similar activities of the club (or national representation team). In this case, it is common in some countries (e.g., in the United Kingdom (UK)) that the right of the club to use the player's apparel applies only to a collective display of the player – that means the display of at least three people (players).[102]

4. Equal Treatment

397. The Universal Declaration of Human Rights of 1948 guarantees equal treatment in its Article 2, the International Covenant on Economic, Social and Cultural Rights in Article 2 section 2 and in Article 3. The principle of equal pay as a part of the principle of equal treatment is enshrined in the ILO Convention no. 100/1951. The Charter of Fundamental Rights guarantees in its Articles 20 and 21 equal treatment and prohibition of discrimination. The Constitution of the SR enshrines the equality in Article 12.

398. In sport, however, this principle is not absolute, either between persons of the same or the opposite sex. It is because of the specific nature (specificity) of sport

102. *Ibid.*, 96–100.

not allowing for competition between the sexes, or for competition of healthy sportsmen with handicaps, and also because the work of various players does not have the same value. Equal treatment, as guaranteed by the ILO Convention no. 111/1958 cannot therefore be applied in sport in the sense that women should be able to compete with men, or foreign nationals in the competitions of national teams and similar. This was also recognized by the European Commission in the White Paper on Sport from 2007.

399. According to the ILO, the standards for equal treatment are also covered by the Convention on workers with family responsibilities (no. 156/1981), who should not be subject to discrimination on the grounds of conflict between their family obligations and work responsibilities. Under the Convention no. 183/2000, motherhood, or pregnancy should also not constitute a ground for discrimination. In sports, it is however questionable as to what extent a sportswoman can combine a career with motherhood and pregnancy, and whether she will meet the performance criteria required for the job, either during pregnancy, after childbirth or after returning from maternity leave or parental leave. The new Act on Sports no. 440/2015 Coll. leaves this issue open for future decisions of courts, so as to establish a case law on whether pregnancy is to be considered a discriminatory or acceptable reason for non-conclusion of a sporting employment contract in cases where the sportswoman is to be hired for a specific sports event while knowing that she is pregnant and will not be able to perform at the event.

400. Under the influence of the European law, the SR has introduced into its legal system a specific anti-discrimination legislation, in the form of Act no. 365/2004 Coll. of 20 May 2004 on equal treatment in certain areas and protection against discrimination (Anti-discrimination Act). This Act prohibits discrimination on grounds of sex, religion or belief, race, nationality or ethnic origin, disability, age, sexual orientation, marital status, family status, colour, language, political or other opinion, national or social origin, property, birth or other statuses. Under §2, discrimination is categorized as direct discrimination, indirect discrimination, harassment, sexual harassment and victimization. Discrimination is also an instruction to discriminate and incitement to discrimination. On the other hand, the Act restricts the prohibition of discrimination *only to equal treatment in employment and similar legal relations, social security, health care, provision of goods and services and in education.* These principles hence now, since 2016, apply undoubtedly also to professional sportsperson performing dependent work under the Act on Sports (being in a specific sporting employment).

401. The Act explicitly *does not apply to unequal treatment relating to conditions of entry and residence of foreigners* in the SR, except citizens of an EU Member State, the European Economic Area Member State and Switzerland, and stateless persons and their families. A particular issue in this context is the *discrimination based on nationality.* Discrimination on the grounds of nationality, although not listed among the prohibited grounds of discrimination in the Anti-discrimination Act, is manifestly contrary not only to the fundamental rights and freedoms under international instruments, but also under European law and the Constitution of the SR. The CJEU expressed its opinion on this matter in the case *Donà v. Mantero*, where exceptionally it admitted the possibility of limiting the participation of foreign players in national team competitions. FIFA and UEFA in cooperation with national associations moreover attempted to limit the total number of foreign players, mainly with the intention to ensure a minimum number of domestic players in the clubs, or at least players who were brought up in the country. The EU is willing to accept the possibility of unequal treatment in this context, but only in the form of indirect discrimination. The already mentioned discriminatory restrictions in the form of UEFA rules on domestic players (*UEFA home-grown player rules*) are therefore probably acceptable for the EU, since they constitute indirect discrimination. On the other hand, the rules proposed originally by FIFA as a 3+2 rule (rejected by the CJEU in the *Bosman* case) and in the form of 6+5 rule (given up in June 2010) represented direct discrimination on grounds of nationality and could not be accepted by the EU. The 3+2 rule meant that the team could consist of up to three foreign players, and two players had to previously operate in the relevant national association for a continuous period of at least five years, including three years in the junior category. The 6+5 rule required that the teams have at least six players who are nationals of the State in which the club is established. The home-grown players rule in contrast sets a condition which requires that eight players from the twenty-five players registered for the club have spent between the ages of 15 and 21 years at least three years in a club operating within the country. There is no condition that these players should have a citizenship of the country.

402. In the individual sports, the situation is worse than in team sports. A lot of explicitly discriminatory provisions on foreign participants in sports competitions can be identified there.[103]

403. The Slovak Anti-discrimination Act also does *not apply* to different treatment on *grounds* of *disability or age, resulting from the provisions of special legislation* (e.g., governing the civil service relationship). According to the Act, there is no discrimination *on grounds of disability* in case of an objectively justified differential treatment, which consists of setting health conditions of eligibility for access to employment or for carrying out certain activities in employment. This could also apply to sports activities, if the Anti-discrimination Act was considered applicable to sports. To what extent, however, in every sport the unequal treatment of disabled is really justified, must be examined on a case-by-case basis, depending on whether biological or psychological differences may favour one group compared to the other (cf. the situation of Oscar Pistorius).

404. Similarly, different treatment *on grounds of age* is not discrimination, if it is objectively justified by a legitimate aim and is necessary and reasonable to achieve this aim. This would be particularly the case of age limits in the sport. Age discrimination could theoretically be invoked by referees (umpires) whose profession is also limited by age. However, in this case, ad hoc exceptions are recognized.

103. Cf. *Study on the Equal Treatment of Non-nationals in Individuals Sports Competitions*, 108 (2010).

405. The mechanism of protection in cases of discrimination involves a right to judicial protection, whereby a reversed burden of proof is applied – the defendant is required to prove that he/she did not infringe the principle of equal treatment, if the plaintiff notifies the court of facts from which it may be presumed that the principle of equal treatment was violated. Under the Anti-discrimination Act, one has the possibility to request that the person violating the principle of equal treatment *refrains* from such conduct, and if possible, provides a *remedy* for the illegal situation or provides adequate *satisfaction.* If the satisfaction is not adequate, especially if non-compliance with the principle of equal treatment has considerably impaired the dignity, social status or social functioning of the injured person, the victim may also seek *pecuniary damages in cash.* Amount of damages in cash is determined by the court with regard to the seriousness of damage and to all the circumstances under which it is incurred.

C. Specific Rights of Employees

406. There are a number of special rights, established by the international ILO Conventions, the EU Charter of Fundamental Rights and also by the Constitution of the SR, that are conditional upon an employment status, and that should thus be considered applicable to sporting employment as well. These rights are as follows.

1. Right to Fair and Decent Working Conditions

407. This right is enshrined in Article 24 of the Universal Declaration of Human Rights. Similarly, it is guaranteed by Article 7 of the International Covenant on Economic, Social and Cultural Rights. Article 31 of the EU Charter of Fundamental Rights likewise recognized the right to fair and reasonable working conditions. The Constitution of the SR guaranteed the right to fair and satisfactory working conditions in its Article 36.

408. Already, the oldest of the ILO Conventions dealt with the issue of working time, which can be considered a part of working conditions. Other ILO convention of interest for athletes is mainly the Convention no. 106/1957 concerning working time in other fields than industry. It requires that non-working day falls on a day, which is considered the country's traditional day of rest. Nevertheless, the matches are often played in Europe on Sundays.

409. Fair working conditions undoubtedly include the payment of fair wages. This is enshrined in the ILO Convention no. 95/1949, which, for example, allows for deductions from wages only under conditions set by national law or collective agreements, or under decision of the competent authority of dispute resolution. This means that the system of fines in sport should also meet these criteria. In Slovakia, however, labour law does not permit to penalize employees by fines at all. Therefore, should Slovakian players be considered employees under Labour Code, the institute of pecuniary fines would constitute a legal problem. Therefore, the new Act on Sports no. 440/2015 Coll. was enacted in 2015, which now allows for fines and other sanctions in sporting employment.

2. Prohibition of Child Labour and Protection of Young Workers

410. The UN Universal Declaration in Article 25 protects motherhood and childhood, but it does not explicitly prohibit child labour. Article 10 section 3 of the International Covenant on Economic, Social and Cultural Rights, in contrast, explicitly speaks of child labour. Similarly, the Charter of Fundamental Rights of the EU prohibits in Article 32 child labour, and in Article 24, it protects children and adolescents. The Constitution of the SR guarantees these rights in the Article 38. Child labour is also prohibited by the ILO Convention on minimum age, no. 138/1973.

411. The importance of this prohibition lies not only in the protection of physical health and moral development of children (under 18 years of age) – young sportsmen – but also in view of the need to ensure quality education for young athletes. Their sporting career often fails, eventually expires when they are aged 30, and they often have no education or special training for any other career.[104] In particular, the status of young African and Latin American players is mostly worrisome in respect of the ILO Convention on worst forms of child labour no. 182/1999, which deals with practices similar to slavery – which is often the situation of young players who are enticed away with the prospects of a career abroad, and end up left on their own in Europe. In the case of football, the fight against this practice took the form of special conditions imposed on players' agents, and also by restricting transfer of players younger than 18 years. International transfer of players younger than 16 years are entirely excluded and transfer of players aged 16–18 years are possible only within the EU under specific conditions laid down in Article 19 of the FIFA Regulations governing the status and transfer of players.

412. Protection of young workers is ensured in the SR through the Labour Code as well as through the 2015 Act on Sports requirement that young workers (sportsperson) aged under 15 years (or older if still subject to compulsory education) be under the supervision of a labour inspection authority and public health authority. Otherwise, their employment is not allowed.

3. Protection Against Unjust Dismissal

413. The ILO Convention on termination of employment no. 158/1982 (ratified by Slovakia on 22 February 2010, making this Convention reach the minimum number of ratifications necessary to become effective) applies to all sectors of labour market, but expressly only to employment contracts of indefinite duration. In sport,

104. Germaine, *Lesportifs et le droit*, 67.

by contrast, mostly fixed-term contracts are used, which may be excluded from the scope of this Convention. According to the Convention, the employee should be allowed to comment on the reasons of notice of dismissal if they are based on the person of the employee and his/her behaviour. The protection against unjustified dismissal is also guaranteed in Article 30 of the EU Charter of Fundamental Rights. In our opinion, the same principle should apply in the event of early termination of employment for a fixed period as well, even in sport, potentially under a broad interpretation of Article 30 of the Charter. Reasons such as lack of effort are thereby often explicitly used as an argument for the termination of employment of athletes (especially in professional football), although the case law of the FIFA DRC considers such reasons as subjective and perceived only by the coach, thus, improvable in an objective manner, and therefore, not recognized as a valid ground for termination.[105]

4. Freedom of Association, Right to Collective Bargaining and to Strike

414. The Universal Declaration of Human Rights in Article 20 enshrines freedom of association, including freedom of association in trade unions, which is expressly guaranteed in Article 23 section 4. The International Covenant on Economic, Social and Cultural Rights provides for this right in Article 8. Further, Article 12 of the Charter of Fundamental Rights enshrines freedom of association, including the trade unions, and Article 28 respects the right to collective bargaining and collective action (strike). The Constitution of the SR provides for these rights in the Article 36 and Article 37 section 4. This issue is also covered by the ILO Conventions no. 87 of 1948 and no. 98 of 1949. Even the member countries that have not ratified the former of them, namely, the Convention on freedom of association and right to organize, are nevertheless obliged to respect these rights in view of the fact that they are enshrined in the Constitution of the ILO from 1919.

415. Thus, athletes as well as other employees, should have the right to associate, thus to create trade unions. In Slovakia, there exists in professional football the already mentioned APFS.[106] Previously, while in Slovakia the players were not considered employees, it was questionable whether their associations are in fact trade unions, and may rely on the constitutional right of association in trade unions. Similarly, it was questionable whether they can participate in collective bargaining and whether athletes united in these associations enjoy the right to strike. According to Article 37 of the Constitution of the SR, the right of association belongs to 'everyone', however, theory and practice assign the right to form trade unions only to employees. Similarly, the right to collective bargaining is limited only to trade unions. Finally, according to H. Barancová, the right to strike is a collective right of an employee, but the right to begin a strike is purely trade union's collective right.

105. Janwillem Soek, *Termination of International Employment Agreements and the 'Just Cause' Concept in the Case Law of the FIFA Dispute Resolution Chamber*, 3(4) The Intl. Sports L.J. 28–45 (2007).

106. *See* www.apfs.sk/, 22 Sep. 2010.

Similarly, the Supreme Court decision in R 1 Co 10/98 states that the right to strike is a subjective right of trade unions.[107] Paragraph 16 section 2 of Act no. 2/1991 Coll. on collective bargaining discerns, besides a solidarity strike, only a strike in view of concluding a collective agreement, thus again, it is actually reserved for employees only.

416. There is an ongoing dispute as to whether there are other forms of strike, apart from a strike with the aim of concluding a collective agreement and a solidarity strike, that are also acceptable. Despite the broadly formulated right to strike in the Constitution, due to another formulation in the Constitution, this right can be invoked only within limits set by an act of Parliament. The only act of Parliament regulating the right to strike is the already mentioned Act no. 2/1991 Coll. on collective bargaining. There is also Article 10 of the Labour Code dealing in general with the right to strike, but some authors refuse to acknowledge the implementing function of this Article.[108] According to a decision of the Czech Constitutional Court (Pl. ÚS 20/05), however, if the legislature failed to exercise the right to strike by an act of Parliament, this does not limit the right to strike itself. A similar argument can also be found in the decision of the Supreme Court of the SR no. 1 Co 10/98. This opinion is also shared by H. Barancová, who also claims that Article 10 of the Labour Code can be viewed as implementation of constitutional right to strike, and pursuant to this Article, the right to strike is not limited only to strikes in connection with collective bargaining.[109] It is also an indispensable fact that the SR respects international law, where a strike has a broader aim than just as a means of collective bargaining.

417. However, even if one recognizes the right to strike as not limited only to collective bargaining, it still remains limited to employees and their trade unions. As long as the athletes in the SR were not considered employees, they had neither the right to create trade unions nor the right to collective bargaining or the right to strike. It was quite a paradox, given that the Labour Code in fact ruled that professional athletes should have had the employee status. Moreover, the ILO Convention on collective bargaining no. 154/1981, in Article 9 requires States to enable and encourage collective bargaining. In sports, it thus appeared that the SR did not meet this requirement. This approach at the same time prevented Slovak players from participation in social dialogue at the European level – namely, in Paris on 1 July 2008, a sectoral committee for social dialogue in professional football was created, without any formal representation of Slovak players.

418. Social dialogue, that is, the so-called tripartite negotiations (consultations), is also regulated by the ILO Convention no. 144/1976. This area is also covered by the ILO Convention on the representatives of employees no. 135/1971, which could

107. Helena Barancová & Robert Schronk, *Pracovné právo* (Bratislava: Sprint, 2007), 787.
108. Ján Drgonec, 'Základné právo na štrajk: rozsah a podmienky jeho uplatnenia v právnom poriadku Slovenskej republiky', *Justičná revue* 59, no. 6–7 (2007): 760.
109. Helena Barancová, 'Štrajk len podľa zákona o kolektívnom vyjednávaní?', *Právny obzor* 91, no. 2 (2008): 98–99.

also be applied to athletes if they are considered employees. They should have the right to workers' representatives, that is, works councils according to the Slovak Labour Code. This is, for example, the situation in the NSC, where athletes have their representative. In the majority of sports organizations, however, this regulation was not applicable since the athletes are not employees.

419. It is therefore clear that in a situation where the Slovak athletes were not employees, their position and protection by trade unions as well as their chances for collective bargaining, including the right to strike, were weak, if not non-existent. Under the new Act on Sports no. 440/2015 Coll., however, the situation has changed dramatically. The Act on Sports now recognizes explicitly that professional sportsperson performing dependent work are to be considered employees and explicitly recognizes even their right to collective bargaining and strike under the Act no. 2/1991 Coll. Nevertheless, the rules on workers' representatives are not applicable in sporting employment due to the fact that the sportsperson themselves are usually too overburdened with other obligations and have no spare time to act as workers' representatives in practice.

IV. Statutory Duties of Sports Subjects

420. According to Article 13 section 1 of the Constitution of the SR, obligations may be imposed by:

(1) act of Parliament or on the basis of an Act of Parliament, within its limits, while preserving fundamental rights and freedoms;
(2) international treaty according to Article 7, which directly establishes rights and obligations of natural or legal persons; or
(3) governmental regulation under Article 120 section 2 of the Constitution.

421. Various categories of statutory duties can be discerned. The individual fundamental rights and freedoms, granted by an act of Parliament (Constitution) and international treaties, usually have their counterpart in obligations of other entities in relation with the rights holders. Since the rights are absolute, meaning an obligation for all persons to respect these rights, the obligation is also an *absolute obligation to respect rights and freedoms of athletes (and other individuals as subjects of sports rights) and sports organizations.*

422. The second category of obligations is the obligations arising from generally binding legal regulations, mostly acts of Parliament, other than the obligation to respect fundamental rights and freedoms. These are the already mentioned obligations related to facilitating the residence of foreigners in Slovakia, obligations related to social security, tax obligations, obligation to keep accounting and similar. Mostly these are *public law obligations imposed by the State*, which *do not necessarily have a direct counterpart in any right of a private entity.*

423. Another, third category encompasses, for example, the basic *duties of employees,* governed in general by §81 of the Labour Code. These are, however, not applicable to sportsperson, since the relevant paragraph of the Labour Code is not enumerated among those paragraphs of the Labour Code, which solely apply to sportsperson under §46 subsection 2 of the Act on Sports no. 440/2015 Coll. Instead, the Act on Sports contains its own regulation of the employee obligations in §32 of the Act. The sportsperson is thus obliged to:

(1) take part in the competitions and events as determined by the sports organization;
(2) apply best effort in a competition to reach the best possible sports results;
(3) prepare for the competition under guidance of the sports organization;
(4) not participate in sports betting in the same sports, either personally or through any third person;
(5) maintain lifestyle as agreed with the sports organization;
(6) observe the internal norms of the sports organization that the sportsperson was acquainted with;
(7) acquaint himself/herself with the rules of the relevant sport;
(8) obey the orders of the trainers and members of the managing team of the sports organization (unless in breach of the generally binding legal regulation or good morals or unless it would directly and seriously threaten the life or health of the sportsperson or any other person);
(9) not perform dangerous activities without the approval of the sports organization;
(10) protect the property of the sports organization entrusted to him/her against damage, loss, destruction and harm and return the entrusted property to the sports organization upon termination of the contract;
(11) notify the sports organization of any injury, disease or loss of health capacity to perform sports;
(12) submit to medical treatment only after consultations with the sports organization, unless the treatment had to be performed without delay;
(13) submit to physical or medical treatment upon a request by the sports organization; and
(14) restrain from acting that could damage good reputation of the sports organization, unless provided otherwise by this or other laws.

424. Other responsibilities of employees are regulated by specific laws – for example, on safety and health at work (no. 124/2006 Coll.), but also, for example, in the work rules.

425. An employer's obligations are also regulated by the Labour Code, but not concentrated in one provision, as it is in the case of employees. In the Act on Sports no. 440/2015 Coll., however, obligations of a sports organization as an employer are specified in detail in §33. These obligations include:

(a) to ensure training of the sportsperson in preparation for the competition, and guidance by an expert trainer in the competition;

(b) to provide the sportsperson with remuneration;
(c) to ensure acceptable conditions for the performance of sports;
(d) to make sure that selected member of a national team can take part in the national team;
(e) to ensure health care, regeneration and relaxation of the sportsperson; and
(f) to allow the sportsperson to prepare for future career, if the sportsperson is a pupil of secondary school or a student of college or university.

V. Contractual Obligations

426. Specific category of obligations is *based on private contracts.* The sports movement mostly used atypical contracts in the past (prior to 2016), the content of which depends solely on the agreement of the parties, with respect to the generally binding legal regulations. In 2016, a detailed regulation of the sporting contracts was introduced (for performance of professional sports, for performance of amateur sports, for training of talented sportsperson, and even sponsorship contract). Still, a relatively broad margin was left to the parties to agree on additional rights and obligations in the contract, unless in breach of the Act on Sports or other legally binding rules.

A. *Creation, Modification and Termination of Contractual Rights and Obligations*

427. For athletes who have the status of employees, whether under the Act on Sports or special laws (on the work in the public interest, eventually on the civil service of the soldiers or police force), specific regulation on the establishment, modification and termination of employment is applicable. Establishment and termination of sporting employment will be paid attention to in the next section.

428. Modification in the employment relationship is permissible basically only upon the consent and agreement of both parties. There are two basic kinds of modifications:

(1) change in the subject (of the employer, in the case of winding up with legal successor, or in the case of the transfer of undertaking or a part thereof); and
(2) change in the content of employment, on the basis of bilateral or unilateral legal act.

429. To modify the content, a written form of agreement is necessary.

430. The Act on Sports no. 440/2015 Coll. contains specific regulation of loan of the players (in §43) – based on the written agreement between the sportsperson, sports organization and other sports organizations, the player may be let on loan to the other sports organization. In the agreement on loan, changes to the original contract on performance of sports have to be agreed upon.

431. In the case of sporting *contractual relations under the Civil or Commercial Code, their creation* under the Civil Code requires that there is an addressed offer to conclude the contract, which is sufficiently definite and indicates the will of the offeror to be bound in case of its acceptance. Acceptance must be made within the prescribed period or within a reasonable time.

432. The content of obligation is the debtor's obligation to give something, to act or refrain from something or to tolerate something, and the creditor is entitled to require this from the debtor (§494). The content of commitments can change. According to §516 subsection 1, the parties may amend by agreement their mutual rights and obligations.

433. Termination of contractual relationship commitment can be achieved *by cancellation*, according to §49 of the Civil Code: 'A party who has contracted in distress under openly inconvenient conditions, has the right to cancel the contract.' (trans. T.G.) This does not apply in the case of commercial law relationships.

434. According to §582, if the contract is negotiated for an indefinite period, the object of which is a commitment to continuous or repetitive activity or undertaking to refrain from certain activities or to tolerate an activity and if the law or the contract does not state otherwise, the contract may be *terminated on notice* of three months as of the end of each calendar quarter.

435. The contract may also be declared *invalid, for example, because of an error or mistake.* According to §49a:

> Legal act is invalid if it is made by acting person in error based on the fact which was crucial for its implementation, and the person to whom the legal act has been addressed, caused this mistake or has known about it. Legal act is also invalid if this person caused the error intentionally. Mistake in the motive does not make an act invalid. (trans. T.G.)

436. Other ways of terminating an obligation is mainly its *solution* or *expiry of the time.* Exceptional way is a termination when *the solution becomes impossible*, or upon *death of the debtor*, if the performance was to be executed personally by the debtor. This case is applicable for athletes whose performance is irreplaceable. *Loss of the right because of its non-application*, that is, prescription is also possible. Another potential way of terminating an obligation, albeit in the sport it is rather rare, is termination upon *merger of right with obligation.*

437. Deviations in the Commercial Code represent, for example, the provision of §273:

A part of the contract may be determined by reference to general business conditions prepared by expert or interest organization or by references to other terms and conditions which are known to the parties concluding the contract, or attached to the draft. (trans. T.G.)

B. Content of Contractual Rights and Obligations

438. From among the rare cases of *athletes as employees* prior to 2016, one may analyse an *employment contract* of sportsmen of the NSC. It is a standard employment contract with a specific job description. Contractual obligations of the athletes in the NSC are mainly the following:

(1) preparation for competition;
(2) training;
(3) compliance with lifestyle rules;
(4) compliance with doping rules;
(5) compliance with the Code of Sports Representation;
(6) compliance with the standards of ethics and especially sporting ethics;
(7) knowledge of rules of sporting disciplines;
(8) undergoing medical checks;
(9) obligation to participate in the representation;
(10) not to engage in actions contrary to good morals;
(11) keeping a training diary (specification of number of hours worked).

439. The duties are to be performed during working hours, in the workplace, in exchange for remuneration from the employer to be paid in the agreed monthly pay period. Peculiarity in comparison with an ordinary employment contract is the absence of provisions on probation period, due to the fact that the athletes conclude a contract based on their previous performance achieved.

440. The sportsmen within the NSC have also signed a collective agreement under which they are entitled to five weeks' holiday, and they have the possibility of supplementary pension savings.

441. In the case of the Centre of National Sports Representation, the responsibilities of sportsmen are defined similarly in the work description. Just like in the NSC, the staff of the Centre is subject to collective agreement, depending on whether they are police staff or non-police employees. Both categories explicitly have their own trade unions and collective agreement. However, these agreements do not show any specificity in relation to sport, since they are applicable to all employees of the Ministry of Interior.

442. For the majority of other athletes in Slovakia who perform dependent work in sports, the new Act on Sports no. 440/2015 Coll. is applicable, replacing the previous (prior to 2016) practice of having their *rights and obligations enshrined in players' contracts* based on §51 Civil Code or §269 subsection 2 of the Commercial

Code. The 2015 Act on Sports specifies the minimum requirement of sporting contracts for both professional sportsperson and amateur sportsperson (and in addition also some specificities of contracts concluded with promising sportsperson). The contracts should now include at least:

(1) identification of the contracting parties;
(2) period of validity of the contract;
(3) type of sports concerned;
(4) remuneration and related issues;
(5) personal rights commercialization;
(6) paid leave and conditions for taking the leave;
(7) the date of beginning of sports performance;
(8) date of contract's entry into effectivity; and
(9) date and signature.

Additionally, the contract may contain:

(1) the place of usual performance of sports;
(2) notice of termination period;
(3) covering of sportsperson's costs;
(4) shortening the paid leave in extraordinary circumstances;
(5) securing the fulfilment of rights and obligations;
(6) sanctions applicable;
(7) applicable law;
(8) applicable language; and
(9) confidentiality clause.

Basically the same elements are presupposed also in amateur contracts, with the exception of rules on remuneration and related rules, if these are not applicable in the specific amateur's circumstances.

443. In addition to the obligations of the club and athlete (player), other sporting subjects, for example, coaches also enter into contractual relationships. The contractual relationship between a club and a coach was usually governed by a contract under §51 of the Civil Code, or in the case of a coach having a trade licence – under §269 subsection 2 of the Commercial Code. Another option was to use Labour Code §228a – an agreement on work activity, or to use a standard employment contract. Yet another option was according to J. Čorba to use an agency contract,[110] or a so-called mandatum contract. An amendment to the Act on Sports, introduced in 2017, brought a new regulation of a contract with a sports expert (including coaches) in addition to all other possibilities enumerated above. It allows to perform up to thirty hours work per week, and can be concluded for a period up to twelve months. In contrast to the contract of sports activity, this regulation does not

110. Čorba, *Obchodnoprávne vzt'ahy v oblasti športu*, 101–102.

specify the content of the contract in greater detail. An example from legal practice offers an overview of the following contractual obligations of a coach:

(1) within their work, to follow the instructions of the association, universally binding rules and regulations of the association, as well as orders, resolutions and decisions of authorities of the club management;
(2) to responsibly prepare for training activities, to organize training according to schedule and to be personally involved;
(3) to lead the team in matches;
(4) to keep a diary of a coach and to present a statement of activity;
(5) during the match of the team to be responsible for order and discipline, and to enforce safety regulations;
(6) to be responsible for entrusted sporting and other material, and to treat it gently;
(7) to comply with the sport and technical regulations during matches and tournaments, and to follow the principles of fair play.

444. Coaches in the Centre of National Sports Representation of the Ministry of Interior (in their capacity as employees) used to have their duties listed in their job description:

(1) ensuring and implementation of coaching when guiding the preparation of top representatives;
(2) professional, methodical and coaching activities, preparation of programmes of physical training and sports activities, guiding the preparation of athletes;
(3) implementation of sports and mentoring activities;
(4) cooperation with the relevant sports association; and
(5) responsibility for entrusted materials.

445. Performance of activities of a *delegate and referee* was similarly usually governed by mandatum contract under §§724 et seq., or a contract under §51 of the Civil Code no. 40/1964 Coll., defining the specific sporting event, where the referees have to carry out their tasks, and reciprocal rights and obligations of the parties. Since 2017, again, an additional option is to use the contract on performance of activities of a sports expert, which lacks any detailed regulation of its contents in the Act on Sports (§49a). Rights and obligations on the one hand usually include the provision of remuneration and provision of the necessary rooms, eventually protection of the safety of the referee and his/her property, and on the other hand, the duty of a referee to perform at his/her best skills and knowledge in accordance with the rules and regulations of the relevant sport and sports organization. A practical example of a referee contract (pursuant to §51 of the Civil Code) governs the obligations and rights of the organization and referee only very briefly:

(1) the referee undertakes to personally carry out the function of referee for the club;

(2) the referee undertakes to carry out the agreed activities according to his/her best skills and knowledge in accordance with the applicable rules of the sport sector;
(3) the club undertakes to pay remuneration to the referee immediately after the completion of the agreed work.

446. Agent's contract is, similarly as the referee contract, often very brief, stating that the agent undertakes to procure for the sportsman a professional contract, and the athlete undertakes to pay the agreed remuneration to the agent, usually a portion from his/her earnings. This type of contract is not regulated by the Act on Sports and a detailed regulation of this profession falls mostly under internal regulation of sports organizations, as is, e.g., the case of intermediaries in football. According to J. Čorba, the activity of agents has the nature of business and agents must be considered entrepreneurs (traders providing intermediary services or representatives of the liberal professions – attorneys-at-law). The agents may be only natural persons despite the fact that, in practice, legal entities are used by the agents (with a sort of 'responsible representative', who owns an agent licence) without any negative consequences.[111] The contract between an agent and athletes should be a civil law contract in nature according to J. Čorba (as a procurement contract under §§774 et seq. Civil Code), since the athlete's sporting activity is not his/her business activity. On the other hand, however, the contract between an agent and the club, which is an entrepreneur, should be concluded under the Commercial Code (as the procurement contract pursuant to §§642 et seq. Commercial Code).[112]

§3. Employment Regulation

447. Previously (until 2016) athletes in the SR in the vast majority of cases did not have employee status, but instead had the status of self-employed persons. However, since the entry into effect of the new Slovakian Act on Sports no. 440/2015 Coll., the situation has changed and sportsperson performing dependent work in sports are now considered to be in a special type of employment – sports employment, based on the contract for professional performance of sports. Should they, however, perform sports maximum eight hours per week, five days per month, or thirty days per year, they can be considered amateurs, under a contract for amateur performance of sports. (Amateurs have in addition to using the option of signing a contract for amateur performance of sports also the possibility to use a contract for training of a talented sportsperson, or a contract for work based on the Labour Code, or finally they do not need to sign any written contract at all.)

448. At the outset, it should be noted that given the former legal nature of the relationship between sports organizations and athletes, previously there were *hardly any collective agreements* that governed the rights and responsibilities of athletes and clubs. The exception is mainly the collective agreement between the NSC and

111. *Ibid.*, 85–86.
112. *Ibid.*, 90 et seq.

athletes employed at the NSC. It was, however, very concise in its content, and no specific issues of the sports occupation were regulated in this collective agreement.

449. Under the Act on Sports, sporting employment arises between a sports organization and a sportsperson. Should the sportsperson be at least 15 years old, a statement of a parent is necessary in addition in order to conclude the professional contract. Under the age of 15, or before the mandatory education of the young sportsperson is finished, administrative approval by a labour inspectorate and a public health authority is required. In that case, the contract is signed by the parents instead of the sportsperson (player) younger than 15 years.

450. Disputes between employees and employers are heard and decided by courts only under the Slovak labour law. It is not permitted to settle employment disputes in arbitration. Since sport is now considered dependent work under some circumstances, this provision is used to argue against the autonomous arbitration by sports organizations, such as was the case of Arbitration Court of the SFA or the CAS in Lausanne. However, exclusion of arbitration in labour disputes is primarily based on a paragraph of the Labour Code, which is not applicable in sporting employment. It may thus be questionable whether the arbitration should be allowed in sporting employment disputes or not.

451. The employment contract must be in writing and must contain the abovementioned essential elements.

452. Sporting employment contract (contract for professional performance of sports) may be contracted for a maximum of five years, unless the sports organization provides otherwise. Employment for a fixed-term may be concluded repeatedly, albeit its repetitive concluding is limited in §48 of the Labour Code.

453. A contract for professional performance of sports expires in the following ways:

(1) By an agreement in writing. The agreement must specify the grounds for termination of employment if the employee (sportsperson) requests this.
(2) By notice – By the employer or employee, the notice period is one month (unless agreed otherwise or unless provided otherwise in the internal rules of the sports association) and starts from the first day of the calendar month following the receipt of the notice. An employer may give notice to an employee only on specified grounds:
  (a) if the employer moved or is winding up in whole or in part;
  (b) if there are reasons based on which immediate termination could be invoked by the employer;
  (c) if the employee lost due to his/her health a long-term capacity to carry out the work;
  (d) if the employee breached his/her basic obligations under §32 and was warned of the possible termination in the previous six months (in connection with the previous breach of obligations).

The employee (sportsperson) may terminate the relationship upon notice if:

(a) the sports organization breached its statutory obligations under §33;
(b) the sports organization did not use the work of the sportsperson for more than two consecutive months;
(c) the sports organization did not use the work of the sportsperson in more than 10% of competitions, despite being in good health.

(3) By immediate termination of employment by the employer if an employee has been effectively convicted of committing a criminal act, or in case of breach of obligations under §32, breach of anti-doping rules, or if the sportsperson took part in a competition on behalf of another sports organization without the approval of his/her original sports organization, or in case of manipulation of sports competitions and their outcomes. An employee may terminate the sporting employment for health reasons, or if the employer failed to pay his/her wages at least for three months within twelve consecutive months despite a warning from the sportsperson, or finally if the sports organization breached seriously its own internal rules in relation to the sportsperson. Immediate termination of employment by both the employer and employee must be executed in writing, it must define the reason so that it cannot be confused with other reasons, and must be delivered within one month from learning of the reasons for termination to the other party, otherwise it is invalid. The reason may not be subsequently changed;
(4) In case of fixed-term employment relationship, by the expiration of the term.

454. Other cases of termination of employment are associated with the death of the employee, an administrative decision or expiration of work permit in case of foreigners.

455. A problem would undoubtedly occur in the event of termination of employment during the sporting season. For this reason, the institute of probationary period is not known in the Act on Sports.

456. *Working time* is regulated in a specific way in the Act on Sports. It is twenty-four hours daily, during which period the sportsperson is at the disposal for the sports organization, e.g., maintaining the standards of lifestyle and diet. Sports activity itself is performed within the twenty-four hour period only in a few hours as required by the employer. The sportsperson has the right to relax at least six hours within the twenty-four hours, and at least one day in a week, or two days in two weeks, exceptionally.

457. Employees are entitled to holidays of twenty calendar days, or one-twelfth of the twenty days for each month of the contractual relationship. Sportsperson are entitled to remuneration even during holidays, since they are obliged to further maintain the healthy lifestyle and diet.

458. In certain cases, the employee is entitled to additional *time-off* due to obstacles at work, either with payment of salary or without any pay. Here the Labour Code applies also to sportsperson.

459. The Labour Code also regulates the issues *of liability*, and these regulations are applicable to sports as well, since the Act on Sports explicitly invokes the relevant paragraphs of the Labour Code, just like it does in case of the time-off for obstacles in work. The employer is responsible to the employee generally for damage occurred under the performance of work duties, and particularly for damage arising from a work accident and occupational diseases, damage to deposited objects and damage incurred when averting risk. On the other hand, the employee is generally responsible to the employer for culpable violation of the obligations, for non-compliance with duty to avert risk, for a deficit of assigned values and for the loss of entrusted objects. Responsibility of the employees is moderated by the statutory provisions, as well as by the possibility of court to reduce the amount of damages.

460. In the case of misconduct, the labour law in Slovakia does not allow to impose fines on the employee. Cutting the employee's wages is possible only if a variable component of wages was agreed upon. However, these limits are not applicable to sporting employment, where any sanctions can be agreed upon in the contract, or regulated in the internal norms of the sports organization (usually the national sports association).

461. An essential limit in Slovakian labour law, which was also the reason for introducing specific regulation of sporting employment in the Act on Sports, is the principle of so-called *numerous clausus of contract types*, which means that labour law does neither recognize atypical contracts nor, for example, arrangements on contractual penalties. There exist two opposing views on this, but the court practice remains restrictive.[113] Slovak labour law does not allow the conclusion of any other type of contract outside of those regulated in detail by the Labour Code (employment contract, contract for work performance, contract for work activity, student work). Therefore, new contractual types had to be introduced in the Act on Sports no. 440/2015 Coll.

462. In the area of *collective labour law*, the legislation of the SR is based on:

(1) The Constitution of the SR (freedom of trade union association enshrined in Article 37 section 1 of the Constitution, the form of such association is governed by Act no. 83/1990 Coll. on association of citizens).
(2) Labour Code (§230 subsection 2 of the Labour Code allows the operation of trade unions in the workplace, unions have the powers of co-decision, consultation, information, control and collective bargaining),
(3) Act no. 2/1991 Coll. on collective bargaining.
(4) And finally the Act on Sports no. 440/2015 Coll. which allows for collective bargaining in professional sports.

113. Cf. Helena Barancová, 'K prípustnosti atypických zmlúv v pracovnom práve', *Právny obzor* 81, no. 6 (1998): 533–538; Karel Kudrna, 'Přípustnost inominátních a smíšených smluv v českém právu soukromém', *Právní rozhledy* 9, no. 11 (2001): 548–551.

463. The system of collective labour law in the SR is built on the principle of dual representation, allowing for both trade unions and work councils (regulated by the Labour Code since 2001) to represent the workers. The work councils are entitled to the right of information and consultation. However, if in the workplace there are no trade unions, the work councils have all the rights of trade unions, except the right to collective bargaining. Under the Act on Sports, however, only trade unions are recognized as entities of social dialogue and collective bargaining.

464. The presupposed outcome of collective bargaining is the collective agreement, which may provide for more advantageous rules for the benefit of sportsperson, going beyond the minimum standards of the Act on Sports.

I. Travel Allowance

465. A separate issue is the compensation of travel expenses to athletes. Travel reimbursements are essentially provided to employees posted on a working trip. The same applies to sportsperson as well – that is the reason why the Act on Sports allows for specification of the usual place of work in the sporting employment contract – in order to better identify the cases of working trips. On the other hand, if a sports association provides the transport – for example, own bus or through hired bus or contracted transporter – the reimbursement of travel expenses is not paid.[114]

466. Athlete posted on a 'working trip' receives:

(1) reimbursement of travel expenses;
(2) reimbursement of documented expenses for accommodation;
(3) meal reimbursement;
(4) documented necessary incidental expenses (e.g., parking);
(5) compensation for use of motor vehicles except vehicles provided by employers.

467. The Ministry of Finance issued a measure no. 401/2012 laying down the basic allowance rates in Euro or in foreign currency for foreign working trips. Allowance rates for domestic working trips are governed by the measure no. 176/2019 of the Ministry of Labour, Social Affairs and Family.

§4. Labour Market Regulation

468. Labour market and employment services are covered by the Act no. 5/2004 Coll. on employment services. The Employment Services Act defines in §11 employment services for the purposes of this Act as a system of institutions and instruments of aid and assistance to participants in the labour market in:

114. 'Vyúčtovanie cestovných náhrad', *Športinform* 20, no. 4 (2010): 28, http://www.sportcenter.sk/userfiles/file/Studovna/Sportinform/04_2010.pdf, 31 Dec. 2010.

(1) job search;
(2) changing jobs;
(3) filling vacancies; and
(4) implementation of active labour market measures, with particular regard to job opportunities for disadvantaged job seekers.

469. Employment services in the SR under this Act are provided by:

(1) headquarters and the Office of Labour, Social Affairs and Family;
(2) legal persons and natural persons who carry out recruitment, provide professional services and implement active labour market measures under an agreement in writing with the competent authority or under a written agreement concluded within a partnership according to §10;
(3) legal persons and natural persons who carry out recruitment for remuneration.
(4) temporary employment agency; and
(5) supported employment agency.

470. The Act also regulates the *employment of foreigners*, when in §21 it provides that a foreigner who is a party to legal relations arising under this Act has the same legal status as a Slovak citizen, if:

(1) he/she was granted the work permit and temporary residence permit for employment purposes, unless stipulated otherwise; or
(2) he/she is an asylum seeker, who entered the labour market on the basis of a special regulation.

471. The work permit can be granted by the competent authority to a foreigner *if the vacancy cannot be filled with employment seekers registered as employment seekers.* In relation to nationals of Member States of the European Economic Area and Switzerland, however, it applies that such a citizen and their family members have equal status as a citizen of the SR in legal relations arising under this Act.

472. In terms of sportsperson and their labour market, however, it is important to note that sporting employment is considered a special type of employment, upon which the rules of the Employment Services Act do not apply. Hence, even with respect to the *players' agents,* with regard to §25 on work placement for a fee, this provision is not applicable, and the agents are not considered as providing work placement services with respect to sportsperson. If the exercise of their activities would be considered job placement, they would have to respect legal norms allowing the provision of employment services for consideration, only under the conditions stipulated by this Act, and only upon licence. It is further stipulated that recruitment for consideration can be performed only by a person who has completed a university degree of at least the first level. Additionally, estimated cost of recruitment would have to be negotiated between the employment service provider and the legal or natural person, for which the employee is recruited. The intermediary might then charge a fee for services related to recruitment only from a natural person who was not registered as an employment seeker as of the date of application for placement. The service provider could collect this fee only after the employment contract becomes effective. These provisions, serving to protect the employment seekers, would hence clearly pose various obstacles to the work placement in sports job market, should the Employment Services Act apply to sports as well.

473. Still, with respect to other jobs in sports, other than the work of sportsperson, the provisions of the Employment Services Act do apply. In such a case, e.g., intermediary, who *arranges* a *work placement for consideration in abroad,* has to enter into a written agreement with the citizen on work placement for a fee. Contract on the work placement for remuneration includes in particular:

(1) name, address, employer identification number and type of economic activities of the foreign employer;
(2) duration of the employment;
(3) type of work, wage or salary and other working conditions;
(4) the manner and conditions of health insurance and social insurance;
(5) the liability of an intermediary for non-compliance with the agreement;
(6) estimated cost of work placement for consideration.

474. Additionally, in terms of the labour market, *minors* have a special status in the SR. It was already indicated above that according to the Slovak Labour Code as well as under the Act on Sports, children and minors under the age of 15 and over 15 years, if they have not completed compulsory school attendance yet, may be employed only with the consent of the Labour Inspectorate and of authority of public health. These issue a certificate with the number of hours a young employee may work, whereby only light work is allowed, provided that the health, safety and school attendance are not endangered.

475. From the age of 15, assuming completion of compulsory schooling, the employee (including sportsperson) can work without restrictions.

476. According to Article 1 of the (repealed) Directive of SFA on the registration of professional and non-amateur contracts, however, a person might have signed a professional contract only if he/she was at least 16 years old. There was therefore a limitation in comparison with the generally binding legal regulation, which allows a person to work from the age of 15 years. A change was brought about in the football system in the Registration and Transfer Rules from 2015. From the same age, 15 years, it should also be allowed to minor employees to move freely within the EU, but in professional football, international transfers within the EU are allowed only from the age of 16 years, and even then, only under certain circumstances. In the case of transfers outside the EU, the age limit is 18 years. This restriction on freedom of movement is intended to protect young athletes.

§5. SOCIAL SECURITY

477. The social security system in the SR consists of three pillars – social insurance (and pension savings), state social support and social assistance.[115] Athletes are not primarily concerned with state social support (it is providing benefits such as child allowance) or social assistance (in case of social need). An exceptional case of state support for sportsperson is a newly introduced contribution to old-age pension for former sports champions (based on the Act no. 112/2015 Coll. and Act no. 228/2019 Coll. on contribution for merits in the field of sports), making sure that the minimum income of former medal holders is not lower than EUR 500 per month. Still, the most relevant for sportsmen are the provisions on social insurance. Social insurance includes sickness insurance, pension insurance, unemployment insurance, injury insurance and guarantee insurance.

I. Social Insurance

478. Social insurance is administered by the Social Insurance Agency, a public institution *Social insurance in Slovakia,*[116] regulated by Act no. 461/2003 Coll., also covers athletes, being either *employees or self-employed persons*, within its personal scope (i.e., as entities insured against certain social events). The new Act on Sports no. 440/2015 Coll. introduced a mandatory social insurance for sportsperson performing dependent work (considered employees), starting from 1 January 2022. There is thus a transition period under which the sportsperson in the position of employees are not covered by mandatory social insurance – in order to leave some time to the sports organizations to accumulate finances to bear the burden of newly introduced obligation of co-financing the social insurance of their employees (sportsperson).

479. Employees are *covered by sickness insurance, pension (old-age and disability) and unemployment insurance.* Insurance arises with the start of employment and ceases on termination of employment. An employee is not a sportsperson outside the employment relationship – e.g., being an amateur.

480. In case of an injury and in insolvency of the employer, it is not employees who are insured, but the *employer*, within the so-called *injury insurance and guarantee insurance.* This insurance commences on the date when the employer began to employ at least one employee and expires on the day when the employer ceased to employ the last employee.

481. The *self-employed persons*, among whom the majority of athletes is counted in Slovakia, are *compulsorily insured within sickness and pension (old-age and disability) insurance,* if their *income* in the previous calendar year is *greater than twelve-fold minimum monthly wage*, which applies as of 1 July. Insurance in

115. Cf. Miloš Lacko, *Slovak Social Security Law* (Plzeň: Aleš Čeněk, 2010).
116. Ján Matlák et al., *Právo sociálneho zabezpečenia* (Plzeň: Aleš Čeněk, 2009).

this case arises from 1 July to 30 June of the following calendar year. If the income in the previous year does not exceed twelve-times the monthly minimum wage applicable as of 1 July, self-employed is not compulsorily insured for sickness and pension insurance for the next year, from 1 July to 30 June.

482. In the case of sickness, pension, and unemployment insurance, there is also a possibility of voluntary insurance. Voluntarily insured may be any person, which has a permanent residence in Slovakia, a temporary residence permit or permanent residence permit, is aged at least 16 years (in the case of voluntary pension, sickness and unemployment insurance), does not receive early retirement pension (for voluntary pension and sickness insurance) and does not receive old-age pension or disability pension because of the decline in ability to perform gainful employment for more than 70% (for voluntary sickness insurance). Other types of insurance, in particular, *injury and guarantee insurance, cannot be concluded on a voluntary basis,* because in these cases it is the employer who is insured, not an employee or self-employed.

483. Premium rates for all types of insurance are as follows:

(1) sickness insurance: employee 1.4%, employer 1.4%, self-employed (4)4%;
(2) old-age insurance: employee 4%, employer 14%, self-employed 18%;
(3) disability insurance: employee and employer 3%, self-employed 6%;
(4) unemployment insurance: employee and employer 1%, self-employed 2%;
(5) injury insurance: employer according to danger classification from 0.3 to 2.1%, however until the coming into effect of the classification a flat rate of 0.8% is applied;
(6) guarantee insurance: employer 0.25%;
(7) the employer also contributes 4.75% to the reserve fund, as well as does a self-employed person, if insured for pension insurance.

484. The basis of assessment is the taxable income of an *employee* for work performed, as well as wage compensation and share of profits. A *voluntarily insured person's* basis of assessment is an amount determined by the person within the provisions on minimum and maximum assessment base.

485. The decisive period for the employee is a calendar month, for self-employed the preceding calendar year for the period from 1 July to 30 June of the following calendar year.

486. The *sickness insurance* benefits comprise:

(1) sickness benefit;
(2) nursing benefit;
(3) equalization benefit;
(4) maternity benefit.

487. The pension insurance benefits comprise:

(1) from the old-age insurance:
  - old-age pension;
  - early old-age pension;
  - widow's pension and widower's pension; and
  - orphan's pension;

(2) from the disability insurance:
  - disability pension;
  - widow's pension and widower's pension; and
  - orphan's pension.

488. The *injury insurance* benefits comprise:

(1) supplementary injury benefit;
(2) injury pension;
(3) one-off settlement;
(4) survivor's injury pension;
(5) one-off compensation;
(6) vocational rehabilitation and rehabilitation benefit;
(7) vocational retraining and retraining benefit;
(8) compensation for pain and compensation for suffering;
(9) reimbursement of medical treatment expenses; and
(10) reimbursement of funeral expenses.

489. The *guarantee insurance* benefit under the conditions stipulated by this Act is a *guarantee insurance benefit.*

490. The *unemployment insurance* benefit under the conditions stipulated by this Act is called *unemployment benefit.*

II. Health Insurance

491. Besides the Social Insurance Act, *health insurance*[117] is of major relevance for the athletes. It is administered by several health insurance companies. These may be owned by private owners (shareholders) or the State. Health insurance is regulated by the Act no. 580/2004 Coll. and similarly as with social insurance, it also concerns athletes, both as employees and self-employed persons.

492. *Mandatory health insurance* explicitly applies to any *employee* – a natural person who has a permanent residence in Slovakia, with the exception of persons who have their residence in Slovakia, but are insured abroad. Persons who do not have permanent residence in Slovakia, but are employed by an employer with a seat

117. Ján Matlák et al., *Právo sociálneho zabezpečenia*, 193–203.

or permanent establishment in Slovakia, are also insured. Finally, asylum seekers, minors, seized foreigners and others are also insured.

493. However, the term employee does not include sportsperson, even if performing dependent work. This is an exception in the status of sportsperson as employees – they have to cover their health insurance on their own, as if they were self-employed.

494. Persons performing sports activities in sporting employment (professional sportsperson under the Act on Sports no. 440/2015 Coll.) thus enjoy the same status with respect to health insurance as any *self-employed* person.

495. *The basis of assessment* for calculation of health insurance payments is the income of natural persons, but some revenues are excluded. The basis of assessment for self-employed is a multiplication of the tax base and the figure of a coefficient.

496. Minimum for self-employed and employee is uniformly 50% of the average monthly wage, maximum is sixty times the average wage in the national economy in the calendar year two years preceding the reference period.

497. *The decisive period* for employees is the calendar year for which premiums are paid, for self-employed it is the previous calendar year. If the self-employed did not carry out self-employed activity or carried it out for less than six months, the amount of the tax base is to be determined by the self-employed on its own.

498. *Premium rate* is for:

(1) employee 4% of the basis;
(2) self-employed person 14%;
(3) employer 10%;
(4) state 4.30%; and
(5) from the share of the profits of the company and cooperative, 10%, and from other income specified in the law, 14%.

499. In conclusion, the athletes in the SR, even if performing dependent work, are insured within the health insurance scheme as self-employed persons. If performing dependent work in sports, within social insurance scheme they will be obligatorily insured (as employees) as of 1 January 2022. Until that day, however, they are temporarily insured in the social insurance scheme only as self-employed, if their income exceeds a given threshold. Below the given threshold of income, they can be insured within the social insurance scheme only voluntarily. However, even in that voluntary case, voluntary insurance is not possible with respect to guarantee and injury insurance, since these serve only to insure an employer, not an employee. In such a situation, the athletes may be insured for injury only commercially, through private insurance.

III. Pension Savings

500. Pension scheme in the SR also comprises, besides the pension insurance administered by the Social Insurance Agency, the so-called second and third pillar pension schemes, which are not insurance, but rather funded savings schemes.[118] Particularly in the case of use of the freedom of movement within the EU, the athlete finds the issues of coordination and transportability of pension entitlements from these pillars important.[119]

A. *Second Pillar*

501. The *Slovak second pillar* pension scheme is governed by Act no. 43/2004 Coll. on old-age pension saving and on amendments to certain acts. It takes the form of a funded scheme, which is complementary to the first pillar (managed by the Social Insurance Agency). In general, it represents *contracting out* from the half of the first pillar in exchange for the possibility of saving on personal pension accounts under State control. Regarding the role of employers in this pillar, nowhere in the Act is an employer mentioned, which makes the scheme appear not as a supplementary pension scheme, which is usually run by employers. This is also indicated by the fact that the second pillar is unlike the supplementary schemes in Western Europe not limited only to employees. Personal scope in the Slovak second pillar is in fact the same as in the case of social insurance in the first pillar under Act no. 461/2003 Coll.

502. For entitlement to a pension, it is necessary that the saver has reached the retirement age (62 years) and was saving for at least ten years. In terms *of substantive scope of* §29, the old-age pension saving benefits consists primarily of a *pension* in the form of:

(1) a programmed withdrawal with life annuity; or
(2) a life annuity.

503. There is also the possibility of *early retirement pension*, in the form of:

(1) a programmed withdrawal with life annuity; or
(2) a life annuity.

118. Tomáš Gábriš, 'Dôchodkové zabezpečenie na Slovensku v kontexte medzinárodného a európskeho práva', *Právny obzor* 93, no. 2 (2010): 101–116.
119. Tomáš Gábriš, 'Transportabilita a zachovanie dôchodkových práv', *Justičná revue* 62, no. 4 (2010): 467–492.

504. Finally, one can also receive *a survivor's pension,* in the form of:

(1) a widow's pension;
(2) a widower's pension; or
(3) an orphan's pension.

505. In comparison with social insurance, a major difference is that the first pillar, due to the absence of personal pension accounts, does not allow for programmed withdrawal. An essential difference compared to the first pillar is also the preservation of property rights, in the event of death. According to §40 of the Act, the assets value is to be transferred to those who are entitled, and they can have the value attributed to their own personal pension accounts. Even before the money is paid to the saver, the pension account assets represent the property of the saver, and the savings company only administers the assets as in a kind of trust.

506. In the case of using the freedom of movement within the EU, *coordination of pension schemes* becomes relevant. After becoming entitled to payment of pension benefits, the payment should be co-coordinated with other schemes in other EU countries, where the person was insured or where the person saved for their pension. In Slovakia, it is necessary to take into account the first as well as the second pillar in the process of coordination. This is suggested by the design of the EU coordination regulation no. 883/2004 as amended by the Regulation 988/2009, where 'compulsory pension saving' is mentioned in the second part of the Annex no. VIII, defining which part of the Slovak social security system is subject to coordination.

507. The possibility of transfer between the funded schemes, possibly also across borders remains questionable. This is a problem of so-called *transportability.* Elimination of the problem of transportability was pursued by the failed proposal of a European directive from 2005 and again from 2007. This issue was not finally resolved and was left to the Member States to regulate. Still, in the future, the fundamental principles of transportability of all pillars of the pension system should be regulated in a new European directive, which would provide for the three basic solutions:

(1) the maintenance of rights in the original scheme;
(2) transfer to the new scheme; or
(3) such national rules, in which the employee is not forced to change the scheme.[120]

508. The Slovak Act no. 43/2004 Coll. currently recognizes only transport between the Slovak pension fund management companies. Under §47, the pension fund management company is a joint-stock company established in the SR, the object of which is the creation and management of a pension fund for the implementation of pension savings under this Act. An authorization for the establishment

120. M.A.B.L. Wienk, *Europese coordinatie vanaanvullenden pensioenen* (Kluwer, 1999), 195.

and operation of a pension fund management company is granted by the National Bank of Slovakia. Moreover, under §98, 'The pension units recorded in a personal account cannot be used otherwise than as provided under this Act.' (trans. T.G.) This would mean that transport abroad is not possible. The savers are only able to pursue voluntary savings on their personal account while working abroad or to suspend and preserve their rights when leaving Slovakia for the purpose of working abroad. However, this solution is obviously not the best and may constitute an obstacle to freedom of movement for the purpose of employment in another EU Member State. Amendment no. 572/2009 Coll. effective from 1 January 2010 responded to the need of foreign transfers in that it added to the text of the Act a new §17a, allowing the *employees of the European Union and its institutions, to transport their rights, but only from Slovakia to the EU pension system,* not the other way around. This need for specific, express provision for the EU staff confirms that *for other categories of employees, that is, savers (including athletes), such an external transport is not possible, either abroad or from abroad.*

B. Third Pillar

509. The so-called *third pillar* in Slovakia is regulated by the Act no. 650/2004 Coll. on supplementary pension saving. Supplementary pension saving is offered only by recognized supplementary pension scheme companies.

510. Within this pillar, one may find the role of collective agreements and employers, and a complementary nature of this pillar as opposed to funded pension savings provided for in Act no. 43/2004 Coll. Thus, the Slovak third pillar represents a true supplementary occupational pillar in the Western European sense. The personal scope covers employees and their families. Other categories of participants are missing. For Slovak athletes, the third pillar is thus relevant only if they are in employment, or if they were employees previously.

511. For the creation of pension rights, a *minimum period of supplementary pension saving may be not less than ten years and the attained age may not be less than 55 years* (in case of special occupations; otherwise the minimum age is 62 years or the moment of entitlement to old-age pension from the social insurance system).

512. According to §15 on the *substantive scope* of the third pillar, one may distinguish the following benefits:

(1) supplementary old-age pension in the form of:
  - lifelong supplementary old-age pension; and
  - temporary supplementary retirement pension.
(2) supplementary service retirement pension, in the form of:
  - lifelong supplementary service old-age pension; and
  - temporary supplementary service old-age pension.
(3) one-off settlement; and finally
(4) severance pay.

513. In terms of ownership of the accumulated funds, the same situation is applicable *mutatis mutandis* as in the so-called second pillar, namely, that it is funded saving on *personal accounts.*

514. In connection with the freedom of movement within the EU, it should be noted that this pillar, unlike the so-called Slovak second pillar, *is not subject to European legislation on coordination* of pension schemes within the Regulation no. 883/2004.

515. Concerning the possibility of international *transports* within the third pillar, it is necessary to note that under §22, the supplementary pension scheme company is a joint-stock company established in the SR, which is engaged in the creation and management of supplementary pension funds, based on the licence granted by the National Bank of Slovakia. Paragraph 6a–6e nevertheless presume an international relevance of both Slovak, as well as foreign 'occupational pension scheme companies'. According to §37a of the Act, the Slovak companies are explicitly able to operate in the EU Member States and similarly, a foreigner employed in Slovakia may remain a member of his/her original scheme. This Regulation, however, allows only to continue saving, not to transport the rights (or at least the saved amounts).

516. In Slovakia, until recently an express provision on transportability was completely lacking between Slovak and foreign occupational pension scheme companies. Amendment no. 557/2009 Coll., effective from 1 January 2010, partially solved this problem. According to §62 subsection 1 of the Act no. 650/2004 Coll., the law now explicitly *permits transfers from abroad.* Albeit the details are not addressed, these will probably be managed by analogy to national transfers. A greater problem is that this Act still *does not regulate transfers from Slovakia.* For athletes, this means that a player who was involved in supplementary pension saving abroad and then becomes an employee in Slovakia, he/she is able to pass on the savings from the foreign supplementary pension scheme to his/her personal account in the so-called Slovak third pillar supplementary pension scheme company. The opposite situation is not possible.

517. To sum up, the issue of transportation of pension saving assets is solved only in relation to employees of the EU concerning the Slovakian second pillar, and in relation to transport from abroad in the case of the Slovakian third pillar, but not vice versa. Transportability is otherwise excluded, and instead the principles of conservation and (in the second pillar) coordination with other pension schemes are applicable. A solution *de lege ferenda* could bring about further amendments to relevant Slovak acts or adoption of a European directive that would explicitly address the transportability of pension rights in the case of funded pension schemes.

§6. Taxation and Accounting in Sport

518. At this point we only pay attention to the taxation of athletes (as employees and self-employed) and of sports organizations with the legal form of a civic association or a business company.

I. VAT

519. From among the indirect taxes (VAT and excise duties), the VAT is the most relevant in sport. The issue of taxable activities of *civic associations* in respect of VAT was addressed in the Case *5 Sž 131/99* by the Slovak Supreme Court. It was a case of a sports club, which had the legal form of a civic association and registered for VAT, although it did not have to register. Being registered does not automatically mean that the subject is obliged to pay tax, was the conclusion of the Court. The activity, which should have been taxed, was carrying out advertising activities that the tax authority treated as taxable. However, the club claimed it had no trade licence and never carried advertisements for profit and also never in fact reached any profit. The then valid legislation (previous Act no. 222/1992 Coll. on VAT) clearly considers any service provided within the business as taxable. The Supreme Court agreed with the applicant that if its activities are not entrepreneurial in nature, thus not aimed to make a profit, only to allow providing sports activities, the revenue is not taxable.

520. The current legislation, Act no. 222/2004 Coll. on VAT no longer requires that an activity must be carried out within the business. Thus, in principle *any independent economic activity* is taxable, regardless of the purpose and of the legal form of the subject (civic association or a business company). At issue here is the nature of sports activities of the *players* – according to some views, this is explicitly not an independent economic activity, even when the contract between players and clubs is concluded under the Civil or Commercial Code and the athlete has the status of a self-employed person.[121] Should their activity be considered dependent work, athletes would not be subject to VAT. However, should their work be considered an independent economic activity, it would be a taxable activity.

521. An exemption from the VAT taxable capacity is very generally worded in §33 of the Slovak Act on VAT no. 222/2004 Coll.:

> *Exempt from the tax are services* that are closely linked to sport or physical education supplied to persons taking part in sport or physical training, if those services are supplied by a legal person or natural person who meets one or several conditions pursuant to §30 subsection 2. (trans. T.G.)

121. Jaroslava Sikorová, *Športovci a športové kluby v procese DPH.*

These conditions are:

(1) acting for a purpose other than profit, and any potential profit must be fully determined to continue or improve delivery of services;
(2) person is established and managed on a voluntary basis by persons who have no direct or indirect interest in the results of its activities;
(3) it applies prices approved by the competent authorities or prices that do not exceed such approved prices for services; in case the prices are not subject to approval, it applies the price lower than is required for similar services by persons aiming to achieve profit from such activities.

522. Under this provision, *services* delivered by a sports entity (athletes or sports organizations), being a civic association and possibly also a company that operates for purposes other than profit (conditions (1) and (2)) or services offered at a lower price than by competitors (condition (3)) should therefore be exempted from VAT. Thus, if the articles of association contain the statement of non-business purpose and a corresponding adjustment of the distribution and use of profit, the club or a business company should qualify for exemption from VAT. Similarly, the services provided by a natural person should be exempted, if any of the three conditions is met.

523. Entrance fee to sporting events is not exempt from VAT because it is a service that is not provided to participants of sport or physical training, but rather to spectators.[122]

524. Final question is the payment of VAT from transfer fees in case of transfers of players and from the training compensations. If the transfer is considered a service supplied to a sporting body, in our opinion in this case there is an exemption under §33 of the VAT Act. However, one can also find the opposite view.[123]

II. Income Tax

525. From among the direct taxes in sports, the most relevant is the income tax. It is governed by the Act no. 595/2003 Coll. of 4 December 2003 on income tax.

A. Natural Persons: Athletes

526. *Athletes* may be taxed from the following aspects:

(1) athlete as an employee (mostly starting from 1 January 2016, since the entry into force of the Act on Sports no. 440/2015 Coll.); or

122. 'Športový spolok a daň', *Športinform* 16, no. 5 (2006): 42–43.
123. Sikorová, *Športovci a športové kluby v procese DPH.*

(2) athlete as a self-employed; and
(3) athlete receiving a one-off payment, for example, a prize in a competition.

527. It must be noted that the performance of sports activities in the SR is not considered a business, an athlete can therefore only be an entrepreneur in other related activities, for example, in advertising (advertising services), on the basis of trade licence issued under the Trade Act no. 455/1991 Coll.

528. In the case of athletes-employees, their *income from employment* is taxed according to §5 of the Act on income tax. In the case of self-employed, their income is taxable as arising 'from activity of a sportsperson or of a sports expert'. Under §6, this income is stemming:

(1) from use of or granting of rights of industrial or intellectual property;
(2) from activities that are neither trade-licensed nor a business activity;
(3) from activities of experts and interpreters;
(4) from activities of intermediaries, which are not trades; and
(5) from activity of a sportsperson or of a sports expert.

529. Other income under §8 of the Act means income from occasional activities, including pursuant to §8 letter j a one-time price from a sport competition, unless the taxpayer performed the sports activities within self-employment. Thus, if an athlete performs sport as a self-employed, winning the contest constitutes taxable income within his/her 'activity of a sportsperson or of a sports expert'. If he/she is not self-employed, it is his/her 'other income', which should also be taxable. However, under §9 subsection 2 letter m, point 3, in case of a prize below the value of EUR 350 in case of a non-professional athlete it is a tax-exempt income.

530. In a clearer manner, this issue may be explained so that the *prizes from sporting competition,* awarded to winning athletes, are taxed as follows:

(1) In the case of a natural person:
   – who does not have the status of self-employed person, a cash price or non-monetary price, the value of which does not exceed EUR 350, is exempt from tax under §9 subsection 2 letter m, point 3 of the Income Tax Act. Organizer of the competition is required to communicate to the athlete the value of the prize. If the *cash* prize value exceeds EUR 350, the organizer is obliged to deduct withholding tax. If a *non-cash* prize value exceeds EUR 350, the organizer does not deduct the tax, and the tax is paid by the athlete. The organizer thus has the only duty – to notify the athlete of the value of the prize.[124]

124. 'Ceny zo športovej súťaže', *Športinform* 20, no. 4 (2010): 35, http://www.sportcenter.sk/userfiles/file/Studovna/Sportinform/04_2010.pdf, 31 Dec. 2010.

  – If the athlete is self-employed, the prize from competition is always subject to taxation by the athlete.[125]

(2) In the case of legal persons in the form of civic association, any prize is tax-exempt, because it is income from the activity for which a civic association has been created.

531. A particular problem is the taxation of *non-cash benefits* other than prize in competition, provided, for example, to a coach or player (borrowed car, accommodation). The Czech Constitutional Court in a Decision II ÚS 686/05 from 25 October 2006 held that in such cases, the provision of non-cash benefits to the coach was not a non-cash taxable income, but only provision in order to allow for better operating conditions. Still, this remains a highly delicate and casuistic issue.

B. Legal Persons

532. With regard to sports clubs not created for business purposes, according to §12, the object of tax of these taxpayers is income from operations which generated a profit, or from which a profit can be obtained, including revenue from sale of property, income from rents, revenue from advertising, revenue from membership fees and income from which withholding tax is paid. The Act expressly stipulates that such taxpayers are the interest associations of legal persons (e.g., CSSF), professional chambers, civic associations, including trade unions and others. What is important is the last sentence of this provision, according to which 'for the purposes of this Act, taxpayers who are not created or established for business, are not companies established for other than business purpose'. (trans. T.G.) The following provisions of the tax exemption therefore do not concern the sports clubs with a legal form of business companies, even when they were set up for other than business purposes.

533. According to §13 of the Act, in the case of taxpayers established for purposes other than business (excluding business companies) *their income from activities for the purpose of which these taxpayers were established or which is their main activity, is tax exempted,* except for income from operations of business, and income from which withholding tax is deducted (§43). This means that the revenue of a civic association is exempt from tax, if that income stems from the activity, which is a fundamental activity of the association (sporting goal) or the purpose for which an association was created, other than a business. Nevertheless, if the civic association is entitled to do business, benefits from business would be taxable under §12. In this context it should be noted that according to the opinion of the Supreme Court raised in its Decision 3 Săf/43/2009, the fact whether any profit was made, can be detected only *a posteriori,* after the tax year, when the total costs of operation of the club will be known.

125. *Ibid.*

534. Income from core activities comprises among others transfer fees and training compensation, as payments for the transfer of rights between the clubs, namely, the rights to exploit the potential of a particular player. Transfer fee shall be paid upon transfer of a player to a new club if the player is still contracted to the original club. After the contract is over, no fee may be required at the European level, which was confirmed by the CJEU in the *Bosman* case. Training compensation, on the other hand, is paid for a player up to a certain age, who concluded his/her first professional contract with a club other than the club by which he/she was brought up. Concerning the question of fixing the amount, in March 2010 the CJEU decided in the *Bernard* case that the amount should equal the actual training costs incurred by the club. Details are governed by internal regulations of the national associations and international federations.

535. *Revenues from training compensation and transfer fees for athletes* were originally taxed, but since 2005 the interpretation of the Tax Directorate has changed in the sense that it is income *from core activity of the civic association* (sports clubs), and therefore *not subject to taxation.*[126] Exemption from income tax was also confirmed by the Supreme Court in Case *3 Sžf/43/2009*:

> exempted income may be the revenue from entrance fees to hockey games, proceeds from the 'sale' of players, revenues from television and radio broadcasting of matches of a hockey club and similar. (trans. T.G.)
> The same would be true in case of a *civic association that has a trade license*, because the transfer of players, as well as the sale of broadcasting rights, is not a trade-licensed activity. Payment for transfers and training of players, as well as for broadcasting rights is always a part of the basic activity of the civic association.

536. As regards the second group of sports clubs, that is, clubs that operate as *business companies*, these are subject to taxation. The exemption does not apply to them, and they are also taxed on income they receive within their main activities.

III. Tax Obligations of a Club Arising from a Contractual Relationship

537. Sports organization that uses the work of individuals other than sportsperson – referees, health professionals, organizing service, etc., usually uses instead of employment contracts the institutes of contract for work performance under §223–§226 of Act no. 311/2001 Coll. – Labour Code, as amended, or the mandatum contract under §724–§732 of Act no. 40/1964 Coll. – Civil Code, or finally the form of an atypical contract under §51 of Act no. 40/1964 Coll. – Civil Code. Since 2017, there is also an option to use the contract on performance of activity of a sports expert under §49a of the Act on Sports.

126. 'Oficiálna informácia Daňového riaditeľstva Slovenskej republiky', *Športinform* 16, no. 2 (2006): 11–13.

538. In the case of natural persons to whom the remuneration is paid, this income is considered as earned from dependent work and is taxed through advance payment of tax.[127]

IV. Assigned Tax

539. Sports organizations in the legal form of civic associations or non-profit organizations may apply annually for 2% or 3% of income tax of natural persons and corporations, in order to support their activities. The list of beneficiaries is drawn up by the Notary Chamber. Details are regulated by the Act no. 595/2003 Coll. on income tax in its §50, limiting the possibility to allocate 2% only to entities to which the taxpayer-legal person has already donated gifts in the amount of 0.5% from the paid tax. If this condition is not met, only 1.5% from the paid tax may be allocated. The taxpayer-natural person may under specific circumstances allocate 3% of the tax, provided the taxpayer provably performed volunteering of at least forty hours in the tax period.

540. If the organization receives over EUR 3,320 from taxpayers, it must within sixteen months from the date of publication of beneficiaries of 2% publish a detailed overview of how these resources were used. It must do so in the Business Journal, where it shall specify the amount, purpose and the use of the resources, and publish an audit statement, if the organization must have audited financial statements. The recipient who received an amount which exceeds EUR 33,000 in the calendar year from the taxes, is required within thirty days of receipt of this amount to establish a special account at a bank or a branch of a foreign bank, serving only to the use of the share from assigned taxes.

V. Sponsorship and Taxes

541. For tax purposes, sponsorship contribution (under contract on provision of sponsorship, regulated by the Act on Sports) represents a special source of taxable income (for self-employed sportsperson under §6, for employed sportsperson under §8 of the Act on income tax, as being 'other income'). The sponsor can deduct the contribution as tax expenditure.

VI. Accounting

542. According to Act no. 431/2002 Coll. on accounting, §9, the entity is obliged to use the double-entry bookkeeping with the exception of (among others) civic associations, if these are not doing business and if their income did not reach

127. 'Dohody a zmluvy s fyzickými osobami zabezpečujúcimi podujatia', *Športinform* 20, no. 4 (2010): 7, 'Výplata a zdanenie odmien', *Športinform* 20, no. 4 (2010): 12, http://www.sportcenter.sk/userfiles/file/Studovna/Sportinform/04_2010.pdf, 31 Dec. 2010.

the amount of EUR 200,000 in the previous financial year. Consequently, a civic association is required to keep accounts in a single entry system, if it did not have income in the previous financial year amounting to EUR 200,000. The majority of civil society organizations (small sports clubs) will therefore keep accounts in a single entry system in line with the Ministry of Finance measure of 1 December 2010, no. MF/24975/2010-74, laying down details of accounting procedures and details of the structure and labelling items in the financial statements, the content of some items and scope of data from financial statements to be published, for entities maintaining accounts in a single entry system, which are not founded or established for business purposes.

543. All other civic associations (sports clubs, associations), which exceeded revenues of EUR 200,000, or if they undertake a business activity (and thus do not fall under the exception of §9 of the Accounting Act), must keep their records in the double-entry bookkeeping, acting in accordance with the measure of Ministry of Finance of 14 November 2007, no. MF/24342/2007-74 laying down details of accounting and chart of accounts for entities that are not incorporated or established for the purpose of business.

544. Another category is organizations established for business purposes and profit. Sporting business companies should be accounted as any other entrepreneurs.

§7. Dispute Settlement

545. According to Reeb,[128] there are three possible ways of settling sports disputes, namely:

(1) national sports organizations;
(2) competent national court; or
(3) arbitration (both at national and international level).

In addition, before using arbitration, mediation can be used (e.g., under the rules of the International Ice Hockey Federation (IIHF)).[129]

546. Reeb's scheme can be simplified into two basic means of resolving disputes – the ordinary courts or out-of-court dispute settlement (either by autonomous sporting bodies, specialized sports arbitration courts or by general arbitration authorities). The role of the courts in resolving sports disputes is only minor – for example, only 0.1% of sports disputes in football were presented before a national

128. Matthieu Reeb, *The Role of the Court of Arbitration for Sports*, in *International Law and The Hague's 750th Anniversary*, 233.
129. Ian S. Blackshaw, *Mediating Sports Disputes: National and International Perspectives* 170 (T.M.C. Asser Press 2002).

court in Germany.[130] It is a manifestation of efforts to deal with sports disputes autonomously. This effort, however, has some unnatural forms, for example, in the past, FIFA and UEFA prohibited a player from going to court in order to have a dispute resolved.[131] The same applies under Article 36 of the Organizing Rules of the SFA. Such a rule is manifestly contrary to the international conventions and the Constitution of the SR, guaranteeing the right to judicial protection.

547. On the other hand, the courts themselves are not too keen on deciding sporting matters. In the UK, courts are generally reluctant to interfere in sport, unless a principle of 'natural justice' is violated. A similar approach can be seen in the United States of America (USA) in the case of *Harding v. United States Figure Skating Association* from 1994, where the court declared that judicial review should concern only the protection of legitimate interests, fundamental rights and principles of justice. Otherwise, the decision-making competence should be left to sports authorities.[132]

548. The decision-making body of a sporting organization should meet the requirement for independence in order to prevent challenging the decision before the court. Furthermore, it is necessary to include aspects of fair trial, for example, public proceedings.[133] Some results of this approach are also reflected in the adaptation of the procedural rules of the FIFA DRC. These include the power of the Chamber to decide only on matters of a contract, which had been registered with the Football Association, the principle of *non ultra petita* (compensation cannot be higher than requested for), the principle of *culpa in contrahendo* (obligation to pay damages incurred due to the failure of negotiations), the principle of res judicata and the principle of *pacta sunt servanda.*[134]

549. In Slovakia, sporting dispute settlement can take place either at the *ordinary courts*, or in the process of alternative dispute resolution through *arbitration* in accordance with Act no. 244/2002 Coll. on arbitration. This Act was used by the sports movement to establish a permanent court – the Arbitration Court of the SFA (repealed by the SFA as of 1 January 2017). Sports organizations also use the services of their own *autonomous arbitration bodies, not being official arbitration courts* on the basis of the Arbitration Act no. 244/2002 Coll. Their authority is based only on the internal rules of sporting organizations. This way of dispute settlement is also recognized by the Act on Sports no. 440/2015 Coll. Before its adoption, the legislator also considered other options for resolving disputes in sport, even in the form of a special National CAS. However, this project ultimately failed.

---

130. Nafziger, *The Court of Arbitration for Sport and the General Process of International Sports Law* 247–249.
131. *Ibid.*, 231.
132. Ian S. Blackshaw, *Mediating Sports Disputes: National and International Perspectives* 2–3.
133. Ian S. Blackshaw, *Should Sports Disciplinary Proceedings Be Held in Public?*, 3(4) The Intl. Sports L.J. 54 (2005).
134. Soek, *Termination of International Employment Agreements and the 'Just Cause' Concept in the Case Law of the FIFA Dispute Resolution Chamber* 31.

I. Resolution of Sport Disputes under the Act on Sports

550. The Act on Sports no. 440/2015 Coll. abandoned the idea of a national tribunal for sports, but, nevertheless, it contains special arrangements for *sporting disputes resolution.*

551. According to the Act on Sports, the rules of national sports associations should also contain methods of dispute resolution in sports, in particular breach of the rules *within a sport performance* (in the game). These disputes are decided by referees determined by the national sports association for the specific sporting event. Disputes are decided by a referee by imposition of sanctions or corrective measures under the rules of the sports competition. The referee's decisions during the game are final. Only in exceptional cases where equality in competition has been undermined, the national sports association may proclaim the outcome null and void and initiate disciplinary action against the referee, athlete or a sports club.

552. In addition to disputes within the games, the Act also presupposes *disputes outside of a particular game.* These are *decided* by *national sports authorities*, under the internal rules of sports association. In terms of types of disputes, one may thereby generally *discern disputes* between:

(1) *organizers* of sporting events *and* sports *clubs* participating in the sporting competition, *or an athlete*, if acting alone in his/her own name;
(2) sports *clubs* which are members of national sports associations, unless the dispute concerns commercial law relationships or their property;
(3) sports *club* which is a member of a national sports association, *and athletes or sports experts.*

II. Disciplinary Proceedings

553. The Act on Sports no. 440/2015 Coll., unlike the previous Act no. 300/2008 Coll. does not discern specific disciplinary proceedings.

554. The Act also does not specify any types of disciplinary measures that may be imposed on athletes and sport experts, unlike the previous Act no. 300/2008 Coll.

555. The types and rates of sanctions are specified only by the national sports associations in their internal rules. These usually take into account the rules of international sports federations, of which the national associations are members.

556. Disciplinary measures may be imposed separately or together with other disciplinary sanctions. Rules on imposing the sanctions usually specify that it is necessary to take into account the seriousness of the misconduct, the consequences caused and the degree of fault as well as the past behaviour of the offender. However, the Act on Sports only specifies that the principles of fair trial should be observed, and everything else is up to the national association to regulate.

557. Because of this level of detail in regulation of disciplinary offences in the Act on Sports, it may be questionable whether these offences are public or private by nature, or whether they stand *at the crossroads between public and private offences,* even though the original explanatory report to the Act no. 300/2008 Coll. referred to private law in this respect. The mixed nature of this Regulation is, however, demonstrated by the fact that the law makes reference to the violation of internal regulations and the details of punishment of offences are regulated by law, unlike in the case of any other civic associations. This reflects a special public interest in appropriate punishment of disciplinary offences in sports.

Chapter 3. Private Regulation

558. Sports organizations, whether superior umbrella organizations or national sports associations, issue on the basis of their statutes various *internal regulations,* binding on their members, that is on persons that voluntarily submit to the competence of the sports organizations. The organizations can enforce compliance with these standards using their monopolistic or dominant position in sports.

559. Another source of private regulation in sports is contracts. In comparison with Western Europe, *collective agreements* are *nearly absent*, since athletes in the SR are generally not regarded as employees. An exception is the collective agreement within the NSC and at the Ministry of Interior, which applies to athletes employed at the Centre of National Sports Representation of the Ministry of Interior.

560. The principal sources of internal regulation concerning status questions in sports are therefore:

(1) internal rules of international federations;
(2) internal regulations of umbrella organizations;
(3) internal regulations of the national associations;
(4) internal regulations of clubs (e.g., disciplinary rules); and
(5) contract (in terms of rights and responsibilities of athletes).

§1. Associations' Regulation of a Club Status

I. Establishment, Transformation and Winding Up of Clubs

A. Establishment of a Club

561. Issues of a club establishment are usually not addressed in the associations' rules. Only in the rules of SFA, one can come across a provision stating that in case of a brand new football club as a separate legal entity (regardless of legal form), its teams start in the lowest provincial association competitions.

B. Transformation of the Legal Status of a Club and Its Winding Up

562. A special section of the Game Rules of the *SBA* prior to 2016 changes used to regulate the issues of modification of legal status of clubs. Under the Rules, the club has a right to *make* modifications in its *official name* registered with the SBA, for example, in case of a new sponsor.

563. *Transformation of legal personality* (e.g., from the form of civic association to a business company) was also regulated, so that if during the playing period there was a change in legal personality, the club was obliged to send a photocopy of the Statutes to the SBA with the new official name, and to prove the takeover of all commitments of the original club.

564. If the new club did not assume commitments from the original club, it was necessary to make transfers of players in accordance with the Transfer Rules of SBA.

565. In the case of *handball,* club's status issues in relation to a possible *merger of the clubs* were addressed in a separate Directive 'How to merge the clubs'. The decision was to be made at the General Assembly of the clubs. Merger contract was to be submitted to the national association with the required essential provisions addressed.

566. The most complex in this respect is the *Directive of the SFA on legal and organizational changes in the clubs*, which seeks to harmonize standards of the SFA with the standards of civil and commercial law in relation to changes in legal personality, legal form, and in cases of termination of legal personality. It provides that if a football club *ceases to exist without a legal successor,* all its teams shall be dissolved and subsequently removed from the competitions.

567. Abolishment of the football club with a successor under the Directive distinguishes between several options:

(1) Termination or winding up of a football club operating as a civic association as a result of transformation into a commercial enterprise: The business company as the new owner takes over a football club and the right to participate in the competitions organized by the SFA and ULC.
(2) Termination or winding up of a football club operating as a business company as a result of a merger or acquisition: In case of *acquisition* with universal succession, the rights, obligations, assets and liabilities pass on to the successor, that is, the acquiring company. When two companies *merge,* all the rights, obligations, assets and liabilities pass through a universal succession to the successor, whereby both merging companies shall be dissolved.
(3) Termination, or winding up of a football club operating as a civic association as a result of the merger: The merger may also take place with football clubs operating as civic associations, with the same effect as in case of business companies.

C. Bankruptcy and Restructuring of the Club

568. Procedure in case of bankruptcy or restructuring of a club is governed by a separate directive of the SIHF 'Procedure in the event of bankruptcy or restructuring of the club'. The club is obliged without undue delay, within three days, to notify the SIHF and the competent body of the competition on the start of insolvency proceedings or on the initiation of restructuring proceedings. The club is then, to a great extent, limited in its activities and rights. Special regulation deals with transfer of the club license in case of bankruptcy.

II. Sport Licensing System

569. Monopoly of international federations and national associations is reflected in the so-called licensing system for clubs, limiting participation in sports competitions. The licensing system is an autonomous means of regulating sports competitions. Its objectives can be formulated as follows:

(1) to ensure proper functioning of the sports competition in the long-term;
(2) to help ensure the stability of sport performance and competitiveness of the teams at the international level;
(3) to strengthen the integrity of the competition;
(4) to build reliability and credibility of competitors;
(5) to improve public image and ability to succeed in the market; and
(6) to improve safety and comfort of spectators.[135]

570. The SFA directive regulating the club licensing system is based on *UEFA Club Licensing Regulations.* In breach of the terms, the club cannot obtain a licence to enter the UEFA competitions, and from the year 2010–2011, to enter the top Slovakian men's competition.

571. The SFA licence is granted in proceedings governed by a licensing authority and an appellate body. According to the Directive of SFA, the essential elements of the licensing procedure are as follows.

572. An applicant for licence *shall be constituted as a joint-stock company* being a member of the SFA or being in a contractual relationship with a member, for at least three years before the beginning of the competitive year for which the licence is granted.

573. In assessing the fulfilment of *conditions*, the following criteria are considered:

(1) sporting conditions (e.g., youth development programme);
(2) infrastructure (according to the Directive on infrastructure of stadiums);
(3) personnel and administrative conditions;
(4) legal conditions; and
(5) financial conditions.

135. Peter W. Heermann, 'Haftungsrisiken des Sportverbandes bei Lizenzierungsverfahren im Ligasport', *Causa Sport* 3, no. 4 (2004): 194.

574. Another requirement is to be found in Article 38 section 9 of the SFA Statutes:

> natural or legal person (including holding and subsidiary companies and their parts) shall not be partner or member of a body in more than one club in the competition and shall not take part in voting rights in bodies of more than one club nor in any way exercise control over more than one club in the same competition. (trans. T.G.)

This is a well-known prohibition of multiple ownership of clubs.

575. Under section 20 of the Licensing Directive of the SFA, the license is non-transferable. In the event of a merger (or acquisition), the license remains preserved.

576. In contrast, the *Directive of the SIHF on awarding competition licences and on managing these licences* allows for transfer of the licence if approved by the Executive Committee and by a commission for transfer of licences. Possibility of disposing of the right to participate is limited, and the transferee may only be another ice hockey team, who is a member of the SIHF, and meets the conditions for participation in the competition. The act is performed under a *written contract.* The contract on transfer of rights and obligations between the club holding the licence and the club interested in the licence, *must contain the specified particulars* besides the requirements of generally binding legal norms (in particular Act no. 40/1964 Coll. Civil Code).

577. The Executive Committee of the SIHF may also, upon a proposal from a governing body of a competition, use its right to *withdraw the licence of a hockey club,* or repeal its validity.

578. A Directive of the Slovak *Volleyball* Federation (SVF) on trading with the licence considers a licence transferable. Although the legal nature and form of contract for the transfer of licences is not regulated in the Directive, special requirements and procedure of its conclusion are regulated. Otherwise, the contract would not be recognized by the SVF.

§2. Associations' Regulation of the Status of Players

I. Registration of Players

579. Under Registration and Transfer Rules of the *SFA*, individual footballers who wish to participate in sports competitions organized by the SFA, regional football associations and provincial football associations have to be registered. Registration of players is only possible in a particular club, through which the player asks for registration.

580. The player can be registered as a professional, or an amateur.

581. The player whose registration was cancelled at the request of the player, *may be re-registered with another club, as well as a foreign club, after two years at the earliest.* A player who was expelled from the football association may *reapply for registration only after five years from the date of exclusion.* In these cases, the question arises as to whether or not this is a disproportionate restriction on freedom of contract of players, that is, a restriction on their freedom of movement and work.

582. Similarly, in *ice hockey,* if a player asks for cancellation of registration at his/her own request, *there cannot be a subsequently issued consent for a transfer* and such a player cannot play in any domestic or international competition *for twelve months* from the date of issuing of a written decision to cancel the registration, unless he/she renews his/her registration at the original club.

583. According to former Article 13 of the Registration Rules of the *Slovak Athletic Association* (SAA), individual membership could have been cancelled by the athletic sports club, of which the athlete was a member. The club could especially indicate individuals in the case of whom it required a *one-year protection period*, during which the athlete was not able to register for another athletic club. Determination of such a withdrawal period could potentially have been considered as deprivation of liberty. The new Registration Rules from 2012 abolished this problematic rule.

584. Similar restriction of freedom of coalition also exists in *karate and martial arts*. The membership in a club runs from the date of establishment of membership until the end of the calendar year following the year in which the contestant asked for transfer or termination of membership and this was rejected by the club. The athlete is therefore considered a member for another year after he/she expressed the will to terminate the membership, which can be understood as a provision contrary to the freedom to join or not to join an association.

II. Contractual Relations Between a Player and a Club

585. The issue of contract between a football player and a club, and the resulting status *of professional footballer was regulated* by the Directive for registration of professional and non-amateur contracts of the SFA, repealed in 2015 by the new Registration and Transfer Rules.

586. A *players' contract* is a written contract between the club and the player on mutual cooperation in carrying out sporting activities with a focus on football. According to the Registration and Transfer Rules, a contract must be in writing. Minimum duration of the contract is a period between two transfer windows and the maximum duration is fixed for five years. This is in conflict with the provisions of the Labour Code, which restricts (in accordance with the European legislation on *fixed-term contracts*) the possibility of (re) contracting the relationship for a fixed period. However, the new Act on Sports no. 440/2015 Coll. allows for this deviation.

587. Registration and Transfer Rules regulate the terms and conditions of the players' contracts in detail, following closely the agreement on minimum requirements for standard player contracts in professional football, signed between UEFA, ECA, EPFL and FIFPro Division Europe.[136]

588. The major problem in contractual practice in Slovakian football represented previously mainly a *unilateral option to prolong the contract* by the Club. If a player raised a claim against the exercise of an option by the football club, he/she was required to submit his/her objections in writing to the presidency of the football club, registry office of the SFA and the SFA Arbitration Court, in a period of seven days from receiving notification on the application of option by the football club. The player's objections were definitely decided upon by the SFA Arbitration court. The new Registration and Transfer Rules have abandoned this practice.

589. *Club commitments* in contractual practice in Slovakia include, in particular, the following obligations:[137]

(1) to provide remuneration;
(2) to create conditions for training, daily regime, rehabilitation and recovery, to provide medical care;
(3) to provide catering and accommodation during journeys and matches;
(4) to lend sports equipment and maintain and exchange it;
(5) on the basis of consultation with the coach to grant the player a time-off in a calendar week, possibly cumulative, if it is not possible to grant leave regularly. Time-off is usually given in the middle or end of the competition period;
(6) to provide continuous holidays for a period of twenty-eight calendar days without reduction in pay;
(7) to compensate the player for damages suffered by a breach of legal obligations by the club; and
(8) to provide the player with a leave for managing private matters, upon written request, without cuts in monthly remuneration.

590. On the other hand, *obligations of players* include:

(1) to participate in training and perform the duties imposed by a coach in connection with participation in training;
(2) to attend meetings and training camps, and perform the duties imposed in connection with these meetings and training camps;

---

136. FIFA Circular No. 1171, www.fifa.com/mm/document/affederation/administration/97/29/01/circularno.1171-professionalfootballplayercontractminimumrequirements.pdf, 16 Nov. 2010.
137. Sluka, *Profesionální sportovec (právní a ekonomické aspekty)*, 126.

(3) within the performance of sporting activities, to make every effort to achieve the objectives of the sports team according to their capacity and abilities, to compete fairly in the matches;
(4) to submit to the timing and organizational arrangements resulting from participation in competitions and in preparation for competitions and training process;
(5) to actively assist in maintaining discipline in the team, speak in public in a spirit of moral principles, to strengthen the reputation of the sports club;
(6) to ensure their health and physical conditions, observe the principles of professional athlete's daily routine, proper nutrition and diet, hygiene, recovery and rehabilitation, to undergo a medical check and avoid doping in any form, prevent injuries and follow doctor's instructions;
(7) to protect the assets of the club, to care for the property of the club, and compensate the club, if they cause damage in violation of their legal obligations;
(8) to participate in community events and speak in public, especially in mass media, while wearing clothing, footwear and other visible parts of clothing, in the way prescribed by the club, in connection with the activities under the contract;
(9) to maintain confidentiality on the facts related to activities of the club, as well as on all matters relating to club activities, disclosing of which the club would not wish;
(10) to recognize and respect the statutes of the club, to act in accordance with them, and to submit to the authority of the club;
(11) to submit to the provisions of the applicable disciplinary rules of the club, whereby the player agrees with sanctions contained in the disciplinary rules of the club;
(12) not to participate personally or through others, in betting, games and contests related to the results of the matches of their teams;
(13) not to perform any other gainful activity without the consent of the club.[138]

591. In respect of *personality rights* of players, the players agree that the club uses the rights of their personality, particularly to disseminate images of the player, to process their original signature as facsimile or printed for promotional purposes, whereby the revenues from ads and promotional activities belong to the club.[139]

592. The SFA Registration and Transfer Rules address both professional and amateur contracts, and have also introduced special rules on contracts with young players.

593. Under the Competition Rules of the *SIHF*, the notion of *player's contract or professional contract means the contract between a club and an ice hockey*

138. *Ibid.*, 124.
139. *Ibid.*, 125.

player. Each player of the Extra league and First League of seniors, juniors and adolescents, who completed 15 years of age, must have a valid player's contract. Obligation to have a contract with a club does not apply to players starting in competitions, which are defined by the relevant provisions (e.g., Second League seniors and below).

594. The fundamental rights and responsibilities of athletes used to be governed by the Statutes of the SIHF, to which the contracts usually referred. The new Statutes from 2016 have abandoned the enumeration of the rights and responsibilities of the players.

595. Guidelines of the SIHF for monitoring and penalties for doping require that ice hockey clubs incorporate into players' contracts *provisions requiring that players familiarize themselves with the anti-doping guidelines* and introduced a duty to communicate every doping control to the club.

596. In *handball*, the Transfer Rules distinguish between two types of players registered in the Slovak Handball Union (SHU) – contractual and non-contractual.

597. Non-contractual players are players who have not entered into a written contract with their club and receive no compensation beyond the costs associated with participation in the match. *Contractual*, i.e., *professional players* are players who have concluded a written contract with their clubs and receive compensation beyond their costs. The registration of *players' contracts* is governed by the 'Registration of players' contracts Directive.

598. According to Article I of the Registration Directive, the contract should meet the standards set by the Act on Sports no. 440/2015 Coll.

III. Contractual Relations Between Clubs with Impact on the Athlete

A. Transfer

599. The Slovak law does not recognize a specific transfer contract governing the transfer of players between sports clubs. It is usually a contract concluded under §51 of the Civil Code or §269 subsection 2 of the Commercial Code. According to J. Čorba:

> transfer contract cannot be assessed under the provisions of the contract for sale or licensing contract for industrial property. There is namely no transfer of ownership or transfer of rights to any intellectual property present, but rather

a sports club undertakes to perform certain acts which result in the registration of an athlete in a new club and the new club acquires the right to performance of the athlete.[140]

600. The nearest similar contracts are agency contracts in their form regulated by the Commercial Code, if the clubs are business companies. In the event that both clubs are civic associations, they may choose between the rules of the Civil or Commercial Code. This applies to all relations arising between clubs in connection with the transfer of players, including loan contracts, transfer fees and training compensation.

601. In professional *football*, a period during which the player cannot make an application for transfer is set at six months after approval of the previous transfer. During one year, a player may be registered in three clubs consecutively, however, he/she can take part in matches of no more than two clubs.

602. Transfer of *ice hockey players* is regulated by the Transfer Rules of the SIHF. Transfer of a player, who has no valid player's contract with the parent club, and wants to transfer without the consent of the club, can do so without any transfer fee being required. This provision is the implementation of the CJEU decision in the *Bosman* case.

603. The SIHF also has a special arrangement that allows for transfer of players without having to formally use the institute of transfer. Each ice hockey club in the SR clearly has a possibility to create – with the aim of easier collaboration with another club – *a farm team* in the senior category. The farm team should be at least one degree lower in the competition structure than the parent club's senior squad is. Creation of the farm team takes the form of a contract establishing a farm team, signed by two authorized representatives of the parent club and two authorized representatives of the club, which produced the farm team.

604. Within *volleyball*, the Transfer Rules of the SVF distinguish between *transit, loan and transfer.* Transit means a change of club affiliation moving from one club to another within the SR. Loan means a time-limited activity in other than the original club, without changing the club membership. Finally, transfer means transfer abroad.

605. Competition Rules of volleyball allow for the creation and use of *farm teams* just like in ice hockey.

140. Čorba, *Obchodnoprávne vzťahy v oblasti športu*, 151.

B. Transfer Fee

606. Transfer of a player is usually associated with a cash transaction, so-called transfer fee, which should compensate the loss of a player, especially since the player is still contractually bound to the club.

607. Rules of the SFA to determine the amount of compensation for professional players served as an auxiliary criterion for determining the amount by the Conciliation Commission of SFA, in case of failed agreement between the clubs. The Rules were repealed by new SFA Registration and Transfer Rules of 2015. Transfer fee upon moving to and from abroad is regulated by the 'FIFA Regulations on the Status and Transfer of Players'.

608. A professional, who ceases to work as football player, remains registered for thirty months with the original club. If such a player would like to play football during that time as a non-amateur or professional in another club, his/her original club is entitled to a transfer fee.

609. The amount of compensation for *a player with a professional contract* is to be agreed upon contractually, and it should take into account the specificity of sports and objective criteria, such as the previous amount of remuneration of the player.

610. In *ice hockey*, according to the interpretation of the Executive Committee of 14 January 2004 on the 'Principles for determining compensation for players', a fee might have been required for a player since the day after completing 15 years of age. If a player transferred from the new club to another club, while it was the second transfer or any other transfer in order, such transfer qualified as transfer with entitlement to *transfer fee*.

611. The amount of fee was derived from the basic value of a player (EUR 0–EUR 17,300), and it was adjusted using the coefficients to increase the value of the player. For players between 18 years and 22 years, upon moving from second league senior competition to a higher competition, the fee was EUR 5,000. For the same category of players moving from regional competition to a higher competition, the transfer fee was EUR 2,500. The new Transfer Rules state that the amount of transfer fee is a matter of agreement between the respective clubs.

612. According to Article 22 of the Transfer Rules of SIHF, when a contract between a player and a club from the National Hockey League (NHL) enters into force, 5% of the transfer fee (including VAT) should be transferred in favour of the SIHF as a solidarity payment.

C. Training Compensation

613. Compensation for training costs incurred by the club raising a young player is justified by the need to promote education of young players in European clubs, as also recognized by the CJEU in the *Bernard* case, stating that although this is a restriction of the free movement of athletes (players), this constraint is acceptable precisely because of the need to support the education of domestic athletes.

614. In *professional football,* according to the FIFA Regulations governing the status and transfer of players, clubs are entitled to a payment within:

(1) training compensation; and
(2) solidarity contribution.

These issues are governed by Articles 20 and 21 of the FIFA Regulations.

615. Training compensation shall be paid to the training club(s) of a player (aged between 12 and 23 years):

(1) when the player signs his/her first professional contract; and
(2) whenever the professional transfers until the end of the season of his/her twenty-third birthday.

616. In case of a transfer before the expiry of a professional contract, every club that has contributed to the player's education and training, receives part of the compensation to be paid to his/her former club as the so-called *solidarity contribution.* Provisions relating to solidarity contributions are listed in Annex 5 of the FIFA Regulations on the Status and Transfer of Players.

617. The provisions of the FIFA Regulations are also reflected in the Slovakian 2015 Registration and Transfer Rules of the SFA. In case of training compensation, the amount ranges from EUR 200 to EUR 10,000.

618. Under the above-quoted interpretation of the Executive Committee of the *SIHF* of 14 January 2004 on the 'Principles for determining compensation for players', compensation might have been required for a player the day after completing his/her 15 years of age, if a player registered in the club transfers to a new club, while it was the player's first transfer. Such transfer qualified as transfer with entitlement to *training compensation.* The new Transfer Rules from 2019 state that the amount of training compensation is to be set by a separate Directive on training compensation.

619. Finally, Article 14 of the Transfer Rules of the Slovak *Tennis* Association (STA) also allowed the original club to require compensation for the costs of training of a player. According to Article 16, *if clubs do not come to an agreement on the amount of compensation, the original club may impose on the player a twelve-month protection period.* During the period, the player was to play for the original club, but he/she might have asked for lifting the protection period. These rules were, however, abandoned and they are not to be found in the new Transfer Rules.

D. Loan

620. Loan of a professional football player can only take place with the consent of the player, for a definite term, and no longer than until the end of his/her professional contract with the original club. Loan of a player *with the status of amateur player* abroad or from abroad is not allowed.

621. Originally, loan was a type of transfer according to the ice hockey Transfer Rules. There were hence two types of transfer in ice hockey: either *unlimited transfer (transfer)* or *time-limited transfer (loan).* This distinction was however abandoned in the meanwhile in the amended Transfer Rules.

622. Under the Registration and Transfer Rules of the *Slovak Federation of Karate and Martial Arts (SFKMA),* two types of loan are discerned:

(1) *absolute* – during this loan the athlete can take part in contests only for the club he/she is on loan; and
(2) *limited* – in team competitions the athlete participates in competitions in the name of the club he/she is on loan, but in individual competitions he/she represents his/her original club.

IV. Accountability

623. Duties of sports subjects and resulting liability are governed by both the players' contracts as well as by the internal regulations of clubs and associations. A special category of rules is disciplinary rules.

A. Disciplinary Liability

624. An athlete is usually made subject to disciplinary rules in his/her contract. If between *the club and athletes* there is a membership relationship, the disciplinary authority arises from the member relationship itself, which may also be considered contractual, or quasi-contractual acceptance of the club's authority, just like in case of registration of an athlete in the club without a specific player's contract.

625. In case of disciplinary responsibility *of clubs towards the association,* this usually arises from the member relationship within the national association. The new Act on Sports no. 440/2015 Coll. introduced in this respect a general 'jurisdiction' of sports association with respect to any natural or legal persons taking part in the activities of the association – hence, membership is not required any longer as a formal legal precondition for the competence of sports associations towards clubs or individual sportsperson.

1. Disciplinary Rules of the SFA

626. The disciplinary proceedings in football are concerned with misconduct of individuals and legal persons.

627. The SFA disciplinary authorities are DCs for competitions managed by the SFA, and territorial authorities for lower competitions.

628. In disciplinary proceedings, according to the SFA Disciplinary Rules, *individuals* may be sanctioned by the following penalties:

(1) exclusion:
   – from the SFA;
   – from national team;
(2) suspension:
   – from function;
   – from sporting activities; or
   – from other than sporting activities;
(3) ban from the dressing rooms, the technical area, including substitutes' bench, spaces of the extra seating or other areas of the stadium;
(4) ban from entering a stadium;
(5) ban on participation in any activities related to football;
(6) community football service order for the benefit of football movement, the SFA or of its member.

629. The following penalties may be imposed upon *legal persons:*

(1) subsidy reduction or refund of expenses or costs covered from the subsidy granted to the SFA by state government, self-government, FIFA or UEFA;
(2) prohibition to apply for grants from the subsidy granted to the SFA by state government, self-government, FIFA or UEFA;
(3) transfer ban;
(4) playing a match without spectators;
(5) playing a match on neutral ground;
(6) ban on playing a match in a particular stadium;
(7) annulment of result of a match;
(8) exclusion from the competition;
(9) forfeit;
(10) deduction of points; and
(11) relegation to lower competition.

630. The SFA Statutes go into greater detail explicitly requiring that the SFA disciplinary procedure to respect the principles of due process and material justice, and the imposed disciplinary measures must be justified and proportionate to the nature and seriousness of the breach of rules or regulations. The SFA disciplinary proceedings is instigated by the DC which shall proceed as quickly as possible, in order to clarify the case. To properly clarify the circumstances of the misconduct, DC is entitled to invite the parties, which may provide important information, ask for written documents and reports or other evidence, as well as to ask an expert panel for opinion. Reimbursement for witnesses is paid by the football association or by the club, of which the offender is a member. After clarifying all the circumstances of the misconduct, DC decides to impose a penalty in the event that the misconduct occurred, or DC stays the disciplinary proceedings in the event that the misconduct did not occur. *Ne bis in idem* principle applies only to disciplinary proceedings, not to any subsequent criminal or civil law proceedings. Criminal sanction for the same misconduct is thus permitted.

631. Given the nature of the misconduct and the person of the offender, DC may waive the sanction. After serving half of the sentence, DC may decide at the request of the punished that the sentence is conditionally suspended for a probation period of two to twelve months.

632. If DC decides simultaneously on various disciplinary offences, it imposes a penalty for the most serious offence and takes into account the other offences as aggravating circumstances. A number of other specific mitigating and aggravating circumstances are recognized.

633. Against the decision of the DC, offender (individual or a club) may appeal to the Appeals Committee. Appeals Committee is authorized to investigate upon a complaint even those decisions that are not final and effective yet, as well as practices of the SFA members' bodies of the first instance.

2. Deviations in Disciplinary Rules of Other Organizations

634. When compared with the disciplinary systems of several other selected Slovak national sports associations, one may refer to the following specificities:

(1) Prescription of misconduct occurs in different time periods – from six months to two years.
(2) Disciplinary Rules of the *SBA* did not give the offender a possibility to be represented by another person in the proceeding.
(3) Disciplinary Rules of *the SHU* previously allowed for the punishment by analogy, when they provided that in case of misconduct which is not explicitly mentioned in the Rules, this should be sanctioned according to the disciplinary offence the most similar by its nature and severity. The principle *nullum crimen, nulla poena sine lege* was thus not respected (*lex* meaning internal rules in this case).
(4) Disciplinary Rules of the *Slovak Swimming Federation (SSF)* provided for specific disciplinary measures for juveniles, but on the other hand, lacked enumerated aggravating circumstances.

B. Other Sporting Misconducts

635. Competition Rules of the *SFA* specifically regulate offences against the Competition Rules, which do not have the nature of disciplinary transgressions. They can be sanctioned by *gaming* effects, that is, a declaration of default outcome, for serious violation of standards and guidelines, and for acting contrary to regularity of the competition.

636. A number of other associations regulate specific offences and sanctions without precisely specifying the nature of these as disciplinary offences and sanctions. For example, the Competition Rules of the *SIHF* separately distinguish offences against the provisions of the Competition Rules, punishable by:

(1) *technical* effects, that is, a declaration of default outcome; and/or
(2) *disciplinary* provisions of the Disciplinary Rules of the SIHF; and/or
(3) deducting the points after the end of competition (which could also be considered a technical effect).

637. Examples of wrongdoings and procedural aspects of their sanctioning are contained in the SFA Competition Rules, for example, and these are mainly: voluntary rescheduling of the meeting to another date, not appearing for a match, players playing in the game on an invalid or other player's registration card, the physical harassment of referees and other officials or spectators by the players – either before the meeting, during the meeting or immediately after the meeting.

638. Violations of rules and of regularity of the competition justify filing a complaint (objection). The opponent is required within forty-eight hours after receiving the objection, to send his/her position statement via internal information system of the SFA to the body that regulates the competition.

639. An appeal can be filed against the decision of the governing body within fourteen days from receipt of the decision, to the second-instance authority.

640. According to the Competition Rules of the *STA*, misconduct and malpractice of clubs and teams are punishable primarily by *a disciplinary sanction.* In particularly justified cases, *gaming effects* may also be imposed. The STA had also issued special norms regulating the conduct of athletes – a code of conduct, which was valid since 1 December 2003 for all tournaments and competitions organized by the STA, its organizational components, clubs and sections. It regulated the issues of clothing, specified inappropriate clothing, laid down the obligation of the best efforts, and to refrain from audible obscenity, obscene gestures and unsportsmanlike conduct. Breach of these obligations was punishable under *the list of penalties.*

V. Dispute Settlement

641. Sports movement is characterized by a special dispute resolution procedure. The rules of sports organizations at national and international levels try to prevent the settlement of disputes in courts. Instead, the athletes and sports organizations turn to special dispute settlement bodies – the arbitration panels, or arbitration courts. However, only rarely do these authorities have the nature of arbitral authority under national law on arbitration. Only in that case, the arbitrator's decision has the legal force of a judicial decision.

A. Arbitration Court of the SFA

642. Until the end of the year 2016, the SFA disposed of a special body for dispute resolution – the SFA Court of Arbitration (repealed and replaced as of 2017 fully by the SFA Dispute Resolution Chamber). Under the Statutes of the Court of Arbitration of SFA, this court was an arbitration tribunal established under the Act no. 244/2002 Coll. on Arbitration. It was a permanent court, the creation of which was published in the Business Journal, and enlisted in the list of permanent arbitration courts kept by the Ministry of Justice.

643. Services of arbitrators may in general also be used outside the permanent court, but always under a written contract and in compliance with the statutory terms of arbitration, under which the arbitrator does not have a competence to decide on ownership rights and other rights in rem in immovable property, status matters, enforcement of awards and insolvency matters (§1 subsection 3).

644. The SFA Arbitration Court decided particularly disputes that arose from the implementation of contracts between legal entities and individuals in areas related to performance of sports activities. The arbitral tribunal was also competent to decide on appeals against final decisions of the SFA bodies, regional and provincial associations, the ULC, and football clubs, where those decisions related to property issues. According to Article 13(1) of the SFA Statutes, members of the SFA had to undertake to refer any dispute to the SFA Arbitration Court.

645. The Arbitration Court consisted of *the executive bodies of* the Court, the *arbitrators* and the *Registrar. The executive bodies* are:

(1) Presidency of the Court of Arbitration.
(2) President of the Court of Arbitration.
(3) Vice President of the Court of Arbitration.

646. The arbitrators had to meet specific conditions under the Act on Arbitration as well as under the Statutes of the Court of Arbitration, which were the following:

(1) completed law degree from a law faculty of a university in graduate level; and
(2) approval by the Presidency of entry into the list of arbitrators.

647. The arbitration procedure took place generally in a *single instance.* It was not public, and it was predominantly written in form. Proceedings began on the date of filing the application with the Arbitration Court. After bringing an action, if the applicant had not designated an arbitrator in the application, the President of the Court invited the parties to choose from the list of arbitrators of the Arbitration Court within a specified period (minimum of fifteen days) after receipt of the call. The applicant and respondent each appointed one arbitrator. Parties to arbitration might have agreed on another person as an arbitrator, unregistered in the list of arbitrators of the Court. Such a person must have met the general conditions for entry into the list of arbitrators of the Court. If the disputing parties did not choose the arbitrators within a specified period, the Court of Arbitration decided upon the arbitrators itself, without delay. The arbitral tribunal, in cooperation with the parties, secured all documents, papers and other evidence, to fully determine the facts. The Arbitration Court, however, carried out only evidence proposed and presented by the parties. If a party failed to submit documents or other evidence within a set period, the Arbitration Court continued with the proceedings and issued a decision on the basis of available evidence only. The procedure was therefore governed by a principle of formal truth, and represented mostly accusatorial, adversarial types of proceedings.

648. The arbitration award is in general binding for the parties to arbitration to the same extent as a final sentence of a regular court. Annulment of an Arbitration Court decision is possible only on the grounds specified in the Act on arbitration, and if an appeal was filed within sixty days from receipt of the arbitral award. The grounds for appeal are mostly procedural. It should be noted that even if a party brings the award before the competent court, the arbitration award still remains valid. The court may only postpone the enforceability of the arbitration award.

649. Albeit the SFA Arbitration Court was repealed in 2016, the SFA members also recognize the CAS as the highest independent legal authority and ensure respect for decisions issued by this authority.

650. The second type of dispute resolution bodies, used by the remaining national associations, are independent arbitral bodies lacking the nature of a permanent arbitration court under the Arbitration Act. The SFA Dispute Resolution Chamber may serve as an example here, following the model of the FIFA Dispute Resolution Chamber. The Chamber is composed of the President of the Chamber, Vice President of the Chamber and an equal number of members for clubs and members of the Chamber for players and coaches, elected by the relevant voters in electronic elections.

B. Arbitration Commission of the SIHF

651. The SIHF used to employ a special Arbitration Commission in order to decide any disputes within the SIHF. It consisted of a chairperson and four other members. In the event that the Commission had an even number of members, the President had two votes.

652. An impetus for the committee proceedings used to be a request of an applicant (club, coach, player, etc.) with a fee of EUR 100 (including VAT) being paid. The Committee was to meet to discuss the dispute within fourteen days from receipt of the request. It discussed the dispute with an attempt to ascertain the actual situation, and to lead the parties to a compromise solution.

653. A final decision of the Arbitration Commission could have been challenged in *a retrial* (not by a general court, but by the Arbitration Commission itself). A motion for retrial must have been submitted within one month since when the party had learned of the reason for retrial. The retrial had no suspense effect.

654. From a legal point of view, the Commission's decisions were not of a binding nature. In order to reach the binding effect of dispute resolution in ice hockey, in 2016, a court of arbitration was inserted into the new SIHF Statutes. However, no actual steps were taken in order to make the Court work in real life. In the 2018 Statutes, a shift back to the Arbitration Commission occurred.

C. International Autonomous Resolution of Sports Disputes

655. The autonomous settlement of sports disputes also has its international dimension. For example, in football, there are particular dispute resolution bodies of FIFA. The highest authority in the world of sport is the CAS based in Lausanne (Switzerland).

1. FIFA Dispute Resolution Chamber and the Players' Status Committee

656. The DRC decides mainly disputes between clubs and players regarding the contractual stability, labour disputes between clubs and players with an international dimension and disputes regarding training compensation and solidarity mechanism, if at the national level there is no independent tribunal.

657. The Players' Status Committee decides cases of international labour disputes between a club or association and a coach, and disputes between an agent and a player/or club, as well as all other disputes. In the event of a competence conflict between the Committee and the DRC, the chairperson of the Committee shall decide.

658. Details of these bodies, as well as the competence and jurisdiction of a single judge within these two bodies, are laid down in rules governing the status and transfer of players. A single judge within the Committee decides in urgent and simple cases, and a single judge of the Chamber decides on matters with a value of up to CHF 100,000 and in simple cases of training compensation and solidarity mechanism.

659. The FIFA rules do not specify whether submission to the competence of these bodies requires a specific arbitration clause or an arbitration contract. Rather, it appears that it is assumed that there is an agreement on the competence of arbitral bodies of FIFA expressed in players' contracts and internal rules of sports organizations.

660. In the case of both FIFA bodies, the procedure is based on the rules of FIFA and national law, including collective agreements and individual players' contracts, taking into account the specificity of sport. The procedure usually takes place in Switzerland, in Zürich, at the FIFA headquarters.

661. Parties may be legally represented. Their representatives must demonstrate a power of attorney. Proceedings are conducted principally *in writing.* In exceptional cases, a hearing will take place with a written record of the proceedings. If necessary, an interpreter will be provided at the expense of the party that requested his/her presence. As *evidence* it is allowed to use: the parties' testimony, witnesses, documentary evidence, expert reports and other related evidences. The Committee and the DRC may also take evidence not proposed by the parties into account. In case of anticipated high costs of carrying out the evidence, parties may be requested to pay an advance payment of these costs.

662. In the case of disputes concerning the training compensation and solidarity mechanism, or cases in which the DRC has already a settled case law, *Players' Status and Governance Department may submit to parties its opinion.* In case that within fifteen days, parties have not submitted a proposal to continue with the proceedings before the DRC, *the consent of the parties with proposals* submitted by the Department is *presumed.*

663. The decisions may lack reasoning. If the parties within ten days from receipt of the notice do not request the reasons for the decision, the original decision will be considered final and binding. However, decisions relating to sporting sanctions must be justified.

664. 664 It was originally planned that the *Arbitral Tribunal for Football* would be an appellate body, which was to be established under the auspices of the International Court of Arbitration for Football. At the end, however, its role is performed by CAS.

2. The CAS

665. The most important arbitration body at the international level is CAS. Although based primarily in Switzerland, it also operates in Australia and in the USA. In addition, always during the Olympic Games a special ad hoc division for the needs of the summer Olympic Games (first in Atlanta in 1996) and Winter Games (for the first time at Nagano in 1998) is created.[141] The main function of CAS is to hear disputes under the arbitration agreement (clause). It may be a dispute relating to sport in general, or financial interests or other interests associated with sporting activity. CAS also acts as an arbitration body for doping cases at the international level.[142] The arbitrators are essentially independent, selected from a list compiled by the International Council of Arbitration for Sport (ICAS) under the statute of CAS.

666. CAS decides in the following types of proceedings.

a. Arbitration

667. Proceedings are conducted principally *in writing*. If necessary, an oral hearing may take place. The parties must propose all the evidence. Later it is no longer possible to submit evidence, unless the parties have so agreed. Parties shall bear their own costs of the evidence as well as that of interpreters. In deciding, CAS uses the substantive law chosen by the parties, otherwise the law of the Swiss Confederation. However, the parties may also authorize the panel to decide *ex aequo et bono*. The final decisions are taken by majority of votes. They shall be justified and made in writing. When the final decision is made, the CAS will calculate all costs, including the initial charge of CHF 500.[143]

b. The Appeal Procedure

668. Another important function of CAS is to decide on appeals against decisions of sports federations. Appeal against the decision of a sports organization is permitted if permitted by the statutes of the sport organization or if the disputing parties agree on this in a separate arbitration agreement. An appeal is also possible against the decision of CAS, if allowed by the procedural rules applied in the first instance. An appeal may be lodged within twenty-one days from receipt of the contested decision. Principally an appeal is decided by three arbitrators, unless the parties agree on a single arbitrator. The applicable law is the law chosen by the parties, otherwise, it is the law of the state in the territory of which is the seat of a sports organization, the decision of which is appealed against. The panel can *completely*

141. Matthieu Reeb, *The Role of the Court of Arbitration for Sports* 236–238.
142. Eric T. Gilson, *Exploring the Court of Arbitration for Sport*, 98(3) L. Lib. J. 504 (2006).
143. Cf. Pavel Hamerník, 'Rozhodčí řízení u Arbitrážního soudu pro sport', *Právní rozhledy* 15, no. 4 (2007): 134–137.

alter the original decision, revoke the decision or return it to the previous instance. A decision is taken by a simple majority. It is always necessary to give reasons for the decision.

c. Consultations

669. CAS also used to offer opinions at the request of sports authorities. Opinions were formulated by a one- or three-member board established by the President of CAS. However, the relevant provisions of the Code of CAS were abrogated in 2012. The CAS is hence not providing consultations anymore.

d. Interpretation

670. Disputing parties may also ask for an interpretation of a panel decision.

e. Mediation

671. Finally, the CAS also provides mediation services.[144]

§3. Specific Issues

I. Health of the Players

672. Competition Rules of the SIHF in Article 23 as valid up to 2016 used to establish responsibility of the players for their health. Alternatively, a guardian or a parent was to be responsible, if the player was younger than 18 years. Before the start of the season, the player was required to submit to the club proof of his/her medical check-ups. The club was obliged to keep records of such medical checks. Moreover, in championship competitions managed by the SIHF, players must have taken a health insurance. The health of the players has in the meanwhile become a target of legal regulation as well – in the Act on Sports no. 440/2015 Coll., emphasizing the need for regular medical checks of the players.

II. Foreign Athletes

673. Restriction on participation of foreign players (foreigners) in sports competitions represents a legal issue that could potentially be challenged before the CJEU as discrimination based on nationality.

674. In this context, within *football*, the current discussion revolves around the issue of 6+5 rule (proposed by FIFA, abandoned in June 2010) and the system of domestic players known as the *home-grown players rule* (proposed by UEFA).

144. Matthieu Reeb, *The Role and Functions of the Court of Arbitration for Sport (CAS)*, 2 The Intl. Sports L.J. 21 et seq. (2002).

675. In the case of Slovak *ice hockey*, Transfer Rules and Competition Rules limit the number of foreign players in the competitions. This limitation represented a potential direct discrimination on grounds of nationality, which could only be justified by arguments on the need for promotion of training domestic players and on support of national identification with the sport.[145]

676. The classification as a 'foreign player' in ice hockey is not based solely on nationality, though. Although the principle is that a foreign player is any player who does not possess the citizenship of Slovakia, an exception is foreign players registered before 15 May 1993. On the other hand, a foreign player is also a player who acquired the nationality of the SR, but in the past, he/she had played in an ice hockey competition in another country for three seasons, whereby he/she had a nationality other than the citizenship of the SR.

677. In *handball*, the requirement for citizenship acts as a prima facie discriminatory provision preventing athletes from *playing for the national team*, since there are the following requirements:

(1) citizenship of the SR;
(2) for three years before his/her first match in a national representation team of the SR, the player has not played for a national representation team of another country;
(3) in the SR, he/she was qualified for the game not less than before twelve months.

678. Accepting the CJEU decision in the case of *Donà v. Mantero* it is clear, however, that such discrimination in terms of nationality is in principle permitted in the case of national teams.

679. In *volleyball*, the allowed number of foreign players depends on the rules of individual competition, thus making space for direct discrimination on grounds of nationality (Article 18 of the Registration and Transfer Rules).

680. In tennis, under the Competition Rules of the *STA*, Article 91, in a team of adults and seniors, only one foreign national may play. However, the number of players under Article 17 of the Registration Rules (i.e., those who have permanent residence permit in Slovakia) is unlimited.

145. Cf. www.iusport.es/images/stories/documentos/REGLA_6+5_iusport-JAVIER_LATORRE.pdf, 29 Dec. 2010.

III. International Relations

681. International (sports) relations are regulated specifically by the Directive on international relations issued by the *SIHF*. According to this Directive, the international relations can only be developed with the written consent of SIHF. International matches can only take place outside the terms for championship competitions.

IV. Release of Players for the Needs of National Representation

682. The *SHU* is one of the rare associations that issued a directive for the release of players for national representative team stating:

> The club, which has concluded a contract with a player who gave his consent to represent the SR, is obliged to release the player for Slovakian national team if called upon to participate in national representative activities of the team of Slovakia. (trans. T.G.)

683. Also, on the basis of §20 of Regulations of International Handball Federation (IHF), the club was obliged to release players for the national team and for the following events:

(1) Olympic Games, World Championships, European Championships.
(2) Qualifying matches for the events enumerated in paragraph (1), including playoffs.
(3) Other activities of the national team.
(4) International matches of the European or International Handball Federation (EHF/IHF).

684. The club, which releases a player, was not entitled to any compensation, under §21 of the international Regulation of IHF. Details of the relationship between the original club and the athlete were to be regulated in an ad hoc 'agreement to ensure representation of SR in handball'.

V. Other Sporting Subjects

A. Coach

685. According to Article 3.6.1. of the Competition Rules of the *SIHF*, in competitions managed by the SIHF, a team can only be trained by a coach with a valid coaching licence. The SIHF in collaboration with other institutions – the Faculty of Physical Education and Sports of the Comenius University in Bratislava, Faculty of Humanities of Matej Bel University in Banská Bystrica, Faculty of Sport of the University of Prešov and Faculty of Education of the University of Constantine the Philosopher, provides for a uniform education system for ice hockey coaches.

B. Organizer/Organizing Service

686. The Act no. 1/2014 Coll. on the organization of public sporting events distinguishes between the organizer and the organizing service (stewards) of the event. In the statutes, rules and directives of the SIHF, the organizer is called 'the meeting organizer'. Under the Competition Rules, Article 3.12.2, the meeting organizer is responsible for the fair and smooth conduct of meetings, for the safety of players, referees, association representatives, regions representatives, and for the safety of spectators. Apart from technical requirements, he/she also ensures the presence of a physician or paramedic, as well as conditions for the exercise of doping control.

C. Referees and Delegates

687. In *handball*, the status of referees and delegates was specifically regulated by the Joint Procedure for the referees and delegates of the SHU. Its provisions stipulated an upper age limit for referees and delegates, which could be seen as age discrimination, particularly in the context of an English court decision of 2010, according to which there is a discrimination in similar situations.[146] Based on Article 3.1, age limit of a referee in all competitions managed by the SHU was 55 years. Exceptions may be proposed to the Commission by referees. An exception is conditional upon meeting the limits for physical and technical competence. Similarly, the age limit of a *delegate* was set at 70 years. Exceptions to the age limit may be proposed by the Commission of delegates, based on the needs. Exceptions are approved by the Executive Committee of the SHU, just like in case of referees. Finally, the age limit for international competitions is determined by the IHF/EHF rules.

688. Minimum age for young referees was set at 15 years.

689. In view of permitted exceptions to the age limits, and also, if it is shown that the age limits are reasonable and necessary for the performance of tasks of the referees and delegates, these cases of apparent discrimination might be acceptable.

D. Players' Agents

690. Agents' activities are not regulated in Slovakia by any legislation. Only some international sports federations such as FIFA and International Federation of Basketball (FIBA) introduced their own internal rules relating to players' agents (in case of FIFA, these were replaced by an institution of intermediaries in the meanwhile). In Slovakia, detailed arrangements on the activities of intermediaries are to be found in the regulations of the SFA. The SFA has explicitly approved its own 'Directive on the activity of intermediaries' in Spring 2015.

---

146. *See* https://www.theguardian.com/football/2010/apr/15/retired-assistant-referees-age-discrimination, 29 Dec. 2010.

691. An intermediary is a natural or legal person who acts as intermediary for a fee or without any fee between a player and a club for the purpose of concluding a player's contract, or who contacts a club with a view of concluding a transfer contract or who provides a consultation service to the players or clubs.

692. Players and clubs are required to use only services of an intermediary registered with the SFA. Violation of this provision is punishable by disciplinary measures, except in cases where an intermediary acting on behalf of the player is his/her parent or spouse, or an attorney-at-law.

693. The SFA intermediary's registration with the SFA shall be granted upon request and upon passing an oral interview with the SFA representatives. The applicant for a registration shall not have a criminal record, may not hold any function in the SFA, or in the bodies of UEFA, FIFA or the club or any organization that is in any way affiliated with the above-mentioned entities.

694. After successfully passing the registration process, the intermediaries are allowed to denote themselves as an 'SFA registered intermediary'.

695. Each applicant for registration must sign the Code of Professional Conduct.

696. The registered intermediary must renew his/her registration each year by submitting a proclamation on meeting all the requirements necessary for being recognized as a registered intermediary.

697. The intermediary may employ employees, but their tasks must be limited to administrative tasks associated with his/her activities. The intermediary is required to send a list of his/her staff at least once a year to the SFA. Each of the employees mentioned in the list must have been an employee of the intermediary for at least three months before submitting the list.

698. In his/her activities, the intermediary is obliged to inform the club and the player on potential conflict of interests.

699. However, it is allowed that the intermediary represents both the club and the player on condition that both parties agree on this in writing.

700. Against the intermediaries who abuse their rights or violate any of the obligations imposed on them in the Rules, sanctions specified in the SFA Disciplinary Rules may be applied.

701. An intermediary has the right to represent or look after the interests of the player or club only if such a player or club concludes a written contract with the intermediary. A.o., the contract must explicitly state who is responsible for payment of remuneration of the intermediary, type of charge and all necessary conditions for its payment. The representation contract must be executed in two copies at least, and must be signed by both parties. The parties send a copy to the SFA for registration within fifteen days from the date of signature. The SFA is obliged to keep a register of contracts it receives. The contract may be concluded for a period of up to two years from the date of conclusion. According to the Rules of the SFA, two years are counted from the date of signing the contract.

702. The amount of remuneration is calculated based on the player's annual gross income (and thus also includes such income as car and housing, bonuses or other types of benefits). If the intermediary and the player cannot reach an agreement regarding the amount of remuneration that the player has to pay to the intermediary, the intermediary is entitled to payment of compensation at 3% of the income that the player receives from the contract negotiated by the intermediary.

703. Intermediaries of a club receive remuneration for their services as a one-off payment in full amount and in advance. However, payment in instalments may be agreed upon.

704. In case of a dispute between an intermediary and a player or a club that are registered with the SFA, the SFA Dispute Resolution Chamber is to be addressed.

Part III. Doping in Sport

Chapter 1. General Issues

705. Originally, the problem of doping was solely a matter of autonomous sports organizations and sporting rules. Only later was it taken over into legal norms enforceable by the State. In the SR, the issue of doping in sport is governed primarily by Act on Sports no. 440/2015 Coll. (replacing the previous Act no. 300/2008 Coll. on the organization and promotion of sports). The use of anabolic substances is, in addition, sanctioned through the means of criminal law, both to protect human life and health, as well as to protect the fair competition.

706. The Act no. 300/2008 Coll. as well as the Act no. 440/2015 Coll. raised several theoretical issues related to the system of doping offences. Generally, legal theory recognizes private and public offences.[147] *Public offences* are:

(1) criminal acts;
(2) offences and other administrative offences;
(3) disciplinary offences; and
(4) constitutional and international law offences.[148]

707. Private offences take the form of contractually agreed penalties, or remedies envisaged in the codes of private law.

708. Specific legal nature of the punishment for doping – being either public or private offences – is of interest for foreign authors,[149] but in Slovakia, this issue has not yet been addressed. The prevailing opinion abroad, in general, is that responsibility in sport (in the broadest sense, especially outside of doping) is of *private nature.* Purely private law character of liability in sport is based on the idea that the conditions of liability, and imposed sanctions and mechanisms of their imposition are based on internal rules of sporting organizations. Their binding force derives in

147. Aleš Gerloch, *Teorie práva*, 3rd edn (Plzeň: Aleš Čeněk, 2004), 183 et seq.
148. *Ibid.*
149. Julia Völlmecke, *Doping As a Crime? The Policy Issue Concerning the Choice of Method to Deal with Doping*, 1(2) The Intl. Sports L.J. 49–56 (2008); Lauri Tarast, *Interplay Between Doping Sanctions Imposed by a Criminal Court and by a Sport Organization*, 3(4) The Intl. Sports L.J. 15–18 (2007).

theory from the contractual relationship between a sports organization and 'its' athletes ('members'). Ian Blackshaw in this context calls attention to the decision of the Civil Department of the Swiss Federal Tribunal of 15 March 1993, issued in the case of *G. v. Fédération Equestre Internationale and Sport Court of Arbitration*, where the tribunal stated that it is generally accepted that the sanctions provided for by sporting regulations represent a form of punishment laid down by contract.[150] Thus, the prevailing view of responsibility in sport is the view of private, contractual liability, accepted by the athlete as well as by the sports organization.

709. However, some authors suggest a possible public understanding, given the public nature of punishment. Public elements consist of:

(1) the public nature of punishment;
(2) direct accountability to fans; and
(3) the existence of independent moral authority of sports organizations authorizing them to punish athletes.[151]

710. This is, however, just a philosophical approach to accountability in sport, which has no practical impact on the sports discipline and sanctions imposed by the sports organizations. In practice, disciplinary rules are considered a private system consisting of penalties under the contract, whereby there is apparently no direct relationship between criminal penalties, civil liability and disciplinary sporting sanctions, which may lead to situations where athletes are punished repeatedly for the same offence.

711. In case of liability for doping, in contrast to other forms of liability in sports, the liability is derived not from internal rules of sports organizations, at least under Slovak conditions. Currently, the regulation of doping is explicitly to be found in the above-mentioned Act no. 440/2015 Coll. The legislation on combat against doping was introduced through a line of attempts starting from the Legislative Intent of an Act on sport from 2004, through a project of a Sports Act from 2007, to the Act from 2008, which finally mastered the inclusion of this issue to the Act on Sport with details to be provided in the form of an ordinance of the Ministry of Education. Responsibility for doping, in accordance with international obligations of Slovakia, thus became a part of *public accountability,* and doping offences, therefore, in our opinion cannot be considered solely private in nature. Still, it is neither classical criminal nor administrative liability.

712. Some classification of doping offences was thereby recognized explicitly in §19 subsection 3 of the Act no. 300/2008 Coll.:

> The violation of the doping ban creates *disciplinary responsibility* of the athlete, who has a doping substance proven in his body, as well as of a sports

150. Ian S. Blackshaw, *Mediating Sports Disputes: National and International Perspectives*, 158.
151. Janine Young Kim & Matthew J. Parlow, *Off-Court Misbehaviour: Sports Leagues and Private Punishment*, 99(3) The J. Crim. L. & Criminology 592 (2009).

> expert, who takes care of preparing the athlete as a coach, a physician or a sports official, if he has given the doping substance to the athlete, directed him to its use, encouraged him or otherwise assisted in the acquisition or use of the doping substance. (trans. T.G.)

713. It was therefore a disciplinary responsibility and a disciplinary offence as a sort of public offence. Still, there are some specificities, such as, for example, the fact that the Act on Sports does not specify which substances should be considered as doping substances. The Act of 2008 in §19 referred explicitly to:

> possession and use of drugs, pharmaceuticals and other chemical substances enlisted by international anti-doping organizations and international sports federations as prohibited doping substances … (trans. T.G.)
> The list is therefore created as an international norm of the WADA. On the other hand, the Slovak Ministry of Education under §4 of the Act no. 300/2008 Coll. published a list of doping substances. In fact, however, even in this case it was not a list created primarily by the State, rather it was based on a list created by WADA. Special regulation on issuing the list was probably intended to legitimize this list as a legally binding document that was relevant for drawing legal consequences under Act no. 300/2008 Coll. in connection with the punishment for doping.

714. However, a question of the public or private nature of liability for doping misconduct arises particularly in a hypothetical case where the Ministry would not have issued a list of doping substances, or would not react in time to the most recent changes to this list. It would then be questionable whether the breach of such a new WADA list constituted a public or a private offence. According to formulation of §19 of the Act no. 300/2008 Coll., this list should have been binding for the Slovak sports movement notwithstanding its transposition into an ordinance of the Ministry. It would therefore still trigger disciplinary responsibility, whereby the basis for sanctions would have been both Act no. 300/2008 Coll. and the list of doping substances drawn by WADA.

715. A kind of *mixed nature of doping disciplinary liability* – at the crossroads between public law and private law – was thus suggested by the wording of Act no. 300/2008 Coll., which implied that sanctions for doping offenders are not imposed by a public authority, but rather by the national association (in the form of civic association) leaning on the regulations of WADA and international sports federations. This is a special principle of the punishment for doping:

> The principle of the separation of deciding on guilt and on the penalties is based on the World Anti-Doping Code which requires that penalties for violation of the prohibition of doping in sport are imposed by national sports

association, which is the disciplinary authority to sportsmen and sportswomen, irrespective of whether or not they are a member of the national sports association. (trans. T.G.)[152]

716. Along this line, both the 2008 and 2015 Sports Act in Slovakia distinguished between assessing the liability (by the SADA) and imposing the penalty (by national association).

717. While the liability is based on the law, with reference to the list of substances drawn up by WADA or an international federation, the penalties are primarily imposed and specified by the autonomous sports movement and its by-laws (albeit also following the standards of WADA and international sports federations).

718. Ultimately, therefore, the penalty and its scale is decided upon by the national association (which in general does not have a nature of public administrative authority in Slovakia), on the basis of outcomes of a doping control performed by SADA (being an administrative authority). Still, since the Act imposes on the sports associations the obligation to impose sanctions for doping offences, i.e., to decide on the rights and duties of sportsperson, this could point to at least partially public nature of such proceedings, which makes us come to the idea of doping being a specific public disciplinary offence. Based on the above arguments, our conclusion is therefore that of a mixed (hybrid) nature of doping liability – at the crossroads between public law and private law – due to the mixed nature of actors and of sources of doping regulation.

719. This conclusion is of importance in connection with the *issue of double liability and sanctions* – athletes can explicitly be punished for doping both based on the Act no. 440/2015 Coll., and for criminal act under the Criminal Code. If the penalty for doping under Act no. 440/2015 Coll. would be considered a public sanction, it would mean that there is a double public punishment of the offender.

720. Double punishment for doping could be considered acceptable in practice, however, since the Act on Sports the State imposes only a sporting (disciplinary) sanction. Therefore, from a criminal point of view it can insist on another penalty. Another argument why double sanctioning under the Act on Sports and the Criminal Code no. 300/2005 Coll. is not in breach of the principle *ne bis in idem,* is also the specific nature of imposing sport penalties for doping, which, although the State insists on this punishment, is not imposed by the State itself. This is due to the separation of decision on guilt from the punishment. Finally, one may argue by the nature of misconduct and of the sanction for doping as being disciplinary, whereby the disciplinary punishment does not exclude subsequent criminal sanction in the Slovak legal theory. Still, it is questionable whether this general theory can be

152. Bill of the Act on Sport from 2008, www.nrsr.sk/Default.aspx?sid=zakony/cpt&ZakZborID=13&CisObdobia=4&ID=335, 29 Dec. 2010.

applied to the specific legal construction of doping misconduct, which may differ from usual construction of disciplinary delicts.

721. Problems remain with the sanction of banning which may be imposed on an athlete based on the anti-doping rules by a national sports association, while the same sentence can also be promulgated on the basis of the Criminal Code: the penalty of prohibition of performance of an occupation pursuant to §61 of the Criminal Code means that for the duration of this punishment the convict cannot pursue certain occupations, professions or functions, or any activity, which otherwise requires a special permit or conditions which fall under special regulation. The length of penalty may vary from one year to ten years if the offender committed the offence in connection with this professional activity. Theoretically, an athlete's doping activity could thus be punished by the prohibition of participation in sports competitions for two years under anti-doping rules, and then, within the criminal proceedings, the court could impose the same penalty again.[153]

722. In this context, one can reflect on whether the sanction imposed on the basis of anti-doping rules could be considered a mitigating circumstance in criminal proceedings, or serve as a reason for reduced sentence, or conditionally suspended sentence. It should explicitly be noted that sporting sanction of suspension (banning participation in competitions) has serious consequences for the athlete and also a serious educational effect. Especially in the case of a professional athlete, who after a temporary suspension may never return to his/her previous sporting condition – in particular, if during the suspension he/she is prevented from the use of training facilities and services.

153. The penalty of suspension has specific limits for the adolescents. The court may impose this sanction on a juvenile only if it does not interfere with preparation for his profession, and the upper limit of this penalty may not exceed five years. It is in our opinion questionable whether a juvenile athlete can speak about his preparation for the profession – particularly in the light of current legal situation in Slovakia, where athletes do not have an employee status. However, we consider that in this case, it would be a preparation for the profession.

Chapter 2. Public Regulation

§1. International Law and Doping

723. The international conventions and documents on doping, whether solely political or legally binding, with relevance to the SR are mainly the legally binding Council of Europe Convention against Doping from 1989 and the policy document of the Council of Europe – European Charter against Doping in Sport from 1984. Within the UN, that is, its specialized agency UNESCO, in 2005 the International Convention against Doping in Sport was signed.

724. The Council of Europe Convention against Doping took effect on 1 March 1990, and in the SR, it came into force on 1 July 1993. The Convention defines the term 'doping in sport' as prescription and use of pharmacological sorts of doping agents or doping methods by athletes, that is, people who regularly participate in organized sporting activities.

725. The UNESCO International Convention against Doping in Sport came into force on 1 February 2007, and in the SR, it came into force on 1 March 2007. In Article 2, among the definitions, doping is not mentioned, but rather an 'anti-doping rule violation' is defined, which includes cases such as failure to report the whereabouts information in order to facilitate doping control. Otherwise, such an omission could not be, strictly speaking, considered doping, just as if it is the case of refusal to submit to doping control. The definition of violation also includes the possession and trafficking with prohibited substances.

§2. National Doping Legislation

726. Already the Legislative Intent of the Sports Act from 2004 pointed out the international commitments of the SR, mainly the above-mentioned Convention against Doping adopted by the Council of Europe, published in the Collection of Laws of the SR under No. 262/1993 Coll., as well as other international conventions (such as a non-binding declaration of the fight against doping adopted in Copenhagen in 2003). Legal regulation of doping should, according to the Legislative Intent, respect the following principles and rights:

(1) fundamental rights of athletes in the detection and sanctioning of the use of dope, particularly;
(2) right to judicial protection (the possibility of initiating judicial review by an independent court in the sense of Article 6 of the European Convention on Human Rights and Fundamental Freedoms);
(3) the principle of presumption of innocence;
(4) adherence to the principle *nulla poena sine lege*; and

(5) principles of independent and impartial proceedings concerning doping sanctioning, respecting the principle of the Article 7 section 2 letter d of the Council of Europe Convention against Doping, which speaks of separation between an investigation and sanctioning authority.

727. The Legislative Intent and the following project of a Sports Act in addition assumed that the athlete would be able to appeal against a decision of sporting association to the joint Arbitration court for sports, which was to have the status of a *cassation* (repealing) authority, meaning it would not be entitled to change the penalty, only abolish it and the sports association would have to start a new procedure following the legal opinion of the Arbitration court for sports. However, this regulation never became valid law.

728. In 2007, in the general part of the explanatory memorandum to the bill on sports it was proposed to regulate the issue of doping in the Act on Sports only in a framework manner and as soon as possible to develop specific legislation – an Act on the fight against doping. This Act would take over the main idea and content of the World Anti-Doping Code (WADC) into national law and create the institutional, organizational and procedural sanctions base for its implementation. The SR would thus become one of the first countries that promoted the fight against doping to the legal level making it a part of public interest of the State.

729. The final draft of the 2008 bill incorporated a relatively detailed arrangement on the fight against doping, including the establishment of SADA, whereby violation of anti-doping obligations was to be sanctioned through the above-characterized disciplinary proceedings. The bill was finally passed by the Parliament as the Act no. 300/2008 Coll. In its §19 it prohibited the use and possession of doping substances, handling of samples to be tested, and specifically provided for the obligation to submit to doping control and an obligation to communicate the place of residence (whereabouts information) for purposes of control. More or less the same approach was taken also in the new Sports Act from 2015. In comparison to the previous Act, it is more abstract, though (e.g., it does not enumerate the sanctions applicable).

730. In order to analyse the *elements of doping rules violation*, one can follow an established system of analysis of subject, subjective aspect, object and objective aspect of doping.

I. Elements of Doping

731. The *object* of the regulation is the goal of ensuring fair competition, and an ancillary object is the protection of life and health of athletes. According to SADA:

> Doping contradicts the ethics of sport and the principle of protecting the health of athletes. In competition and training it is therefore prohibited to the athlete himself, or with the participation of others:

1. to use prohibited substances, belonging to groups such as pharmacological stimulants, narcotic analgetics, anabolics, diuretics and peptide hormones and their analogues,
2. to use different doping methods such as blood doping, pharmacological, chemical and physical manipulation. (trans. T.G.)[154]

732. The objective aspect is characterized by a ban on the use and possession of medicines, pharmaceuticals and other chemical substances listed by the anti-doping organizations and international sports federations as prohibited doping substances – both in sports competition and in training for the competitions. This does not apply if the doping substance is intended for medical purposes for the athlete.

733. The objective aspect is thereby not only ingestion of doping but also other forms of prohibited conduct under section 88 of the 2015 Act on Sports. This detailed regulation is thereby essentially in line with the definition of doping violations in the UNESCO International Convention, as well as with the principles formulated by the WADA in its Code.

734. The *subject* is primarily an athlete or another person, who committed an anti-doping rule violation under section 88 of the 2015 Sports Act.

735. The *subjective aspect* is construed as an objective (strict) liability for the outcome, without fault being taken into account. National sports association takes into account the athlete's degree of fault only when choosing from the range of penalties.

736. The fault is usually treated in standard legal distinctions between intention (direct, indirect) and negligence (conscious, unconscious).

737. The athlete must always be punished, at least by a warning.

738. If the athlete proves that the doping substance got into his/her body without his/her fault, sports federation can reduce by half the maximum penalty.

739. A *circumstance precluding unlawfulness* is under §88(4) of the 2015 Act the use of doping substances for therapeutic purposes, if the health conditions of the athlete require their use for medical purposes and the athlete was allowed to use them.

740. Only SADA can authorize the use of doping substances for medical purposes in accordance with the WADC, on the basis of the request of the athlete, with a medical expert opinion attached, and upon a recommendation by the national sports association. The athlete, who has been allowed to use doping substances for

154. *Vrcholový športový výkon bez dopingu (otázky a odpovede)* (Bratislava: ADA, 2005).

therapeutic purposes, is obliged to notify the national sports association and the international sports federation of this fact.

741. Request of an athlete takes the form of application for a so-called Therapeutic Use Exemption (TUE). Criteria for granting a TUE are as follows:

(1) if the athlete would not use the prohibited substance or method, he would suffer health problems that are not negligible;
(2) use of prohibited substances or methods will not increase performance beyond the natural performance without the condition being treated;
(3) there is no possibility of treating a disease or condition without the use of prohibited substances or methods. (trans. T.G.)[155]

742. Athlete should apply for a TUE no later than twenty-one days before its approval is needed (e.g., before the event). The Commission for TUEs, which consists of independent experts, decides on granting or refusing a TUE on the basis of the athlete's application and attached medical documents. The Commission shall issue a certificate of consent to the use of prohibited substances, or a certificate to reject the use of banned substances. The Slovak standard norm for granting a TUE is based on the International Standard for TUE, which was adopted in 2004, with effect from 2005, revised in 2009, 2010 and 2011. The revised International Standard for TUE is effective from 1 January 2015.

743. Besides those substances for which the exemption is necessary, a further category of substances used to be distinguished which did not require authorization, but were only subject to a disclaimer of the application. In this case, although medical evidence was necessary just like for the TUE, the athlete did not need to wait for a reply and approval by SADA, or international federation. However, since 1 January 2011, this option was abolished.

II. Penalties

744. In Slovakia, sanctions for doping rules violations are not determined by the Act No. 440/2015 Coll.

745. When determining the sanctions, the international sporting rules apply instead, mainly the WADC.

746. Under the Code, taking into account various mitigating circumstances, a national sports association can change a general sanction of temporary ban of four years if this was the first detection of doping rule violation, into a reprimand or a ban on participation in sporting competitions for two years. However, the athlete must always be punished, at least by a reprimand.

155. *See* www.antidoping.sk/?antidoping-ADA-SR=terapeutickÉ-vÝnimky&ada=93, 16 Jan. 2011.

747. In addition to the basic penalty imposed by the national association, doping has some other *side effects* for the athlete, arising from the Act on Sports or from the WAD Code, namely:

(1) *financial:* throughout the duration of the temporary ban, the punished athlete or sport expert cannot be allocated funds from the State budget for training and for taking part in a competition;
(2) *sporting:*
   - if the athlete violated a doping rule during or in connection with sports competition or a sporting event, the organizer will not accept the sporting result achieved by the athlete;
   - athlete is obliged to return to the organizer all remuneration and prizes received;
   - sporting consequence can take a form of collective responsibility of the sports team – if the athlete who had violated a doping rule, was a member of a team sports, all members may be punished by disqualification from competition and the sporting event, if it is found that another member of the team had also violated doping rules.
(3) *other:* if the athlete has been sanctioned by a temporary ban on participation in sporting competitions, he/she must be available throughout the period of the ban for testing, outside of competitions.

III. Mitigating and Aggravating Circumstances in Doping Legislation

748. While the 2008 Act on Sports provided for various *mitigating circumstances*, copying the WAD Code, this is not the case with the new Act on Sports from 2015.

749. The same is true with respect to *aggravating circumstances.*

750. No rules on doping contained in the 2015 Act on Sports regulate the liability of *sports specialist,* unlike in the 2008 Act on Sports.

IV. Doping Control Procedure

751. The specific *procedure of the doping control* was regulated by ordinance of the Ministry of Education of the SR no. 542/2008 Coll. of 25 November 2008 on the procedure in implementing doping control and management of biological samples of athletes. This was repealed by the Act on Sports from 2015. However, the principles applicable to doping controls are still the same, based on the WADC. The SADA plays an important role in the doping controls. It carries out independent doping controls, plans and performs the in competition doping controls and out-of-competition doping controls, especially in the case of athletes who have significantly improved their performance. In European countries, the doping tests are conducted primarily out-of-competition, just like in Australia, Canada and the USA.[156]

752. The request to make a testing may come from:

(1) an international sports federation or national sports association;
(2) the organizer of a sporting competition or sports event organizer; or
(3) it may be decided upon by the SADA itself.

753. In order to plan controls, the organizers of competitions and events are obliged to present to SADA every year by 20 December a list of sporting events to be held in the following calendar year.

754. A doping control is exercised under the authority of a Commissioner, authorized by the SADA statutory body. The Commissioner shall present a call for doping control to the athlete, to be confirmed by the athlete's signature. If an athlete refuses to accept the call or refuses to acknowledge its acceptance by signing, the Commissioner shall indicate this fact in the invitation. The athlete must attend the place of competition for doping control immediately, no later than one hour after receiving the call. In carrying out doping controls of a minor athlete, his/her legal representative or any accompanying person, who may be a member of the team of the athlete, must be present.

755. The Ordinance also provides for how the spaces where the inspection takes place should look. No photographs or video recordings, sound recordings or audio-visual recordings can be made in this area. Soft drinks provided to the athlete can be opened only by the athlete. Throughout the time of leaving the place of doping control, the athlete must be supervised by a doping Commissioner or Assistant Commissioner. When the sample is urine, the athlete follows the instructions of the doping Commissioner and the collected urine sample is divided into samples 'A' and 'B'. The doping Commissioner shall submit the sealed samples to SADA. Other than urine samples, blood samples may be collected only by a physician or a nurse in the presence of the doping Commissioner, or by a doping Commissioner, who is a physician or nurse himself/herself. The Commissioner is responsible to SADA for the delivery of intact biological samples taken from the athletes. Upon receipt of samples, SADA determines a laboratory to carry out the analysis.

756. If the analysis of the sample 'A' shows positive testing, the athlete has the right to ask the SADA to perform the analysis of sample 'B', and to receive a copy of the documentation of the analytical results of sample 'A'. If the analysis of the sample 'B' is negative, the outcome of the whole doping control is negative.

---

156. *Vrcholový športový výkon bez dopingu (otázky a odpovede).*

V. Whereabouts Information

757. An out-of-competition control of athletes is possible only if the residence of athletes can be monitored, or if the Commissioners are informed about the athlete's place of stay. An Athlete Monitoring Form (for both individual and team sports) is designed for all athletes – representatives of the SR falling under the competence of sports organizations in the SR. The selection of these athletes is made by the sports organizations themselves. Failure to provide information on places of residence for the purpose of doping control constitutes a violation of the standards of the WADC and other rules governing the performance of doping controls. It may lead to a suspension or a permanent ban of professional sporting activities.

§3. Criminal Law and Doping

758. In addition to sporting sanctions prescribed by the rules of sports movement, another result of doping may be criminal sanctions imposed by a court in criminal proceedings. Doping explicitly meets elements of several criminal acts. An athlete may therefore be punished for the same offence by a sporting sanction on the basis of anti-doping rules, and also by a criminal sanction under the Criminal Code. Under the Criminal Code, however, it is mainly other persons besides the sportsperson that can be punished directly with respect to doping – §176 namely specifically provides for punishment of those who provide anabolic substances to other persons, especially to sportsperson.

I. Mitigating and Aggravating Circumstances under the Criminal Code

759. In this place, we pay particular attention to mitigating and aggravating circumstances applicable to doping. These are regulated in §36 and §37 of the Criminal Code.

760. *Mitigating factor* that could be applied to cases of doping constituting a criminal act could be, for example, that the offender:

(1) committed a criminal act due to a lack of knowledge or experience;
(2) committed a criminal act in connection with the negative consequences of his/her illness, while the disease is also considered a circumstance precluding unlawfulness according to the doping regulations;
(3) committed the act in the age near minority or as a person of old-age, if this had an impact on his/her intellectual or volitional capacity;
(4) committed the act under pressure of dependence or subordination; in the case of doping, this could be pressure from the coach, other sports specialists or parents;
(5) committed the act under threats or coercion; this may also originate from sports specialists or parents;
(6) was leading a proper life before the act;

(7) confessed to committing the offence and sincerely regrets the act;
(8) reported the act to the competent authorities;
(9) assisted in detecting a criminal act by the competent authority; or
(10) contributed to the detection and conviction of an organized group, or criminal group.

761. An aggravating circumstance related to doping is, for example, that the offender:

(1) committed the act with especially abject motive;
(2) misused his/her employment, occupation, function or status to gain illegal or improper benefit, which may have a form of victory of the athlete in competition;
(3) has committed more criminal acts;
(4) used a person which is not criminally responsible, to commit a criminal act;
(5) induced a minor person to commit the act;
(6) committed the act as an organizer;
(7) has already been convicted of a criminal act, while the court may, however, disregard this fact due to the nature of prior convictions.

II. Criminal Acts Related to Doping

762. Paragraph 176 provides for the most important criminal act in connection with doping – 'illegal handling of anabolic substances', which means that someone procures or administers another person anabolics or any other agents with anabolic or hormonal effects (specified in the Act no. 397/2015 Coll.) for other than a therapeutic purpose, shall be liable to a term of imprisonment of up to three years, and if this was committed in relation to a sporting competition, up to eight years.

763. This means only the person administering the doping substances is punishable, not the athlete who ingested the substance.

764. Should the perpetrator thereby cause grave bodily harm or death, or act in large scale or as a member of a network of criminals, the punishment can be raised up to fifteen years of imprisonment.

765. The most serious criminal act that can be connected with doping is *manslaughter* (§149), defined as causing death by negligence. It is conceivable, if administering of some doping substances (other than anabolics or hormonal substances) is likely to cause death. The means used to enhance performance often have significant side effects, which can lead to fatal consequences.

766. Bodily harm in general may be another criminal act connected to doping. For clarification of the terms used, *bodily harm in general* comprises bodily harm and grievous bodily harm. *Bodily harm stricto sensu* for the purposes of Criminal

Code means such a harm to another, which objectively required medical examination, treatment or therapy, during which the damaged person was for longer than a short time hindered in the normal way of life. *Grievous bodily harm* (*severe injury to health*) for the purposes of this Code means serious disorder or serious illness, which may be:

(1) mutilation;
(2) loss or substantial reduction of working capacity;
(3) limb paralysis;
(4) loss or substantial weakening of the functions of sensory organs;
(5) damage to an important organ;
(6) disfigurement;
(7) inducing abortion or killing the foetus;
(8) excruciating suffering; or
(9) health disorder lasting for a longer period (at least forty-two calendar days during which the normal life of the victim was seriously affected).

767. Intentional damage to health may take the form of *intentional grievous bodily harm* (§155) or *intentional bodily harm distinct from intentional grievous bodily harm*. Using doping may clearly, for example, cause severe liver damage, and thereby reduce the fat metabolism, which may result in severe disease with long-lasting or permanent consequences.[157]

768. A negligent grievous bodily harm (§157) is to be distinguished from the *negligent bodily harm* (§158).

769. The *intent* may be:

(1) direct, where the offender wanted by his/her actions to cause injury;
(2) indirect, if the offender knew that his/her action can cause injury and the offender was reckless as to whether the harm will be caused.

770. Negligence may be:

(1) conscious, where the offender knew that his/her actions can cause injury, but without reasonable grounds he/she relied that no injury will be caused; or
(2) unconscious, if the offender did not know that his/her actions can cause injury, but given the circumstances of the case and his/her personal circumstances he/she ought to know and was able to know.

771. Another criminal act related to doping is the *harm to health* (§162), which covers cases of incorrect indication of medicines by a person without professional qualification, which occurs as a result of negligence and causes immediate danger

157. *Ibid.*

to life or a bodily harm. Similarly, §170a punishes *illegal handling with medicines*, e.g., import or production of illegal medicines.

772. Similar category of cases is covered by §170 as 'endangering the health through illegal medicines, medical devices and supplies'. This section is used to punish a person who either intentionally or by negligence causes or increases the risk of harming human health through the handling of medicines.

773. Another possible criminal act in connection with doping is 'unauthorized production of narcotic drugs and psychotropic substances, poisons, or precursors, their possession and trafficking' (§171). The substances are further specified in the Act no. 139/1998 Coll. The possession of such substances for own use (in an amount corresponding to a maximum of triple usual single dose, and only for personal consumption) is punishable separately. The possession for own use on a larger scale (in an amount corresponding to ten times the usual single dose, for personal consumption) is also separately punishable. This paragraph further punishes those who unlawfully:

(1) manufactured;
(2) imported, exported, transported or caused to be transported;
(3) bought, sold, exchanged, procured; or
(4) harboured for any length of time a narcotic drug, psychotropic substance or precursor, or mediated such activity.

774. Another criminal deed is 'promoting drug addiction' (§174). The objective aspect is inducing another to abuse addictive substances other than alcohol, or supporting or encouraging abuse of such substances, or their dissemination.

775. Exposing a person to the influence of doping substances could also theoretically fall under the elements of criminal deed specified in §208 – 'abuse of close and entrusted person', if the athlete was in such a relation with those who gave him/her dope. Physical or mental suffering can clearly also be caused through exposure to the impact of substances that could harm the health of a person. This deed requires, however, a higher degree of brutality and ruthlessness, which would probably, in modern doping, not be common.

776. In the case of a victory with the help of doping substances it would be possible to consider the criminal act specified in §221 – 'fraud'. It is defined as being committed by a person who, to the detriment of foreign assets, enriches himself/herself or other person, by causing someone to err, or using someone's mistake, which results in a small loss (EUR 266) to the foreign assets.

777. The last criminal deed which is applicable is 'damaging foreign rights' (§375), consisting of the fact that someone causes serious injury to the rights of another in that he/she causes someone to err, or uses someone else's mistake.

778. In the case of fraud and harming foreign rights, the damage occurs particularly to athletes, who due to doping have not gained victory and have not received the related awards (prizes). Similarly, a sports club or national association may be damaged, for example, as to its reputation. It is also damaging to the organizer of the competition and the sponsors.

§4. Administrative Offences and Doping

779. The Offences Act no. 372/1990 Coll. can be invoked in relation to doping only in the field of protection against alcoholism and other addictions according to §30 subsection 1. This offence is committed by a person who has:

(1) sold, given or otherwise allowed consumption of alcoholic beverages to a person obviously affected by alcohol or other addictive substance, a person younger than 18 years or to a person with the knowledge that he/she will work or exercise other activities which could endanger human health or harm property;
(2) illegally sold, or given or allowed to another person harmful use of addictive substances other than alcohol; and
(3) intentionally allowed to enjoy an alcoholic beverage or to take other addictive substances to a person younger than 18 years, if it endangers his/her physical or moral development.

780. These offences are punishable by a fine.

Chapter 3. Private Regulation

781. The issue of doping is regulated at the international level by international conventions and the WADC, and at the national level mostly in the internal regulation of doping as issued by individual sports organizations.

782. For example, in the case of *football*, Disciplinary Rules of the SFA read that the sanction is to be imposed based on the WADC.

783. Additionally, under the Disciplinary Rules of the SFA, other sanctions may be imposed on the individual or a legal person as recognized by the Disciplinary Rules.

784. Examples of autonomous regulation of doping controls and sanctions may also be found in the Directive for monitoring and penalties for doping of the *SIHF*. Under its Article 1:

(1) The SIHF considers as doping any presence of a prohibited substance in a bodily sample of a player, use by a player of a prohibited substance or use of a prohibited method from the list of prohibited substances and prohibited methods or any breach of anti-doping rules of the WADA, the IIHF, the IOC, the SOC and the SADA. Doping is prohibited in competition and in preparation for competitions.
(2) The use of prohibited substances or methods is detected in a doping control.
(3) Directive for monitoring and penalties for doping within the SIHF as well as relevant legal norms of the SR and the WADC apply to all ice hockey players of both sexes (hereinafter referred to as 'player') who participate in competitions of SIHF and IIHF, their coaches, officials of sections, clubs, and other utility and support staff (hereinafter 'staff') and organizers of individual competitions and matches. (trans. T.G.)

785. Other provisions state in accordance with the rules of WADA and SADA that refusal or failure by the player to submit to doping control is considered a doping rules violation and is punished under the SIHF Disciplinary Code. However, the Directive on Anti-Doping takes precedence before the Disciplinary Code in cases of conflict.

786. Collecting the samples for analysis is the task of authorized commissioners of the IIHF, the IOC and the SADA.

787. The Directive also determines specific responsibilities of the different entities:

> Every player is required to inform the medical doctor about any prohibited substances, prohibited methods and effects of the use of medical substances in terms of doping. The physician is required to be familiar with the prohibited substances and prohibited methods, including supplements, as specified in the

World Anti-Doping Code (WADC), the relevant directives of SADA, regulations and directives of the IIHF and SIHF. Coach and staff must be familiar with these directives and see to it that a player does not use banned substances and methods. Officials of the SIHF, of regions and clubs are obliged to familiarize themselves with these directives and in the scope of their competence to prevent the misuse of banned doping substances and methods by a player. (trans. T.G.)

788. Doping control may be imposed on a player even outside the territory of the SR, based on decisions of the doping control body of the host country, eventually third country under an international anti-doping convention.

789. The outcome of the test has to be passed on by the player to the statutory body of his/her club and to the main coach of the team. These are obliged to inform immediately the managing body of the competition, and this communication is strictly confidential. Competition managing authority shall immediately inform the Executive Committee of the SIHF.

790. The Directive also requires that ice hockey clubs incorporate into players' contracts provisions on the obligation of players to become familiar with the anti-doping directives and to communicate any doping control to the bodies as described above (Article 6 of the Directive).

791. Offences and penalties are regulated in the Directive as follows:

If the presence of a prohibited substance in a bodily sample of a player was demonstrated or a player has used the prohibited substance or prohibited method, or refused to undergo any part of a doping control, or if a player or another person has attempted to manipulate or falsify the results of the doping control, or if he/she is suspect of manipulation, or has administered the prohibited substance or method, or illegally traded with any prohibited substance or prohibited method, the sanction is following:

1. temporary suspension until the results of analysis of the 'B' sample are exposed;
2. for the first transgression, suspension for four years is imposed; for the second transgression, a lifetime ban is imposed;
3. if a player illegally trades with, or administers the prohibited substance or prohibited method, he/she will be punished by suspension for a minimum of four years, and maximum of a lifetime ban;
4. if the use of specified substances (under Article 10.3 World Anti-Doping Code) will be proven, the sanction will be:
   – for the first transgression warning and reprimand, and maximum of one year disqualification;
   – for the second transgression suspension for two years;
   – for the third transgression lifetime suspension.

5. if a player fails to report his/her whereabouts information, or misses a doping test, he/she shall be punished by a ban of at least three months and a maximum of two years;
6. if a member of the staff breaches anti-doping rules, that member will be sanctioned by a lifetime suspension;
7. in case the outcomes of analysis are not yet known, the main couch is competent to decide on whether the athlete will take part in the competition.

Collective responsibility is reflected in that if three players from one team have in any season positive testing in the A sample or B sample, or committed any wrongdoing under the Article 1, letter a of the Directive, the whole team is to be punished under the provisions of Disciplinary Rules of SIHF. Disciplinary Rules in Annex 2 B – Penalties for teams – in point fourteen, called 'violation of the prohibition to use doping', punish doping by the exclusion of the team from the competition, or by a return to competitions of the SIHF (however, this invocation of Disciplinary Rules is now obsolete since the new Disciplinary Code of SIHF valid since 2016).

792. From among other sports associations, rules of the *Slovak Canoe Association* used to explicitly mention the duty of all competitors in the race, but also during sports training, to submit to doping control upon invitation under the directives on the doping control issued by the Slovak Canoe Association, SADA, WADA or the International Canoe Federation. Currently, only the general rules on Anti-Doping by the Act on Sports and WADC are applicable.

793. Rules of the *Slovak Cycling Association* invoke the SADA rules on monitoring and penalties for doping in sport, and the Anti-Doping Rules (Anti-doping Examination Regulation (AER)) of the International Cycling Union.

794. Competition Rules of *volleyball* also refer, apart from the sportive-technical documents of SVF, to SADA regulations as well as to the generally binding legislation of the SR.

795. In swimming, Disciplinary Rules of the *SSF* used to contain the principle (now reformulated in Article 38 of the 2016 Disciplinary Code) that:

> For a violation of the doping rules bears disciplinary responsibility the athlete, to whom it has been proven that in his body is a doping substance, as well as sports specialist, who is in charge of the preparation of the athlete as a coach, medical doctor or sports official, if he gave the doping substance to the athlete, induced him to use it, encouraged him or otherwise helped him in the acquisition or use of doping substances. Equally responsible is the athlete who:
>
> 1. tried to take a doping substance with intent to affect his athletic performance,
> 2. refused a doping control, or failed to take part in testing without a serious reason,

3. exchanged or tried to exchange biological samples intended for doping control,
4. manipulated or attempted to falsify any part of doping control,
5. did not notify his whereabouts information for the sake of a doping control, and in this way prevented a doping control. (trans. T.G.)

796. According to Article 38 of the current Disciplinary Code, penalties for the use of doping are to be imposed based on the WADAC foremost or based on the Disciplinary Code itself.

797. Disciplinary Rules of the *SHU* govern various disciplinary offences together with prescribed penalties in their Part C.

798. In addition to sportsperson, also *coaches and officials* can get punished for anti-doping rule violations.

799. Under the Statutes, the SAA is bound as far as doping is concerned by the WADC of WADA, anti-doping rules of the International Association of Athletics Federations (IAAF) and the IAAF Procedural Directives, specified in Chapter 3 of the applicable rules of athletic competitions of IAAF.

800. Athletes are further obliged to comply with the SADA rules regulating the method of control and punishment of doping in sport, including any later amendments. All members of the SAA are bound to respect the above-mentioned rules and comply with them. Disciplinary Rules of the SAA specify in detail sanctions for breach of anti-doping rules.

801. Under the SAA Statutes, the SAA in relation to the control and sanction of doping in sport additionally:

(1) has the right to exert controls in competition and out-of-competition through authorized bodies or persons; reports on the inspections are to be annually submitted by the SAA to the IAAF;
(2) undertakes to allow the IAAF to carry out doping controls at competitions organized by the SAA;
(3) recognizes the right of the IAAF to make unannounced doping controls of individuals who are members of the SAA.

Part IV. Sport and Business

Chapter 1. General Issues

802. The exercise of sports activities by athletes, activities of sports clubs or national associations, and their relations with third parties show several aspects of for-profit activities. This may be a trade or business under the Trade Act or Commercial Code, but also a gainful activity outside the realm of business, resulting from civil contracts.

803. A specific combination of sport and business is the area of competition. At the European level, the *Piau* case (namely, the decision of the Court of First Instance in Case T-193/02 *Laurent Piau v. Commission* of the European Communities (EC) from 22 April 2004) stated that for purposes of competition law, sports clubs and international federations constitute business companies (or associations of businesses[158]), and therefore they are participating in the economic competition, although with some exceptions resulting from the fact that the objective of competition in sport is not to completely ruin a competitor, but rather to create and maintain a certain balance in the competition to ensure the uncertainty about the scores. The same is the purpose of prohibition of personal links between sports clubs (prohibition of *multiple ownership* – laid down also in §15 subsection 6 of the Act no. 440/2015 Coll.), which therefore should not be considered an unlawful restriction of competition.[159]

804. From among the individual sports activities, activities of sports clubs, associations and other entities participating in sports, one can give the following examples related to business and trade:

(1) *Transfer contracts,* namely, contracts on the transfer of players (athletes), but also contracts on loan and training compensation, which have in the SR a nature of atypical contracts under §51 of the Civil Code or §269 subsection 2 of the Commercial Code. According to J. Čorba, their basis is a commitment of a sports club to terminate or to establish a contractual relationship with the player, and to pay in exchange for a player's know-how, knowledge, abilities

158. Čorba, *Obchodnoprávne aspekty športovej činnosti*, 97.
159. Čorba, *Športové kluby a ich právny život*, 90.

and talents,[160] eventually, in case of a training compensation to compensate the original club for the costs associated with bringing up a player.

(2) *Trading with licences* allowing start in the competition; this issue is usually treated by internal rules of sports associations, as well as by contracts under the Civil and Commercial Code – either as an atypical contract or a contract for sale, depending on the internal rules of an association.

(3) *Sponsorship contracts, advertisement and gifts*, whereby sponsorship must be distinguished from advertising. Advertisement is used to support activities of the advertiser (sales promotion of their product) and not to advertise the producer himself/herself unlike in the case of sponsorship. Sponsorship differs from a donation in the way that the sponsor expects consideration – self-promotion. Sponsorship contract is regulated under §§50 and 51 of the Act no. 440/2015 Coll., and the contracts for advertising are atypical contracts concluded in practice under the Commercial or Civil Code.[161]

(4) *Sale of broadcasting rights,* whereby it can be questioned whether it is performance of individual athletes that is being broadcasted, or the performance of the whole team or the whole competition, and to whom the rights belong and who can exploit them.

(5) *Merchandising,* which is a contractual relationship between sports organizations (athletes) and manufacturers of merchandising goods (souvenirs), using the popularity of sportsmen or clubs.

(6) Relationships between owner or user of sports facilities and cafeteria operators.

(7) Relations between sporting event organizer and private security services contracted to ensure order and others.

805. From another perspective one can divide the above-mentioned business relations in the field of sport into *the relations which arise between entities of the sports movement,* which are largely governed by *internal regulations* of the sports organizations, and the other categories of commercial (gainful) relationships between *sporting entities and their* business *partners operating outside the realm of the sports movement.* This latter group of relationships is almost exclusively subject to the official legislation governing commercial and civil relations, and only rarely is it regulated by internal rules of sporting organizations.

§1. Legal Forms of Doing Business in the SR

806. Business activity in the SR is split *into two main forms – trade activity and business activity.*

160. *Ibid.*, 91–92.
161. *Ibid.*, 93.

807. Trade *licences* are granted and issued under the Trade Act no. 455/1991 Coll., which in §2 stipulates that 'the trade is a sustained activity operated independently in their own names on their own responsibility for profit and under conditions stipulated by this act'. (trans. T.G.) In §3, activities are excluded that are not trades. Sporting activities are not excluded. The law thereby recognizes three types of trades:

(1) crafts, under condition of competence gained by apprenticeship (listed in Annex no. 1 of the Trade Act);
(2) bound, if the condition is a competence acquired otherwise (the list is attached under Annex no. 2);
(3) free, if there is no condition of competence whatsoever (there is a list of recommended designation of trades).

808. When examining the individual trades in Annexes to the Act, as well as a list of recommended designations of free trades one cannot find any trade focused specifically on sporting activities. Athletes can thus not possess a trade licence to perform a sporting activity (this is precluded under §3 explicitly). The Trades Offices did not accept this type of trade even previously – with reference to the uncertainty of the term 'sporting activity'. Athletes can thus become tradesmen only when providing other services, for example, advertising. The same applies to the sports organizations – clubs and associations. Nevertheless, some trades are closely related to sporting activity. These are the following:

(1) mountain guiding activities including guiding and escorting people on the hiking trails and routes;
(2) massage services.

809. A condition for their operation is special education, proof of eligibility and possibly a certificate of accreditation under special regulations. It should be noted that the trainers and masseurs need not necessarily be tradesmen in order to carry out their activity for a club.

810. The second option of performing business activities in Slovakia is *entrepreneurship under the Commercial Code.* According to §2, 'Entrepreneurship means sustained activity performed independently by an entrepreneur in his/her own name and on his/her own responsibility for profit.' (trans. T.G.) Entrepreneur under this Act is:

(1) a person registered in the commercial register;
(2) a person conducting business under a trade licence;
(3) a person who operates business on the basis other than a trade licence pursuant to special regulations;
(4) a natural person who carries out agricultural production and is registered in a register under a special regulation.

811. Athletes performing primarily a sporting activity do not fall into any of these categories, unless they dispose of a trade licence, for example, for the provision of advertising services. Sports clubs, as far as they are civic associations, also do not fall into any of these categories, unless they have a trade licence for any of the trades.

812. In contrast, sports clubs, which are business companies, are registered in the commercial register, and they are entrepreneurs, although *established for other purposes than profit.*

813. *Competition* between the various business entities in the market of the SR is governed by Title V of the Part 1 of the *Commercial Code,* differentiating between unfair competition and restricting competition.[162] Restriction of competition is specifically dealt with in Act no. 136/2001 Coll. on protection of economic competition. Legally binding rules of competition are however not contained only in the generally binding legislation, but may also result from business customs, good morals and in the case of sport from the rules of sporting organizations.[163]

§2. Sports Organization as an Entrepreneur

814. While sports associations must have a form of civic association due to the Act no. 440/2015 Coll. on Sports, sports clubs may have pursuant to the same Act the form of both civic associations under the Act on association of citizens no. 83/1990 Coll. and the form of a business company based on the Commercial Code no. 513/1991 Coll. (mostly as limited liability companies and joint-stock companies).

815. However, irrespective of legal form, a sports organization can be authorized to do business – either under the Trade Act or the Commercial Code. It is even easier if a sporting organization has a provision in its Articles of Association, under which the association operates a trade for the purpose of economically supporting its core mission.[164]

816. As long as a civic association does not have a trade licence, it is not an entrepreneur, and the contractual relations entered into are not falling under the legal regime of the Commercial Code. However, the parties can voluntarily agree to apply the Commercial Code.[165]

817. In the case of clubs having a form of business companies, even if these are not established for the purpose of business, still, their relations are subject to the

162. Marek Števček, 'Hospodárska súťaž v právnej reglementácii Obchodného zákonníka (stručný komentár)', *Obchodné právo* 9, no. 11 (2008): 31–34.
163. Čorba, *Obchodnoprávne vzťahy v oblasti športu*, 160.
164. Cf. 'Športový spolok môže mať živnosť', *Športinform* 19, no. 9 (2009): 9, http://www.sportcenter.sk/userfiles/file/Studovna/Sportinform/09_2009.pdf, 29 Dec. 2010.
165. Čorba, *Obchodnoprávne vzťahy v oblasti športu*, 62–63.

Commercial Code, although according to §261 of the Commercial Code, it is to be applied only to contractual relations between businesses, if they arise within their business activities.

818. According to §261 subsection 3 of the Commercial Code, there also are 'absolute businesses', which are situations where the Commercial Code is to be applied, whatever be the nature of the parties. On the other hand, under section 6, there also are 'absolute non-commercial relations', which are governed only by the Civil Code.

819. Under §262, in addition, the parties may agree in writing that their relationship, which does not fall into the group of relationships mentioned in §261, shall be governed by the Commercial Code. The Commercial Code thus can also be used by non-entrepreneurs, if agreed upon.

820. Under some circumstances, the sports clubs as business companies enter into civil law rather than commercial law relationships. Clubs, for example, often act as organizers of sporting events and come into relationship with the spectators. This relationship, although it is a relationship with economic impact, is civil in its nature, and it can be considered a relationship between entrepreneurs and consumers.[166]

§3. Athlete as an Entrepreneur

821. In practice, Slovakian in individual sports are mostly self-employed persons. They can become entrepreneurs, or tradesmen, if they obtain a trade licence to perform, for example, advertising and marketing activities.

822. De lege ferenda, however, it could be appropriate to formulate a specific trade, consisting in sporting activities, for the purposes of professional sportsperson doing individual sports.

823. Athletes as self-employed persons are entering into contracts with entities within the sports movement (clubs, agents) as well as outside of this sphere. From among the second category, one can mention the contractual relations with sponsors and marketing partners, or managers. In the event that the athlete has a trade licence for a performance, for example, for advertising activities, contracts should be according to J. Čorba, concluded under the Commercial Code. J. Čorba also paid special attention to the contractual relationship between the athlete and his/her manager, who is a person different from the players' agent (recognized in some sport sectors). The managers and the athletes sign agency contracts, procurement contracts or atypical and mixed contracts, with a commitment of the manager to arrange for matters relating to participation of the athlete in sports competitions, contact

166. *Ibid.*, 142–143.

with the media and contact with fans, negotiation of advertising contracts, sponsorship contracts, advertising the person of the athlete, construing his/her image, on the one hand, and on the other hand, the commitment of the athlete to pay a compensation for the manager's services.[167] This agreement, if the athlete performs the activity as an entrepreneur within the object of his/her trade licence should be, according to J. Čorba, concluded under the Commercial Code, otherwise under the Civil Code. In the event that there would be only one of the activities for which the athlete has a trade licence, the whole relationship should be subject to the Commercial Code.[168]

167. *Ibid.*, 80.
168. *Ibid.*, 80–81.

Chapter 2. Public Regulation

§1. Broadcasting Rights

I. Ownership and the Use of Broadcasting Rights

824. Broadcasting rights to sporting events and their commercial exploitation is a lucrative source of revenue of sports organizations in Western Europe and the USA, particularly in the case of the Olympic Games.[169]

825. Sale of broadcasting rights is neither a trade in Slovakia within the meaning of §3 subsection 1 point b of the Act no. 455/1991 Coll. on trades (Trade Act) nor an entrepreneurship under the Commercial Code no. 513/1991 Coll.[170]

826. In practice, the use of broadcasting rights takes the form of the organizer of the match allowing an operator to use the facilities on-site for the purpose of recording and broadcasting of sporting events. This happens usually based on an atypical contract, which is in the case of competitions at the national level concluded by a sports association, or a designated company to which the right to authorize broadcasting transmission of a particular sports competition was transferred. These companies sell broadcasting rights to individual broadcasters.[171]

827. The most fundamental legal question of who actually owns the broadcasting rights has no straightforward answer.[172] The most widespread concept claims a co-ownership of clubs and national association, and possibly of an international federation in case of an international event. However, national authorities dealing with competition, as well as the European Commission itself, still reject the idea of collective ownership of those rights, which is the position of FIFA and UEFA.[173]

828. Act no. 440/2015 Coll. on Sports attributes to a sports organization the right to decide on television and radio broadcasting rights to sporting events in competence of the sports organization. The issue of 'ownership' of these rights is not addressed here.

829. Previously, the Legislative Intent of Sports Act from 2004 provided that the use of revenue from television and radio broadcasting rights is the responsibility of sports associations, which will be required to adopt an internal regulation on contracting the broadcasting rights, as well as the method and the ratio of dividing the revenue from the use of these rights among members of sports associations. It also seems to have inclined to the idea of a sort of collective 'ownership' (in Slovakia,

---

169. Mary Still, Kate Jordan & Toby Ryston-Pratt, *TV Rights Related to Major Sports Events: The Example of the Olympic Games*, 1 The Intl. Sports L.J. 15–23 (2003).
170. Čorba, *Športové kluby – podnikatelia pro forma?*, 273.
171. Čorba, *Obchodnoprávne vzt'ahy v oblasti športu*, 136.
172. Cf. a number of articles in The Intl. Sports L. J. no. 3 (2003).
173. Luca Ferrari, *Legal Aspects of Media Rights on Football Events under Italian Law: Ownership, Exploitation and Competition Issues*, 3 The Intl. Sports L.J. 5 (2003).

only material thing can be owned in the proper sense, though). The use of television and radio broadcasting rights to sporting competitions, that are not organized by a sports association, was to be left to the disposal of the organizer of the competition. In cases where the organizer is an international sports federation, the rights in question should fall within its jurisdiction. However, at the end of the day this question was not regulated in the final version of the Act no. 300/2008 Coll. We can only assume that the broadcasting rights belong to clubs participating in competitions organized by sports organizations and also to the organization (national association, international federation), whereby the rights are exploited by the authority governing the competition, that is, by the organizer or an authorized legal person (company) that licenses the broadcasting rights to the television channels.

830. In 2010, broadcasting rights to the highest Slovak national football league competition (Fortuna League), as well as to the matches of the Slovak national team, falling under the competence of the SFA, were licensed to a Romanian cable television company, operating on the territory of Slovakia with only a small market share (i.e., with limited coverage). The operation took place with intermediary services of a marketing partner of the SFA, UFA Sports Slovakia, and the licensing to the television company was executed by the Sport Five company, disposing of the rights on the basis of their previous acquisition from the SFA. Subsequently, a heated debate as to the admissibility of licensing the rights to a cable television with low coverage started.

II. Right of Public Access to Broadcasts of Sporting Events

A. *European Regulation*

831. A case similar to the situation that occurred in 2010 in Slovakia in connection with the sale of broadcasting rights was addressed already in 2001 by the British House of Lords. It was a case of *TV Danmark*.[174] National British legislation in the Broadcasting Act of 1996 under section 97 authorized the Secretary of State for Culture, Media and Sport to compile a list of sporting and other events of national interest. Organizers of sporting events in those limited cases could not contractually commit themselves to grant exclusive rights to broadcast the events. Section 98 explicitly divided broadcasters into two groups, which roughly correspond to the pay-TV and public television, whereby a provision of §101 provided that a broadcaster of one category cannot broadcast an event from the event list, if it is not transmitted at the same time by at least one broadcaster from the second category.

832. Similar concerns of other Member States regarding the availability of sporting events of public concern led to the adoption of Directive 97/36/EC of the European Parliament and the Council on 30 June 1997. It was an amendment of the

174. *Regina v. Independent Television Commission (appellants) ex parte TV Danmark 1 Limited (On 25 July 2001 [2001] UKHL 42)*, www.publications.parliament.uk/pa/ld200102/ldjudgmt/jd010725/dan-1.htm, 9 Nov. 2010.

broadcasting directive (89/552/EEC), known as the Television Without Frontiers Directive, and it introduced a new Article 3a. On the basis of this Article, it was ensured that the British TV company broadcasting in Denmark with a low coverage, TV Danmark, had to offer to the Danish public broadcasters the opportunity to broadcast the matches, to which TV Danmark had bought the exclusive rights.

833. Since the times of the decision in *TV Danmark* case, the European legislation in this matter has changed, and currently broadcasting of sporting events is governed by a Directive of the European Parliament and Council 2010/13/EU of 10 March 2010 – Audiovisual Media Services Directive. Its Article 14 is thereby almost identical with the original Article 3a ensuring that any Member State may take measures in accordance with EU law to ensure that broadcasters who are under their jurisdiction do not broadcast on an exclusive basis events that the Member State considers of major importance for society in such a way that a substantial proportion of the public in that Member State is excluded from the possibility of following such events. For this sake, the Member States should draw up a list of national or external events of major importance for society.

834. The term 'important event', also referred to as a 'major event', is specified in the Recommendation R (91) 5 of the Committee of Ministers of the Council of Europe directed to Member States, on the right to short reporting on major events in the case of acquisition of exclusive rights to their cross-border television broadcasting (adopted on 11 April 1991). Two types of events are discerned: organized and unorganized events. Organized event is any sporting, cultural, social, or political event, held as a result of the decision of the organizer and organized by a public or private natural or legal person. Unorganized major event is usually associated with current events similar to those usually presented in news or current affairs programmes (e.g., accident, natural disaster, armed conflict, etc.).

B. Slovak Regulation of Broadcasting Sporting Events

835. Domestic legislation of the SR has implemented the original Council Directive 89/552/EEC of 3 October 1989 as amended by the European Parliament and Council Directive 97/36/EC of 30 June 1997 into the form of Act no. 308/2000 Coll. on broadcasting and retransmission.

836. Ensuring public access to the major events under this Act is done through two rights. The first is the *right to short reports* (§30), which ensures that the television programme service broadcaster may record and transmit events inducing increased public interest, whereby the right to broadcast the event is an exclusive right of another broadcaster. The event, however:

(1) may be broadcasted only within the broadcasting of a regular news programme;
(2) shall not exceed ninety seconds;

(3) must not be broadcasted before the broadcaster owning the exclusive right could use his/her right and broadcast the event of increased public interest in his/her own news programme; and
(4) must be broadcasted with an indication of source (broadcaster) which has the exclusive right to broadcast the event inducing increased public interest.

837. Such a method was used by private Slovak televisions while broadcasting matches of the football World Cup in 2010, whereby the exclusive rights were owned by the Slovak Television as a public medium.

838. Another way to ensure the right of public to access information is the so-called *right of public access to major events* (§31). Major event is a political, social, cultural or sporting event, which meets at least two of the following conditions:

(1) its outcome has a special general resonance and is of interest also to that part of the public that usually does not follow events of this nature;
(2) it has a unique cultural importance to the people and, in particular, contains elements of their cultural identity; and
(3) it is a major international event, and it involves the State representation.

839. Public access to major events through television broadcasting service is to be ensured by the Council for Broadcasting and Retransmission in cooperation with the Ministry of Culture and Ministry of Education of the SR, as well as with the right holders and broadcasters. This is to be executed by drawing up a list of important events. The list of events, after being approved by the European Commission, shall be notified through the website of the Council for Broadcasting and Retransmission and also on its official board at the place of its residence, and delivered to the affected broadcasters.

840. Provisionally, the Council for Broadcasting and Retransmission prepared a *list of significant events,* subject to approval by the European Commission. This list includes:

(1) Summer Olympic Games.
(2) Winter Olympic Games.
(3) Semi-finals and finals of FIFA World Cup, as well as all matches of the Slovak national team at this World Cup.
(4) Semi-finals and finals of UEFA EURO Championships in football as well as all matches of the Slovak national team at the Championships.
(5) Semi-finals and final match of UEFA Champions League and UEFA Cup in case of participation of Slovak team.
(6) Matches of the Slovak national team at the World Ice Hockey Championships.

841. Major events of the Member States that have already been approved of by the European Commission can be found on the website of the Commission.[175]

842. The Council for Broadcasting and Retransmission also compiled *a list of all broadcasters,* in which broadcasters are divided into groups of:

(1) broadcasters whose mode of transmission allows without paying a separate charge access for more than 80% of the population; and
(2) broadcasters with limited public access.

843. A broadcaster in group (2), who obtains exclusive rights to broadcast a major event is obliged to enable access to a substantial part of the public through a broadcaster from group (1) under *fair, reasonable and non-discriminatory market conditions*, in the manner determined by the Council. A substantial part of the public for the purposes of this Act means more than 80% of the population. The broadcaster from group (2), who obtains the exclusive right to broadcast a major event, is especially required to inform all broadcasters from group (1) of an option to broadcast the major event. This information must be provided in sufficient time before the event and must contain information about event, in particular, time and place *and the price which the broadcaster requests.* Broadcaster from group (2) is entitled to broadcast this event only after conclusion of a contract ensuring public access to that major event with at least one broadcaster assigned to group (1) or after none of the broadcasters from group (1) showed interest in broadcasting within fourteen days from receipt of written information on broadcasting of the event under the terms specified in the information on broadcasting of the event.

844. Finally, for cross-border situations, where the broadcaster acquires the right to broadcast events which are on the list of major events in one of the Member States of the Council of Europe or EU Member States, is to apply them in accordance with the rules *of that Member State* and in *such a manner that a substantial part of the public in that Member State will not be hindered in watching the event live or recorded.*

845. The Act on broadcasting and retransmission also includes penalties for breaching the rules on broadcasting of major events. According to §67, the Council may impose a fine in the range from EUR 1,659 to EUR 99,581, if the conditions for broadcasting major events were breached.

III. Broadcasting Rights and Competition Law

846. The basic feature of the sale of broadcasting rights by the autonomous sports organizations is their collective selling (by one company, for example, Pro-Hokej), whereby the broadcaster acquires exclusive rights for several years. This

---

175. *See* http://ec.europa.eu/avpolicy/reg/tvwf/implementation/events_list/index_en.htm, 9 Nov. 2010.

leads to certain restriction of competition. In Slovakia, the sale and purchase of broadcasting rights to sporting events has not yet been subject to any judicial proceedings in relation to competition law. One can only use the decisions of the European Commission as a basis and possibly adjust the current contract practice in Slovakia to meet the European standards.

847. The European Commission is willing to accept collective selling of broadcasting rights, while all broadcasters have a fair access to broadcasting the sporting events for consideration, and as long as possible exclusive contracts with broadcasters are not concluded for a longer period than three years. It also recognizes the possibility of blocking hours when the transmissions should not take place in order to ensure physical participation in national matches. However, it rejects the concentration of broadcasting rights and restrictions of their purchase.

A. *Collective Selling of Rights*

848. The issue *of collective sale of broadcasting rights* was dealt with by the European Commission in several cases, which include *UEFA Champions League* case, the *Bundesliga* case, and the case of *FA Premier League*. In the *UEFA Champions League (2003)*, the Commission accepted for the first time collective sale of broadcasting rights for football matches. It was based on an understanding of collective selling as creating a special product intended for European consumers, whereby this product is being sold in a single place, otherwise it would not be produced efficiently and evenly distributed. An idea of solidarity between clubs was also emphasized.[176] Still, the broadcasting rights should be divided into several packages, so it should be possible to acquire them by several broadcasters, and the competition among broadcasters must take place under fair and non-discriminatory terms.

849. In cases of *German Bundesliga (2005)* and the *FA Premier League (2006)* both leagues agreed to divide the broadcasting rights into several packages for television, as well as for mobile methods of broadcasting. Furthermore, each club was allowed to use unsold and unused rights and the right to recordings of events, the right of Internet broadcasting and telephone transmissions. Moreover, it was expressly stated that exclusivity could not take longer than three seasons (three years). It was also ruled that one purchaser could not acquire all rights to live broadcasting. In this way, the Commission sought to limit the monopoly of British television company British Sky Broadcasting Group, regarding broadcast rights of the FA Premier League.

850. Individual requirements of the Commission which followed a goal to exclude a possibility of a single buyer and to exclude the possibility of long-term exclusivity sales were the following:

176. Stephen Weatherill, *European Sports Law: Collected Papers* 314 (T.M.C. Asser Press 2007).

(1) distribution in packages;
(2) reasonable composition of packages;
(3) packages adapted to the needs of different distribution platforms (mobile operators, Internet providers, etc.);
(4) exclusion of any conditions and reservations when purchasing packages;
(5) return of unsold right to clubs for their own use; and
(6) limitation of the period of exclusive broadcasting rights to the maximum of three years.[177]

B. Blocked Hours While Broadcasting Sporting Events

851. In another case – of review of the UEFA rules on broadcasting of sporting events (2001/478/EC, OJ 2001 L 171/12), the Commission addressed the issue of UEFA rules allowing *to restrict the broadcasting of football matches* at a time when in the Member States national competitions and matches take place, in order to avoid reduction of interest and of number of spectators in stadiums. This was not an issue of sales of broadcasting rights as in previous cases, but rather the regulation of broadcasting through the so-called blocking of hours. Some broadcasters opposed these rules and argued that in the case of broadcasting across Europe, national restrictions make it impossible or very difficult for a single broadcaster to broadcast throughout Europe. Preliminary investigations of the Commission, however, showed that broadcasting football on TV really affects the target group of men in age categories, which could be directly present at matches as spectators (paragraph 40). UEFA moreover argued that the restriction on television broadcasting is too limiting, and therefore it does not represent a significant intervention in the competition (paragraph 49). The Commission accepted this argument of the absence of significant intervention, and therefore did not find it necessary to closely examine the extent to which television has indeed had a negative impact on participation in sporting events. Accordingly, the Commission rejected the complaint of broadcasters.

C. Collective Acquisition of Broadcasting Rights

852. From another perspective, in terms of *joint acquisition and exchange of broadcasting rights between broadcasters*, the issue of broadcasting rights was dealt with by the European Commission and Court of First Instance in cases of *Eurovision I and II*, in relation to the original Article 85(3) of the EC Treaty. They examined whether or not the status and activities of the European Broadcasting Union (EBU) is in breach of competition rules of the EC Treaty (today's TFEU).

177. Torben Toft, *Developments in European Law*, http://ec.europa.eu/competition/speeches/text/sp2006_003_en.pdf, 9 Nov. 2010; Parrish & Miettinen, *The Sporting Exception in European Union Law*, 146–149.

853. The EBU, established in 1950, is a non-profit organization of radio and television broadcasters, which initially grouped only public service broadcasters, and did not accept as members any commercial broadcasters. The EBU has developed a framework for joint acquisition and exchange of programmes called Eurovision. Non-members have been at a disadvantage by the fact that access to broadcasted events could be obtained only if a member of the EBU had no interest in broadcasting the event in question. Exemption from applicability of competition rules could be granted only if the Eurovision system could be understood as necessary for the fulfilment of tasks of public broadcasters. An argument in this sense could be that the Union actually reduced transaction costs, supported smaller members and allowed for exchanges between the countries.

854. When the Commission first recognized and accepted the existence of the EBU, the Court subsequently rejected the decision, and expressed the belief that the Eurovision system does not allow non-members to sufficiently benefit from the rights not used by the EBU members, or to acquire sublicences for broadcasting. Subsequently, the Commission in 2000 adopted again a decision to allow the functioning of the system of joint acquisition of sports broadcasting rights, their exchange and sharing, with safeguarding sublicences that would allow non-members of EBU to access the broadcasting rights. In fact, this system did not work properly, and therefore the Court of First Instance annulled the Commission decision again. Subsequently EBU allowed to even greater extent the membership of non-public broadcasters.

D. Merger of Television Broadcasters

855. Another angle from which the European Commission examined the broadcasting rights is the restriction of competition by a *merger of television broadcasters,* who own the exclusive broadcasting rights. This problem occurred in the European Commission's decision in the case *Newscorp/Telepiù* (2004/311/EC, OJ 2004 L 110/73). In this case, an Australian television company The News Corporation Limited had acquired a stake in an Italian pay-TV companies Telepiù Spa and Stream Spa, which were to be merged together and provide a paid broadcasting channel by satellite. The Commission in this matter expressed its doubts as to the compatibility of the merger with the competition rules, and therefore opened a special procedure under the Merger Regulation.

856. Newscorp relied on the assessment of the television market in Italy as a single market, without distinguishing paid broadcasting and free TV broadcasting, which would mean a smaller market share for Newscorp. The Commission's investigation, however, showed a clear difference between the two markets. Accordingly, the Commission considered the merger a threat to competition, but in the interest of viewers allowed that Newscorp could make proposals to change the attitude and the final decision of the Commission.

857. Newscorp proposed to allow the football organizations to unilaterally terminate contracts concerning broadcasting rights with television. Newscorp also gave up exclusivity in favour of Internet broadcasters. Moreover, it undertook to enter into future contracts concerning exclusive broadcasting rights only for a maximum of two years, ensuring the possibility of unilateral termination. After presenting these proposals, the Commission decided that the merger would not establish a dominant market position in relation to broadcasting rights to sporting events.

858. A similar case was solved by the European Commission, known as Audiovisual Sport (AVS), which also concerned a merger, finally authorized by the Commission, on condition that:

(1) AVS will cancel options for continuing a contractual relationship.
(2) Third-party access to broadcasting rights will be guaranteed under fair and non-discriminatory terms.
(3) Company resulting from the merger will not own exclusive rights.
(4) There will be an agreement under which access to the broadcasting rights will be subject to an arbitration mechanism.

§2. Advertising and Sponsorship

859. Sponsorship and advertising were in the recent decades closely connected to sports since they represent an important source of income. Advertising is to be distinguished from sponsorships, although this distinction is complicated in Slovakia due to the lack of legal regulation of sponsorship.

I. Advertising

860. Slovak Act no. 147/2001 Coll. on advertising and amending certain acts in its §2 subsection 1 letter a defines advertising as product presentation in any form to introduce the products to market. It limits advertising of drugs, weapons, alcoholic beverages and tobacco products. Tobacco advertising is restricted more than the advertising of alcoholic products, because according to §6 tobacco advertising and marketing is prohibited even if it represents presentation of the trademark, emblem, name or other distinctive features of tobacco products only, except for placing the advertising on the points of sale of tobacco products. In particular, advertising is limited in connection with TV programmes intended for minors, according to the Audiovisual Act no. 343/2007 Coll. The EU and its law does not prevent Member States to impose restrictions on advertising alcohol or tobacco products, as confirmed by earlier decision of the CJEU from 13 July 2004 in Case C-262/02 – *Commission v. France* – and the Case C-429/02 – *Bacardi France SAS v. Télévision Française 1 SA*. Advertising restrictions are therefore permissible due to reasons of public order *(orde public).*

861. Private relations between a client and recipient of advertising are not regulated in Slovakia by any specific contract type and therefore mostly an atypical contract under §51 of the Civil Code or §269 subsection 2 of the Commercial Code is used. The content of such a contract is, on the one hand, a commitment of the recipient of an advertisement to promote the advertiser's products, and on the other hand, commitment of the client to pay for advertising, thus for promoting the product. The essence is the idea of promoting products (goods and services) of the advertiser, to be placed on the market, which will increase the client's profits. Unlike sponsorship, advertiser aims not to improve his/her image and reputation in the market or in the public opinion. A common feature with sponsorship, however, is reciprocity of the performance – the advertiser obtains the possibility to present products, and the recipient receives a monetary payment for advertising.

II. Sponsorship

862. Sponsorship in sports is regulated in the SR by a special type of contract under the Act no. 440/2015 Coll. on Sports, §§50–51.

863. Sponsorship is understood as a relationship between the sponsor and the sponsored, in which the sponsor provides direct or indirect pecuniary or non-pecuniary support to the sponsored sportsperson, sports expert or sports organization, and this in turn helps the sponsor to achieve his/her marketing objectives by connecting the sponsor (his name, product) with the sponsored.

864. Unlike advertising, sponsoring is not a product presentation, but it links the sponsor or a product with a (sporting) partner. The goal is to influence the company's image. Sponsor's objectives are in fact mainly publicity and the growth of the reputation of the company or brand.[178]

865. Sponsorship differs from donation by the fact that sponsoring includes certain consideration – for example, connection (and refining) of the image with the sporting event.[179] Applied to sports, in the sponsorship contract, the sponsored party undertakes to place a sponsor's logo visibly on clothing and sports equipment of their athletes, on advertising panels around its sports fields, or on tickets, or to ensure the presentation of the sponsor in the local press or audiovisual media, to ensure participation of their athletes in the advertisement campaigns of the sponsor, or even accept a sponsor's name as the club name.[180]

866. The sponsored party can be a club or an individual athlete, or a sports expert. In the latter cases, one can speak of personal sponsorships, in which the

---

178. Sluka, *Profesionální sportovec (právní aekonomické aspekty)*, 83.
179. Zuzana Magurová, 'Sponzorstvo, darcovstvo alebo reklama?', *Právny obzor* 82, no. 1 (1999): 58–60.
180. Čorba, *Obchodnoprávne vzt'ahy v oblasti športu*, 122.

sponsor promotes himself/herself and his/her products through links with the popular name of a particular athlete. The various forms are advertising on the clothes of an athlete, athlete's inclusion in a media campaign or direct integration of athletes into sales promotion – for example, book signing, drawing the lottery prizes and so on. Finally, it is also possible to integrate the athlete into personal communication with clients.[181]

867. In the absence of legislation on sponsorship, sports organizations and sportsperson had the complete freedom to modify their contractual relations. Under the new Act on Sports, there are certain limitations introduced: the sponsorship cannot be used as a salary or remuneration for the athletes, costs of displaying the name or logo of the sponsor cannot exceed 10% of the sponsorship, the contract has to take a written form with certain requirements as to the content of the contract (§50 subsection 3 of the Act), and it has to be made public in the electronic information system of sports run by the Ministry of sports. There is even an obligation stipulated in the Act to return the unused sponsorship at the end of the sponsorship period, and to provide the sponsor with information on how the sponsorship was used in detail. This detailed regulation is similar to previous proposals for introducing a sponsorship contract – e.g., the draft Act on sport from 2005 included a proposal of a sponsorship regulation in its §74, which defined the sport sponsorship as:

> any service provided by a legal entity or natural person under the sponsorship agreement, which is intended for direct or indirect funding of sport in order to promote the name, trademark, reputation or activities of a legal person or natural person. (trans. T.G.)
>
> Exemption from taxes was also proposed, while sponsors could deduct the amount of the contribution from their tax base. A special contract of sponsorship should have been introduced by the same Act into §630a of the Civil Code as:
>
> a contract concluded for the direct or indirect promotion of the name, trademark, reputation or other sponsor activities on the one hand and the direct or indirect financing of the activities of sponsored on the other. (trans. T.G.)
>
> The contract should have been concluded in writing and include in particular:
>
> 1. designation of the contracting parties;
> 2. the duration of the sponsorship contract;
> 3. way of terminating the sponsorship contract;
> 4. the type of sponsorship, including a timetable;
> 5. the time and manner in which the sponsor may obtain information on the use of the funds;
> 6. the manner, aim and extent to which the sponsorship is to be given;
> 7. if there are reasons for establishment of conditions to be fulfilled by the sponsored, specification of these conditions, including the period for notification of compliance;
> 8. other issues on which the parties agree.

---

181. Sluka, *Profesionální sportovec (právní a ekonomické aspekty)*, 85–87.

868. However, as indicated above, this proposal was never submitted to the Government or to the National Council (Parliament). The specific content and form of the sponsorship contract is thus still a matter of agreement between the parties.

869. From among the older cases, when there was still no regulation of sponsorship in the Slovak legal system (prior to the Act no. 440/2015 Coll.), an example of *a sponsorship contract* with a biathlon club can be offered, concluded under §51 in conjunction with §§628 et seq. of the Civil Code (as the club in this case was a civic association, not a business entity). Paragraph 628 concerns the donation, and the contract is thus a mixed type of contract that has elements of gift, which is in contradiction with the basic idea of sponsorship, and probably was chosen due to tax advantages, since gifts are not subject to tax. Mutual rights and obligations under the contract state that 'sponsor' (donor) is committed to periodic financial support of the recipient. Obligations of the recipient ('sponsored', the donee) are formulated in a broader manner: to use the funds only for the purpose intended by the sponsor, in this case, namely, for the purchase of training equipment, and for participation in a national contest. The beneficiary undertakes to select appropriate professional participants from among its athletes and provide funding for their participation in the events as provided by the sponsor. Similarly, the beneficiary should procure the evidence for the use of financial support in terms of object and purpose of this contract. The specific forms of presentation of the sponsor to be implemented are the following:

(1) placing the sponsor's logo on clothes of the athletes in the form as proposed by the sponsor;
(2) mentioning the sponsor while evaluating the competitions organized by the club, evaluating the results of the championships and other competitions, on the club website, in print, radio and other telecommunications means;
(3) in the case of providing sponsorship of more than EUR 2,000, the sponsor will be marketed as the general sponsor of the club.

870. Formal denoting of the partner (sponsor) may have had various forms, given the formerly complete contractual freedom in this regard. The example of the SOSC and its marketing activities show the development in previous years in this field. For example, at the end of the twentieth century, the SOSC offered to its partners the possibility of sponsorship in four programmes, consisting of the following types of sponsorship:

(1) the official outfit provider;
(2) friend of Olympic thought;
(3) sponsor; and
(4) Top sponsor (exclusive in the industry).

871. Currently, the SOSC offers the following categories of sponsor partnerships:

(1) Exclusive Partner.
(2) General Partner.
(3) Main Partner.
(4) Partner.
(5) Supplier.
(6) Media Partner.
(7) Project Partner.

872. Another document of the SOSC previously offered a slightly different categorization of sponsor partnerships, depending on the amount of annual contributions:

(1) Exclusive partner (EUR 320,000 per year).
(2) General partners (EUR 200,000 per year).
(3) Main partners (EUR 100,000 per year).
(4) Suppliers (barter cooperation up to EUR 16,000 per year).
(5) Supporters (single financial contribution up to EUR 16,000 per year).
(6) Media partners.

873. Sponsorship also has certain *competition aspects* – exclusivity should therefore be granted solely on the basis of objective selection criteria.

874. It is also necessary to pay attention to the unfair practices relating to sponsoring called *ambush marketing,* which means joining brand image with a theme (sports event) without a contract with the owner of the theme and often with an effort to assert oneself against a competitor from the industry, who is an official partner (sponsor) of the event.[182] It is therefore an effort to stimulate an idea of connection to the sporting event, even though a party is not a sponsor. In doing so, the sponsor suffers damage through not being exclusively associated with sponsored competition, and the sponsored may incur damage in the form of lost profits due to reduction in the interest of the sponsors.[183] Examples of such a practice come from Fuji and Kodak at the Olympic Games in 1984 and 1988. Kodak sponsored the TV transmission of the games and the USA athletic team, even though Fuji was an official sponsor of the games, and in 1988 it was vice versa. At the Olympic Games in 1992, the official partner was Reebok, but Nike sponsored the US American basketball team. This type of marketing is also referred to as parasitic marketing, and its aim is to attack the exclusive sponsor. Examples from Slovakia included the use of symbols of Ice Hockey Championship, World Cup and European Cup in advertising products to increase their sales.[184]

182. Libor Duchoslav, 'Analýza ambush marketingu v športe na Slovensku', in *Humanistické podoby športu atelesnej výchovy* (Bratislava: Slovenská vedecká spoločnosť pre telesnú výchovu a šport, 2006), 24.
183. Sluka, *Profesionální sportovec (právní a ekonomické aspekty)*, 83.
184. Duchoslav, *Analýza ambush marketingu v športe na Slovensku*, 25.

875. Finally, in terms of legal evaluation of sponsorship, it is necessary to draw attention to the opinion of J. Čorba, according to whom:

> the actual extraction of funds from sponsors is not a business activity – the sponsored club may have no trade license for doing advertisements … as long as this is done in order to obtain funds to cover its costs. Only if the activity of an entity is focused on making a profit through leasing advertising space or other dissemination of advertising, then such an entity has to have a trade license for such activity. With regard to sports clubs, advertising is usually only an ancillary activity connected to the performance of their duties … not representing an action performed in order to make profit. (trans. T.G.)[185]

§3. Merchandising

876. Merchandising means using the name (registered trademark) of a sports organization or athlete in combination with items sold, intended for use by supporters of the organization or fans of the athlete. According to J. Švidroň and J. Čorba, the essence lies in commercial use of values, which the names and likenesses of sportsmen acquire with their popularity. Their value allows to be used to promote the sale of goods or services in other business fields. In the context of individual athletes, one may speak of the so-called *character merchandising.*[186]

877. According to J. Čorba, both in cases of the athlete and the organization this is a business activity. Athlete should therefore have a trade licence and the contract signed with his/her trading partners should be governed by the Commercial Code. Similar considerations apply in the case of organizations, for example, so-called club merchandising, being understood as the commercial exploitation of the popularity of a club, which takes forms of sales of souvenirs with motifs of the sports club or individual athletes (e.g., T-shirts, hats, scarves, mugs, pens, etc.).[187]

878. Financial profits from merchandising are generally very low in Slovakia, because of the low value of sport as a product on the Slovak market.[188] Therefore, the legal aspects of merchandising are not considered worthy of special attention, unlike in other countries. There is no specific merchandising contract type. In practice, atypical contract under §269 subsection 2 of the Commercial Code no. 513/1991 Coll. is being used.

185. Čorba, *Obchodnoprávne vzt'ahy v oblasti športu*, 124–125.
186. Švidroň, *Základy práva duševného vlastníctva* (Bratislava: Juga 2000), 208.
187. Čorba, *Obchodnoprávne vzt'ahy v oblasti športu*, 143.
188. Peter Dedík, 'Organizácia a financovanie profesionálneho futbalového klubu v prostredí tržnej ekonomiky na príklade FC Nitra, a.s.', in *Sport a kvalita života 2007* (Brno: Masarykova univerzita, 2007), 35.

879. In drafting the contract, it is to be advised to use the recommendations of foreign experts recommending that a merchandising contract should contain particulars of a licence contract for use of a trademark, and therefore to specify:

(1) what rights are granted;
(2) what the other contracting party may do with them;
(3) in which territory;
(4) for what reward;
(5) whether in awarding a 'licence' the licensor reserves the right to control the use of trademark and quality of materials used; and
(6) possibility of termination of the merchandising relationship.[189]

§4. Limitation of Club Ownership

880. Competition law aspects of sport are reflected in efforts to ensure a free and balanced sports competition. A specific feature of competition in sport as opposed to the standard economic competition is an effort to maintain comparability and competitiveness of the teams in the competition in order to maintain spectator interest.[190] Competition in sports also works differently because sports clubs are usually regionally oriented and their supporters identify with the region, which reduces the likelihood of transition to a competitor.

881. Objectives in this area are ensured by the sports movement, first, through the so-called licensing system allowing competition only with a licence, and second, through a special transfer system with training compensation.

882. Some practices, such as *corruption* (bribery as unfair competition practice under §49 of the Commercial Code) or an agreement on *joint action* may constitute anti-competitive practices that are prohibited by both the Commercial Code, and by the Act on Protection of Competition no. 136/2001 Coll. Coordination between the clubs is to be prevented through the restrictions on ownership and control of sports clubs. The ownership of sports clubs may explicitly be transferred just as any other property right, while it could theoretically be taken over by an owner of another sports club. Given the special nature of sporting competition, however, such multiple ownership poses a threat to fair competition, as it was stated in 1998 when in a UEFA competition two clubs – Slavia Prague and AEK Athens – had the same owner, company ENIC.

883. It may be questioned, however, whether the mere interconnection of clubs through the same owner (prohibited under §15 subsection 6 of the Act on Sports no.

189. Ian S. Blackshaw, *Sports Licensing and Merchandising – The Legal and Practical Aspects*, 1 The Intl. Sports L.J. 22–25 (2002).
190. Cf. Jozef Čorba, 'Regulácia a autoregulácia športových súťaží v Slovenskej republike', *Justičná revue* 62, no. 11 (2011): 1195–1205.

440/2015 Coll.) is a practice contrary to the internal sporting rules as well as statutory provisions governing competition in the SR. The Commercial Code in §42 provides that 'abuse of participation in the competition is any unfair competition and illegal conduct restricting competition'. (trans. T.G.) According to §44, 'Unfair competition is an act in competition, which is contrary to morality of competition and is likely to cause harm to other competitors or consumers. Unfair competition is prohibited.' (trans. T.G.) The Act also contains examples of such a competition.

884. Illegal *restriction of competition* represents another type of misuse of participation in the competition. It is governed by the Act on protection of economic competition no. 136/2001 Coll. According to §2, this Act applies to all activities and conducts of the undertakings, which restrict or may restrict competition. According to §3 subsection 1:

> Restriction of competition is any restriction on freedom of action of the entrepreneur in the market, particularly the exclusion of existing or potential competitive activities, actual or potential reduction of the scope of competitive activity or distortion of competition. (trans. T.G.)

885. The Act further identifies three specific types of restriction: agreement, abuse of dominant position and concentration. Paragraph 9 understands the concentration as acquisition of control over other businesses (in our case the club), but only in excess of the limits of turnover which are too high for sports clubs. That means concentration is not applicable, only an *agreement between the clubs, or abuse of dominant position* of clubs could be invoked.

886. Thus, in very general definitions of abuse of competition, the mere fact of ownership of two teams or clubs participating in a competition might be interpreted as a restriction of competition or unfair competition, as it is *able to reduce the extent of competitive activity* or distort the competition. It is also an activity that is 'contrary to morality of competition and is likely to cause harm to other competitors or consumers'. One must thereby necessarily take into account the relevant market, which in this case, is a very specific sports market. It is precisely because of the specific character of a sport competition that one can argue that even the mere fact of ownership or control of several clubs that participate in the same competition or the participation of several teams of the same club in one competition, may pose a substantial threat to the integrity of competition.

887. Explicit rules prohibiting the so-called *multiple ownership,* that is, the ownership or control of several clubs, or the participation of several teams of the same club in one competition, were therefore introduced in §15 subsection 6 of the Act on Sports no. 440/2015 Coll. in all-sports sectors in Slovakia.

Chapter 3. Private Regulation

888. Business and competition relationship between athletes and sports organizations on one hand and extra-sporting entities on the other are predominantly governed by generally binding legal regulations rather than by internal rules of sporting organizations. The exceptions are the following restrictions of competition, which are (or at least originally were) primarily regulated by internal rules:

(1) collective selling of broadcasting rights since this takes place under standards advocated by FIFA and UEFA, and also by the national autonomous regulation;
(2) blocked hours of broadcasting sporting events, resulting from the internal regulation of UEFA;
(3) sale of tickets to sporting events (which has to meet the terms of equal access to ticket market); and
(4) limitation of multiple ownership of clubs.

889. The internal regulation must not deviate from the framework given by the generally binding legal regulations of the EU or the Member States.

§1. Marketing

890. For commercial use of broadcasting rights, but also of the rights deriving from advertising and sponsorship contracts, the individual Slovak national associations as well as the SOSC created their own marketing companies as business entities controlled by the sports organizations. From their profit, the main activities of sports organizations as formulated in their statutes should be financed.

891. In the case of the *SOC,* it is the company SLOVENSKÁ OLYMPIJSKÁ MARKETINGOVÁ, a.s. The *SPC* has created a company called, Paralympijská marketingová spoločnost', s.r.o., with the Paralympic Committee as the sole owner. The *SFA* exploits its marketing rights on its own through the SFZ Marketing, s.r.o. company, after terminating relationship with its marketing partner – UFA Sports Slovakia, s.r.o. Member of the SFA, *ULC,* is also active in the field of marketing, advertising and audiovisual rights, connected to competitions managed by the ULC. For the needs of the *SAA*, to ensure all activities of marketing, advertising, sponsorship and media, the company ATLETIKA s.r.o. was created, as a marketing agency of the SAA. Finally, the *SBA* created for the same purpose a company called Slovak sport agency a.s.

§2. Broadcasting Rights

892. The issue of broadcasting rights to sporting events is by its nature primarily an internal issue of sports organizations. From a legal point of view, the question of ownership of broadcasting rights is vague and an idea of collective holding of rights by clubs and organizers of the competition prevails. Still, the Act no. 440/2015 Coll. on Sports attributes the right to decide on broadcasting rights to sporting events only to a sports organization which organizes the competition, and it does not address the relationship between the organization and the clubs taking part in the competition at all.

893. The commercial exploitation of broadcasting rights, which is largely entrusted to the competition organizer (the national association, the international federation), thereby follows the goals of the most profitable sales, not of providing public access to broadcasting of the event. To ensure the access, generally binding legal norms of the EU and the SR are applicable. Public access to the transmission is also governed by UEFA and its internal rules,[191] though, but rather in the negative sense – via so-called blocked hours, restricting the possibility to broadcast sports on television in specific time windows, in order to ensure spectator presence in stadiums.

894. According to Article 68 of the Statutes of the *SFA*, SFA is the original and exclusive owner of all rights arising from contests and other events that fall within its competence, without any restriction in terms of content, time, place and law. These rights include especially all kinds of rights to objects of intellectual property rights, property rights, rights to producing audio, visual, audiovisual recordings, rights of reproduction and broadcasting, retransmission, dissemination through the Internet and other electronic networks, or through data carriers, data use within databases, spread on data carriers, multimedia, marketing and promotional rights, merchandising, intangible rights and rights under the law on copyright and related rights (Copyright Act). SFA is responsible for granting authorization for the dissemination of video, audio and other data carriers of football games and activities that fall within its competence.

895. Broadcasting rights to football matches were in accordance with this provision of the Statute until 2009 contractually transferred to company Šport progress, in which SFA held shares for 34%. In 2010, however, SFA bought the rights back, although the Šport progress owned the rights until 2016. The redemption took place with the support of UFA Sports, which has become a new marketing partner of the SFA. The new contract guaranteed an annual compensation for the broadcasting rights, in the amount of EUR 2.3 million payable by the company UFA Sports. Half of this amount was payable to the SFA, and the second part of the same value of EUR 1.15 million should go to the ULC, the governing body of two highest Slovak football competitions. Assuming an increase of the annual amount to an amount higher than EUR 2.3 million, the profit was to be redistributed so that the SFA would receive 70% and the remaining 30% would go to the company UFA Sports. In the summer 2011, the contract with UFA Sports was terminated, though. This arrangement, however, concerns only the exploitation of broadcasting rights, which fall within the competence of SFA and the ULC. Exploitation of broadcasting rights

191. *Regulations governing the implementation of Article 48 of the UEFA Statutes*, www.uefa.com/newsfiles/88494.pdf, 7 Jan. 2011.

to other competitions that do not fall within the competence of SFA and the ULC, belongs to an organizer of the competition.

896. Similarly, according to the Statutes of the *SIHF*, Article 6.2, the SIHF is the owner of all the rights related to the competitions organized by the SIHF. The issue of broadcasting rights in ice hockey has recently also been addressed by J. Čorba, who pointed to the fact that all participants in the highest ice hockey competition of Slovakia established a governing body – Pro-Hokej, a.s., which disposes of the broadcasting rights for the Extra League matches. The company issued exactly the same number of shares as there are participants in the ice hockey Extra league, and each club, which operates in the Extra league owns a share. In case of relegation to a lower competition, the club is required to transfer this share to the club that has replaced it in the Extra league. A club, which gets into the league, is obliged to buy the share, but always only for its nominal value.[192]

§3. Ownership of Clubs

897. Limiting participation of related clubs or teams in the same competition has its origins in the rules introduced in 1998 by the Executive Committee of UEFA in order to avoid any suspicion of influence on the results of sports competitions. In 2000, ENIC challenged this measure of UEFA before the European Commission, but the Commission gave the right to UEFA, claiming it is an internal measure of a sports federation, which has an impact on competition, but its aim is not to distort competition, but on the contrary, to ensure the integrity of competition.[193] Such a restriction of competition is therefore allowed.

898. The same regulation was also contained in the Slovak association's licensing rules. In *volleyball,* it was explicitly excluded in the Directive for selling licences that an entity with the right to participate in a competition may acquire a competition licence in the same category. Similarly, the *football* club will not be granted a licence under the provisions of Article 38 section 9 of the SFA Statutes: 'natural or legal person (including holding and subsidiary companies and their parts) shall not be partners or members of a body in more than one club in the competition and shall not take part in voting rights in bodies of more than one club nor in any way exercise control over more than one club in the same competition.' The same principle was finally also laid down in §15 subsection 6 of the new Slovakian Act on Sports no. 440/2015 Coll.

---

192. Jozef Čorba, 'Zmluvné vzt'ahy pri vysielaní TV prenosov zo športových podujatí', in *Tradície ainovácie vsúkromnom práve*, ed. Ján Husár (Košice: UPJŠ, 2009), 43.
193. *See* http://europa.eu/rapid/pressReleasesAction.do?reference=IP/02/942, 1 Jan. 2011.

Selected Bibliography

Barancová, Helena. 'Antidiskriminačný zákon a zásada rovnakého zaobchádzania v pracovnoprávnych vzt'ahoch'. *Právny obzor* 88, no. 4 (2005): 335–348.

Barancová, Helena. 'K prípustnosti atypických zmlúv v pracovnom práve'. *Právny obzor* 81, no. 6 (1998): 533–538.

Barancová, Helena. 'K vymedzeniu pojmu pracovného pomeru. Pracovný pomer alebo obchodnoprávny vzt'ah?'. *Právny obzor* 87, no. 1 (2004): 28–44.

Barancová, Helena. 'Štrajk len podl'a zákona o kolektívnom vyjednávaní?'. *Právny obzor* 91, no. 2 (2008): 94–108.

Barancová, Helena. *Zákonník práce: Komentár*. Prague: C.H.Beck, 2010.

Barancová, Helena & Robert Schronk. *Pracovné právo*. Bratislava: Sprint, 2007.

Blaho, Peter & Pavel Holländer. *Postavenie práva v systéme metód štátneho riadenia spoločnosti*. Bratislava: Univerzita Komenského, 1989.

Cirák, Ján. *Ochrana osobnosti v slovenskom občianskom práve*. Bratislava: VOP-FUK, 1994.

Cirák, Ján & Svetlana Ficová et al. *Občianske právo: Všeobecná čast'*. Šamorín: Heuréka, 2008.

Csach, Kristián. *ÚS SR: Výklad contra proferentem a preferencia platnosti právneho úkonu ako všeobecné výkladové pravidlá,* www.lexforum.sk/240, 30 December 2010.

Čorba, Jozef. 'Obchodovanie s bielym mäsom? Právne aspekty zmluvných vzt'ahov pri prestupoch športovcov'. In *Právo a obchodovanie: Zborník príspevkov účastníkov vedeckej konferencie doktorandov konanej 7. júna 2007 v Košiciach*, edited by Ján Husár. Košice: UPJŠ, 2008.

Čorba, Jozef. *Obchodnoprávne vzt'ahy v oblasti športu* (unpublished PhD. dissertation). Košice: UPJŠ, 2008.

Čorba, Jozef. 'Regulácia a autoregulácia športových súťaží v Slovenskej republike'. *Justičná revue* 62, no. 11 (2010): 1195–1205.

Čorba, Jozef. 'Slovenský zákon o organizácii a podpore športu ako nevyužitá šanca?'. In *Olomoucké debaty mladých právníků: aktuální otázky normotvorby, právo na spravedlivý proces: sborník příspěvků: 8.-10.september 2008, Olomouc*, edited by Ondrej Hamul'ák. Olomouc: Iuridica Olomoucensis, 2008.

Čorba, Jozef. 'Športové kluby a ich právny život'. In *Otázky sportovního práva*. Plzeň: Aleš Čeněk, 2008.

Čorba, Jozef. 'Športové kluby – podnikatelia pro forma?'. In *Naděje právní vědy: sborník z mezinárodního setkání mladých vědeckých pracovníků: 12.-14.október*

2007 na Zámeckém statku Býkov, edited by Vilém Knoll. Plzeň: Vydavatelství a nakladatelství Aleš Čeněk, 2008.

Čorba, Jozef. 'The Slovak Act on the Organization and Support of Sport; a Missed Opportunity?'. *The International Sports Law Journal* 3, no. 4 (2009): 65–70.

Čorba, Jozef. 'Ťažký život legionára – pojednanie o možnostiach vykonávania športovej činnosti v zahraničí'. In *Míľniky práva v stredoeurópskom priestore 2007: zborník z medzinárodnej konferencie doktorandov a mladých vedeckých pracovníkov konanej v dňoch 16.-18.4.2007 v priestoroch ÚZ NR SR Častá-Papiernička*. Bratislava: Univerzita Komenského v Bratislave, 2007.

Čorba, Jozef. 'Zmluvné vzt'ahy pri vysielaní TV prenosov zo športových podujatí'. In *Tradície a inovácie v súkromnom práve*, edited by Ján Husár. Košice: UPJŠ, 2009.

Dedík, Peter. 'Organizácia a financovanie profesionálneho futbalového klubu v prostredí tržnej ekonomiky na príklade FC Nitra, a.s.' In *Sport a kvalita života 2007*. Brno: Masarykova univerzita, 2007.

Dobrovičová, Gabriela. 'Rozhodnutia Ústavného súdu Slovenskej republiky a pramene práva'. *Právny obzor* 78, no. 5 (1995): 401–407.

Dolobáč, Marcel. 'Pracovné vzt'ahy v športe'. In *Otázky sportovního práva*. Plzeň: Aleš Čeněk, 2008.

Dolobáč, Marcel. 'Právne postavenie športovcov'. *Justičná revue* 62, no. 6–7 (2010): 796–801.

Drgonec, Ján. 'Základné právo na štrajk: rozsah a podmienky jeho uplatnenia v právnom poriadku Slovenskej republiky'. *Justičná revue* 59, no. 6–7 (2007): 759–780.

Duchoslav, Libor. 'Analýza ambush marketingu v športe na Slovensku'. In *Humanistické podoby športu a telesnej výchovy*. Bratislava: Slovenská vedecká spoločnosť pre telesnú výchovu a šport, 2006.

Gábriš, Tomáš. 'Dôchodkové zabezpečenie na Slovensku v kontexte medzinárodného a európskeho práva'. *Právny obzor* 93, no. 2 (2010): 101–116.

Gábriš, Tomáš. 'Princípy a zásady tzv. športového práva'. *Acta iuridica olomucensis* 5, no. 2 (2010): 53–67.

Gábriš, Tomáš. 'Professional Football and the EU Law: Bernard Award of the ECJ from March 16, 2010'. In *Rozhodovacie procesy EÚ a ich dopad na vnútroštátne právo*. Bratislava: Univerzita Komenského v Bratislave, 2010.

Gábriš, Tomáš. 'Transportabilita a zachovanie dôchodkových práv'. *Justičná revue* 62, no. 4 (2010): 467–492.

Gerloch, Aleš. *Teorie práva*. 5th edn. Plzeň: Aleš ČenĚk, 2009.

Grexa, Ján. 'Občiansky atribút v športovom hnutí na Slovensku'. In *Občan a občianstvo 2002*. Bratislava: FTVŠ, 2002.

Grexa, Ján. 'Šport na Slovensku – štát versus občianske združenia'. *Telesná výchova a šport* 10, no. 3 (2000): 35–40.

Grus, Zdeněk. 'Švarcsystém v rozhodovací praxi a nový zákon o zamĚstnanosti'. *Právní rozhledy* 13, no. 1 (2005): 18–22.

Hamerník, Pavel. 'Rozhodčí řízení u Arbitrážního soudu pro sport'. *Právní rozhledy* 15, no. 4 (2007): 134–137.

Hamerník, Pavel. 'Rozsudek Evropského soudního dvora Simutenkov – definitivní konec cizineckých kvót ve sportu v EU?'. *Právní rozhledy* 13, no. 21 (2005): 795–799.

Hamerník, Pavel. *Sportovní právo s mezinárodním prvkem*. Prague: Auditorium, 2007.

Hamilton, Mark. 'Elective Performance Enhancement Surgery for Athletes: Should It Be Resisted?'. *Acta Universitatis Palackianae Olomucensis. Gymnica* 36, no. 2 (2006): 39–46.

Hora, Jiří. 'K otázce trestní odpovědnosti hráčů při sportovních úrazech'. *Acta Universitatis Carolinae Gymnica* 15, no. 1 (1979): 15–24.

Hurdík, Jan. *Zásady soukromého práva*. Brno: Masarykova univerzita, 1998.

Hurdík, Jan & Marian Jeřábek. 'Freedom of Will and Legal Order'. In *Freedom of Contract Conference*. Brno: Masarykova Univerzita, 1997.

Hurdík, Jan, Petr Lavický & Ivo Telec. *Občanské právo hmotné: Obecná část. Ochrana osobnosti*. Bratislava: Bratislavská vysoká škola práva, 2008.

Ivor, Jaroslav, et al. *Trestné právo hmotné 1*. Bratislava: Iura Edition, 2010.

Ivor, Jaroslav, et al. *Trestné právo hmotné 2*. Bratislava: Iura Edition, 2010.

Knap, Karel, et al. *Ochrana osobnosti podle občanského práva*. Prague: Linde, 2004.

Kolárik, Jozef. 'Trestnoprávne predpisy v prvých rokoch existencie Československej republiky'. In *Acta Iuridica Sladkoviciensia I*. Sládkovičovo: Vysoká škola v Sládkovičove, 2010.

Koudelka, Zdenk. *Samospráva*. Prague: Linde, 2007.

Králík, Michal. 'Civilněprávní odpovědnost sportovců za sportovní úrazy ve světle evropské a světové judikatury 20. a 21. století'. *Soudní rozhledy* 12, no. 8 (2006): 285–295.

Králík, Michal. 'Několik poznámek k právní odpovědnosti sportovců za sportovní úrazy'. *Právní rozhledy* 14, no. 15 (2006): 539–548.

Králík, Michal. 'Právní odpovědnost za sportovní úrazy'. In *Otázky sportovního práva*. Plzeň: Aleš Čeněk, 2008.

Králík, Michal. *Právo ve sportu*. Prague: C.H.Beck, 2001.

Králík, Michal. 'Trestněprávní odpovědnost sportovců za sportovní úrazy ve světle evropské a světové judikatury 20. a 21. století'. *Soudní rozhledy* 12, no. 10 (2006): 365–373.

Králík, Michal. 'Zamyšlení nad tzv. sportovním právem'. *Právní rozhledy* 6, no. 10 (1998): 485–495.

Križan, Ladislav. 'Analýza vybraných ustanovení zákona NR SR č. 300/2008 Z.z. o organizácii a podpore športu a o zmene a doplnení niektorých zákonov'. In *Medzinárodná vedecká konferencia Atletika 2008*, edited by Jaroslav Brod'ani & Martin Miškolci. Nitra: KTVS PF UKF, 2008.

Križan, Ladislav. 'Mal by mat' profesionálny futbalista na Slovensku postavenie zamestnanca?'. *Bulletin slovenskej advokácie* 15, no. 3 (2009): 28–34.

Križan, Ladislav. *Právne aspekty profesionálneho futbalu a povolania profesionálneho futbalistu na Slovensku po roku 1989* (unpublished PhD Dissertation). Bratislava: Univerzita Komenského v Bratislave, Fakulta telesnej výchovy a športu, 2010.

Križan, Ladislav. 'Právne postavenie profesionálnych futbalistov pôsobiacich vo vybraných krajinách EÚ z hl'adiska ich vnútroštátnej legislatívy'. *Notitiae ex Academia Bratislavensi Iurisprudentiae* 4, no. 1 (2010): 61–78.

Križan, Ladislav. *Právo v športe v Čechách a na Slovensku – časť 3.: 'Športové právoa' siet'ová štruktúra systému práva prof. Holländera.* http://jinepravo.blogspot.com/2009/08/ladislav-krizan-pravo-v-sporte-v.html, 10 September 2010.

Križan, Ladislav & Tomáš Gábriš. 'Výchovné za mladých športovcov – Rozhodnutie Súdneho dvora EÚ vo veci Bernard'. *Športinform* 20, no. 8 (2010): 20–21.

Kudrna, Karel. 'Přípustnost inominátních a smíšených smluv v českém právu soukromém'. *Právní rozhledy* 9, no. 11 (2001): 548–551.

Lacko, Miloš. *Slovak Social Security Law.* Plzeň: Aleš Čeněk, 2010.

Lazar, Ján, et al. *Základy občianskeho hmotného práva 1.* Bratislava: Iura Edition, 2004.

Libenský, Jan. 'Patnáct let zákona o státní péči o tělesnou výchovu'. *Teorie a praxe tělesné výchovy* 12, no. 7 (1964): 289–292.

Lyčka, Martin. 'Rien va plus – právní úprava loterií v Evropské unii a aplikace těchto zásad na právní úpravu v České republice'. *Právní rozhledy* 15, no. 16 (2007): 586–597.

Magurová, Zuzana. 'Legislatíva tretieho (neziskového) sektora na Slovensku'. *Právny obzor* 79, no. 3 (1996): 198–223.

Magurová, Zuzana. 'Sponzorstvo, darcovstvo alebo reklama?'. *Právny obzor* 82, no. 1 (1999): 55–65.

Machajová, Jozefína, et al. *Všeobecné správne právo.* 4th edn. Bratislava: Eurokodex, 2009.

Matlák, Ján, et al. *Právo sociálneho zabezpečenia.* Plzeň: Aleš Čeněk, 2009.

Nápravník, Čestmír. 'Smrtelné úrazy ve fotbale'. *Teorie a praxe tělesné výchovy* 35, no. 11 (1987): 674 et seq.

'Oficiálna informácia Daňového riaditel'stva Slovenskej republiky'. *Športinform* 16, no. 2 (2006): 11–13.

Peráčková, Janka. *The Slovak Republic and Its Sport Sector.* Bratislava: Faculty of Physical Education and Sport, 2006.

Petoová, Andrea. 'Olympijský marketing'. In *Manažment v športe,* edited by Libor Duchoslav. Bratislava: Slovenský olympijský výbor, 1997.

Poruban, Andrej. 'K otázke náhrady za výchovu mladých hráčov futbalovým klubom'. *Justičná revue* 62, no. 5 (2010): 691–694.

Potůček, Martin. 'Výsledky obsahové analýzy dokumentů vrcholového řízení tělesné kultury v ČSSR za léta 1945–1981'. *Teorie a praxe tělesné výchovy* 32, no. 5 (1984): 288 et seq.

Prusák, Jozef. 'Problém surovej hry (súť'aže) a prenikanie právneho princípu non laedere do športových pravidiel'. *Teorie a praxe tělesné výchovy* 33, no. 6 (1985): 374 et seq.

Prusák, Jozef. *Šport a právo (Úvod do dejín, teórie a praxe právnej zodpovednosti v športe).* Bratislava: Šport, 1985.

Prusák, Jozef. 'Teoreticko-metodologické otázky skúmania vzájomných vzt'ahov medzi športom a právom'. *Teorie a praxe tělesné výchovy* 32, no. 9 (1984): 558 et seq.

Průcha, Petr. *Veřejná správa a samospráva*. Prague: Vysoká škola aplikovaného práva, 2004.

'Registrácii daňových subjektov podliehajú aj športové spolky'. *Športinform* 16, no. 4 (2006): 33–35.

Sakáčová, Zuzana. 'Niekoľko pohľadov na vzťahy medzi športom, právom a medicínou'. *Telesná výchova a šport* 17, no. 2 (2007): 32–35.

Sakáčová, Zuzana. 'Právne aspekty vzdelávania v športe'. In *Vzdelávanie odborníkov pre telesnú výchovu a šport v tradícii a perspektívach: Vedecký zborník*. Bratislava: ICM Agency, 2006.

Sakáčová, Zuzana. 'Právo a šport v súčasnosti'. In *Šport a spoločenské a humanitné vedy 2009*. Bratislava: ICM Agency, 2009.

Sakáčová, Zuzana. 'Šport a právo'. In *Športová humanistika 98*. Bratislava: FTVŠ, 1998.

Sádovský, Stanislav. *Boj proti dopingu a právní garance lidských práv* (unpublished PhD Dissertation). Bratislava: Comenius University in Bratislava, 2008.

Sádovský, Stanislav. *Právní aspekty násilí ve sportu*. Prague: Karolinum, 2010.

Síkorová, Jaroslava. *Športovci a športové kluby v procese DPH*.

Sluka, Tomáš. *Profesionální sportovec (právní a ekonomické aspekty)*. Prague: Havlíček Brain Team, 2007.

Stloukalová, Brigita. 'Profesionalismus a amatérismus v zrcadle socialistického sportu'. *Tělesná kultura* 31, no. 1 (2008): 68–84.

Surmajová, Žaneta. 'Právna úprava eliminácie násilia na športových podujatiach v Slovenskej republike'. *Notitiae ex Academia Bratislavensi Iurisprudentiae* 3, no. 1 (2009): 82–97.

Škultéty, Peter, et al. *Správne právo hmotné*. Bratislava: VO PF UK, 2004.

'Športový spolok a daň'. *Športinform* 16, no. 5 (2006): 42–43.

Števček, Marek. 'Hospodárska súťaž v právnej reglementácii Obchodného zákonníka (stručný komentár)'. *Obchodné právo* 9, no. 11 (2008): 31–34.

Števček, Marek, et al. *Občiansky súdny poriadok: Komentár*. Prague: C.H.Beck, 2009.

Števček, Marek. 'Right to a Fair Trial in Relation to Judiciary System of the Slovak Republic'. In *Prawa czlowieka*. Katowice: Oficyna Wydawnicza Waclaw Walasek, 2008.

Števček, Marek. 'Základné teoretické problémy a východiská rozhodcovského konania v Slovenskej republike'. In *Aktuálne problémy vo vývoji práva SR a ČR*. Bratislava: VO PraF UK, 2008.

Štumbauer, Jan. '40 let zákona o státní péči o tělesnou výchovu a sport'. *Teorie a praxe tělesné výchovy* 37, no. 11 (1989): 689 et seq.

Švidroň, Ján. 'Veda a prax pri ochrane osobnosti'. *Právny obzor* 86, no. 6 (2003): 626 et seq.

Sýkorová Chmelárová, Katarína & Denisa Kováčová. 'Športový arbitrážny súd – CAs'. *Notitiae ex Academia Bratislavensi Iurisprudentiae* 3, no. 3 (2009): 113–118.

Tobiášová, Lýdia. 'Alternatívne tresty'. In *Development and Construction of the European Legal System*. Bratislava: VO PraFUK, 2007.

Tobiášová, Lýdia. 'Domáce väzenie – nový trest v rekodifikovanom Trestnom zákone'. *Justičná revue* 58, no. 10 (2006): 1373–1385.

Selected Bibliography

Tobiášová, Lýdia. 'Trest povinnej práce'. *Justičná revue* 60, no. 8–9 (2008): 1167–1180.

Topinka, Jiří. 'Dopady daňových předpisú na sportovce a sportovní kluby'. In *Otázky sportovního práva*. Plzeň: Aleš Čeněk, 2008.

Vozár, Jozef & Lukáš Lapšanský. 'Reklama z pohľadu práva proti obmedzovaniu hospodárskej súťaže'. *Právny obzor* 87, no. 6 (2004): 506–524.

Index

The numbers here refer to paragraph numbers.

Index

Made in the USA
Monee, IL
13 September 2026

62974280R00142